THE
RESTAURANT
DREAM?

An inside look at restaurant development, from concept to reality.

LEE SIMON

THE RESTAURANT DREAM?

ISBN-13: 978-0-910627-83-2 • ISBN-10: 0-910627-83-5

Library of Congress Cataloging-in-Publication Data

Simon, Lee.
  The restaurant dream? / Lee Simon.
     p. cm.
  Includes index.
  ISBN-13: 978-0-910627-83-2 (alk. paper)
  1. Restaurant management. I. Title.

  TX911.3.M27S56 2006
  647.95068--dc22
                         2005034556

ART DIRECTION & INTERIOR DESIGN: Meg Buchner • megadesn@mchsi.com
FRONT COVER & BOOK PRODUCTION DESIGN: Lisa Peterson • info@6sense.net • www.6sense.net
EDITOR: Jackie Ness • jackie_ness@charter.net

Printed in the United States

TESTIMONIALS

"Every person who has the dream of opening a restaurant must read this book. A priceless detailed description of making a plan prior to what will be the most bank withdrawals ever made in one year."

Tim Rosendahl, CEC, CCE, AAC, President - Executive Chef, Dakota Food Group

"At last we have a book that allows students and other would-be restaurateurs to make informed decisions about entering the restaurant business. Lee's detailed account of real-world restaurant development experience is a useful companion to what we teach in the classroom."

Stephani Robson, Cornell University School of Hotel Management

"A must-read for anyone who plans on starting their own restaurant company. *The Restaurant Dream?* helps eliminate the nightmares."

Rob Foraker, Director of Equipment Purchasing, Max & Erma's Restaurants, Inc.

"In his journey through the development of a restaurant concept, Lee identifies the trials and tribulations that all restaurateurs experience. A must-read for anyone contemplating entry into the always crazy, sometimes unexpected, but never boring world of restaurant development."

Brian Wright, Development Principal - Partner, Corinthian Restaurant Group, DBA Earl of Sandwich

"Having had the pleasure to work directly with Lee on our new commissary confirms the practical skills articulated in this incredible book actually work in the real world. A mandatory cover-to-cover read for anyone planning to invest time, resources, and funds into the food and beverage industry."

Warren Dietel, President, Puff 'n Stuff Events Catering

"*The Restaurant Dream?* is a refreshingly honest and incredibly informative look into Lee's journey as a restaurateur. He clearly addresses and answers many of the questions fledgling owners and partners don't want to talk about, or even think about, in all the planning and operating insanity that comes with the business. This book is a must-read for anyone interested in opening their first establishments; and learning about the *Business of Restaurants*."

Jacob Hamburger, Managing Partner, Prey Bar and Lounge, New York, New York

"Lee presents a real-life view that recognizes the many details that must be dealt with as a developer of a restaurant concept. His personal experiences with all aspects of the development process are clearly evidenced in this blend of classroom theory and real-world practicality."

Frank Zorc, Senior Director of Development, Ginn Clubs and Resorts

"In *The Restaurant Dream?*, Lee chronicles his roller coaster ride of developing a restaurant from the initial idea through the grand opening. His experience will benefit anyone who thinks they want to open a restaurant."

Carolyn Lambert, Associate Professor, Pennsylvania State University
School of Hospitality Management

"An interesting twist from the "How To" tome, the "How Did" methodology for being in the *Business of Restaurants* provides the reader with a flavor of the journey, tasting both the bitter and the sweet along the way. An intriguing and invaluable perspective for anyone in the hospitality industry."

Stephen C. Lipinski, Restaurant Veteran and Hospitality Real Estate Specialist

Why Buy This Book?

Have any of the following questions ever crossed your mind:

- I have never opened a restaurant before. What is the process *really* like?

- What is involved in developing a restaurant *concept*? What do I need to know?

- What the heck is EBIDTA, and why should I care?

- How hard is it to find the right location for a restaurant? What should I look for in a restaurant location?

- What are the pros and cons of taking over an existing restaurant location? How about the pros and cons for leasing a space that is under construction?

- What are impact fees, and who is expected to pay for them?

- What can I do to make sure I am getting a good deal on a lease? What should I avoid?

- What are TI dollars? Who provides them, and when are they provided?

- What is design-build, and is it right for me?

- What kinds of contracts can I sign with my general contractor? What are the options? Which one is best, and why?

- As I begin to design my restaurant, what are some of the things I should be thinking about?

- What can I do to make sure that my restaurant is built within budget?

- What kinds of things can go wrong during the construction phase?

- What are lien waivers, and who is responsible for them? Why does this matter?

- What is life like as a restaurant owner?

This book contains the answers to these questions, and much more. This is a real story, about real people and real events, that will give you an insider's look at an actual restaurant development process. *The Restaurant Dream?* is filled with educational information and strategy, all intertwined within a story highlighting the successes and failures that our team experienced in developing a new restaurant concept, from the ground up. You can steal some of our ideas and apply them to your own efforts. You can learn from our mistakes — without having to *pay* for those mistakes yourself. If you have looked at other books on the shelf, I think you will see that this one is different. It is full of specifics and short on generalities. It provides you with an in-depth look at all phases of the development process, from the initial idea through the first several months of operation. Regardless of whether you are considering opening a restaurant, you know someone who is, you are a veteran restaurateur, or you are just interested in the subject, this book has something for you.

Table of Contents

Introduction:
The Business of Restaurants

There is a difference between those who are in the RESTAURANT BUSINESS and those who are in the BUSINESS OF RESTAURANTS. Stated another way, the latter represents a far more sophisticated approach and relies on data and complex operational systems, whereas the former tends to operate on limited information and gut feel. I hope that doesn't sound too abstract, because I believe that this critical differentiation is at the center of potential success or failure for aspiring restaurateurs. You are probably thinking suspiciously to yourself, *Here comes one more guy touting some "theory" based on fancy terminology that just won't hold up in the real world.* Well, although I have spent my fair share of time in the academic world, I am—and always have been—a businessperson first. I am an entrepreneur with enough scars and stories to tell you that it was my real-world experience within the hospitality industry that confirmed for me the difference between those in the *Restaurant Business* and those in the *Business of Restaurants*. Now, I cannot take credit for creating this catch phrase, but I certainly have adopted it wholeheartedly.

The world, and particularly American society, has been on a track toward wide-scale homogenization for years. Variety in the form of numerous smaller, more independent retailers has been replaced in many cases by fewer larger, more dominant retailers. The success of these "chains" is evidenced in virtually all markets. Whether it is The Gap, The Home Depot, Wal-Mart, or Circuit City, it is clear that the average consumer has been conditioned to gravitate toward a known brand or experience in favor of an unknown brand or an unknown experience. Smaller, more localized retailers in industries such as hardware, electronics, clothing, and sporting goods have been pushed around by the "big-box" retailers for years now, with many of the independents having to perform the one act every entrepreneur fears: hanging the "closed" sign in the window for the last time, knowing that there isn't another opening scheduled. It is a thought that keeps many an owner up at night.

The sheer number of eateries in the United States has delayed this same pattern in the restaurant industry. However, the chains are gaining ground. Recently several industry periodicals have reported that chain restaurants account for more than half of all restaurant revenues. The chains bring with them sophisticated systems, purchasing power, brand awareness, and a wealth of other resources that many independent restaurateurs simply cannot obtain. These chains, many of which are part of a larger portfolio owned by a parent company, have altered the way that the entire industry does business. Some of these companies have billions in annual sales. Many of them are public companies that must answer to shareholders and boards of directors. They are actively tracking their stock performance and same-store sales from quarter to quarter. It is fair to say that these chains have changed the game. Handwritten "dupes" (industry lingo for a customer's order) hanging in the window with a call out of the order to a short-order cook have been replaced with sophisticated hand-held wireless electronic ordering devices that can place orders from anywhere in the restaurant, provide detailed nutritional information on specific menu items, and even allow customers to pay by credit card table side. It is a whole new ballgame, with unprecedented levels of sophistication surfacing throughout the restaurant industry. These chains are in the *Business of Restaurants*.

Whether they like it or not, every independent restaurant owner — or aspiring restaurateur — is competing with the chains and their sophisticated systems and resources. Now, if you are an independent or thinking of opening a new restaurant concept, do not be discouraged. In fact, local independent restaurants actually have many advantages over the larger, national restaurant chains. With a direct pulse on the community and a smaller, more agile structure, independents are in a position to move quickly and capitalize on opportunities faster than many of the larger chains. Independents typically have opportunities for more specific, personalized marketing, which, if executed properly, can yield very effective results. However—and this is a big condition—the independent or small regional chain must be able to think and act in a sophisticated manner. They must be in the *Business of Restaurants* as well. Unfortunately, many restaurateurs are still in the *Restaurant Business*.

There is no specific definition for those in the *Restaurant Business*. It is not as though there is a standardized test that classifies you into one category or the other. Rather, it is a general mindset. These operators rely on a more primitive and often-outdated approach to doing business. It typically involves less hard data and a greater reliance on estimation and guesswork. If you ask someone in the *Restaurant Business* what their "average check" is (in the restaurant industry, average check is typically the total amount of food and beverage revenue divided by the total number of patrons, resulting in an average amount of revenue per person), they may or may not know. Someone in the *Business of Restaurants*, however, will likely be able to tell you not only what their average check is, but how it fluctuates by season and key reasons for the differences between one year and the next. There are countless other examples illustrating the differences between these two groups. One will view a case of tomatoes as nothing more than a case of tomatoes, whereas the other will view the food product as *inventory*. The more sophisticated operation will tend to pay closer attention to equipment features, maintenance records, and warranties when making decisions as to which piece of equipment is right for their operation, thereby taking the long-term view. The less sophisticated operator, however, will tend to focus more on short-term issues such as the initial purchase price. I could go on and on.

Perhaps you are thinking that I am promoting the larger chains over the independents and trying to warn aspiring restaurateurs that they have no chance of succeeding as a little fish in shark-infested waters. That is not the case. What I am trying to stress is that the independents will have to compete with the larger chains, whether they like it or not. Because the playing field has already been set, it is important for the independent to fully understand the rules of this game and adequately prepare for the battle. Thus, I am hopeful that the awareness of these two different approaches—the *Restaurant Business* versus the *Business of Restaurants*—will enhance the aspiring restaurateur's likelihood of success.

So what is this book about, and why did I invest the time to tell the story of one team's efforts to establish a new restaurant concept from the ground up? Well, I was presented with a unique opportunity to join a team that consisted of several individuals with impressive credentials and advanced degrees in each of the areas of expertise required to open a restaurant. Given the anticipated sophistication of both the team and the process that was being established, I thought that there was a unique opportunity to document the creation of a restaurant concept, from the initial idea through construction and opening for business. I enjoy teaching, and hope that, by sharing our story, others will benefit from reading about our successes and failures, learning from what we did right and avoiding what we did wrong.

This is not a tale about a celebrity chef opening a $5 million restaurant, where the celebrity chef has an almost-unlimited budget and is guaranteed success from previous publicity and notoriety. Neither is it the recounting of a large national chain's success story where you know that the story will have a happy ending. This is not a book that provides a number of checklists, implying that addressing every item in a particular list will ensure success. You will not find many magic formulas or rules of thumb in the pages that follow. This is a story about what can *really* happen during the course of developing a new restaurant concept from the ground up—the good, the bad, the worse than bad, and the ugliest of uglies. This is a *real* story, based on actual events. It is not a dry textbook. It is numerous case studies all rolled into one *long* tale. This is about a real process carried out by a group of first-time restaurant developers. It is our story. It is the documentation of one approach, not a "how-to."

I must admit that the story that actually occurred is far more intriguing than any story I could have ever fabricated, even in my wildest dreams. This book documents the ever-winding path our development process took over the course of several years. There are other books available that offer guidance for opening a new restaurant, but I believe this book is different. It is not my intention to tell you what to do or what not to do. Rather, I want to tell you what we did and, most importantly, *why*. If some of our stories will assist you in creating, or re-creating, your establishment, by all means use them to your advantage! Steal the ideas! Certain decisions that our team made provided negative results, but in a different scenario or set of environmental conditions, they might have resulted in success. That is why throughout this book I stress the reasoning behind our approach, and not just the approach itself. The logic and processes used to arrive at the answer are far more important than the answer itself. I should tell you that some of the names and details in this book have been altered. The objective of this book is to educate, not denigrate. I can assure you, however, that where such information has been modified, the sincerity and authenticity of the situation has remained.

This is a story and, to some extent, a class. I want to take you along for a ride and share an experience with you—an experience with extreme highs and extreme lows. Satisfaction, jubilation, frustration, and utter disappointment. Opening a restaurant is, after all, a very emotional process. There is an almost unimaginable investment of time, money, resources, reputation, and—most importantly—heart, or at least there should be. It is still a business, but a business that requires all of the above and so much more to realize success. This book is full of specifics and short on generalities. It is not intended to be all things to all people. It is not intended to address the development process for each type of restaurant, from quick service to fine dining. Rather, it is intended to provide an in-depth look at the development of one specific restaurant concept, allowing you, the reader, to become intimately engaged with the process. I believe that information can be gleaned from our efforts, even if your situation is slightly different. For instance, in this story we discuss a restaurant that was approximately 4,000 square feet in size. You may be looking at opening or renovating a restaurant either half that size or twice that size, but many of the issues that must be considered and addressed will be similar to those that we had to address ourselves. The lease rate may be higher, for instance, but the components of the lease and many of the potential negotiating tactics will be transferable.

If I have done my job right, this book should be useful to several different groups. First, and most obvious, is the current or aspiring restaurateur who is looking to develop, revitalize, or expand a restaurant concept. This book starts with the assembling of a team, even before the concept was fully defined, and continues through the development process to opening day and beyond. I also believe that students engaged in hospitality education programs will benefit from this story. They will be able to experience the development process through the eyes of a couple of college instructors. Again, if I have done my job correctly, this should be a unique combination of theory and real-world experience applied to a real-life venture—a very powerful mixture. This book offers several topics for discussion on numerous aspects of the development process. In addition, many of the lessons contained within this book are about more than just opening a restaurant; they are lessons about business and about life. Be creative. Set yourself apart from the crowd. Take a risk. Be passionate about what you do, whatever it is that you do.

Finally, I believe that the general public can benefit from our story as well. I hope to demonstrate that it takes more than grandma's secret family recipe to open a restaurant. In no way am I trying to be disrespectful to grandma or talk anyone out of opening a restaurant. Rather, I hope to share the level of commitment and dedication required to actually open a restaurant. It may encourage a new concept or prevent a doomed effort from ever getting off the ground. Either way, ever so humbly, I hope that this book will somehow help the industry as a whole.

With a few exceptions, this book is set up chronologically so that you can follow the development process in the order in which it happened, as it happened. You have an invitation to come along for the ride. You will be able, I hope, to experience our story in much the same way that we did. There were surprises, both positive and negative. There were decisions that, at the time, seemed like the right decisions to make but would prove to be detrimental to our efforts. There were other decisions that were, we thought, not in our best interest but proved to be advantageous in the end. Live and learn—we lived it, and now I hope that you can learn from our story.

So what, specifically, can you expect to read or learn about in the next several hundred pages? I have tried to capture the restaurant development process in its entirety. Our story starts even before the idea of opening a restaurant really came to be. It progresses through the formation of our team, the development of our *concept* (a specific industry term to be discussed in detail), the development of the menu, securing a site for the restaurant, negotiating the lease(s), the entire design and construction effort, opening the doors, and the early months of operations. As you can see, this book focuses on the development process, or the creation of a restaurant from the ground up. It is not a book on menu development, though the subject is covered briefly. It is not a book on operations. It is not a book offering legal guidance on lease negotiations, though again, the subject is discussed. This *is* a book on the restaurant development process and all that it encompasses.

And now, our story. I hope that you will find the account of our efforts enlightening, inspiring, educational, and entertaining all at the same time. It certainly was for me.

1

Doctor Knows Best

It was another dark, gray, cold morning in Ithaca, New York. As with every year in Ithaca, the sun had set in October and wasn't due to return again until May. I was in my junior year at Cornell's School of Hotel Administration. I rolled out of bed that day with a mix of emotions. On one hand, I was not overly excited about facing another dreary, overcast morning. On the other hand, I was on a mission. I had a meeting scheduled to try to get out of a class that was required but not directly related to my area of concentration, hospitality facilities planning and design.

Cornell offered a class that we called TCAB, which stood for the Terrace Café and Bistro, the facility where this class was held. In this class, the students were required to break into teams of two or three and "open a restaurant" in a simulation that was as close to real life as a classroom would allow. Each team was responsible for developing the theme, creating the menu, producing the financial projections, evaluating and justifying the food costs, ordering the food, and finally preparing, cooking, and serving the meals to actual guests in an authentic restaurant setting. Each week, a different team "opened" their restaurant, while the other class members would fill the roles of server, cook, dishwasher, greeter, and other essential staff positions. We rotated weekly, allowing each student the opportunity to work in each staff position. The restaurants created each week were vastly different. One week might be a French fine-dining theme with an average check of $20, while the next might be a southern barbecue theme with an average check of $8. Each team's efforts varied in virtually every aspect of a restaurant's composition from volume to menu to ambiance. The patrons consisted of other Cornell students, as well as local residents who had come to learn that the food at these TCAB events was usually pretty good and offered at a rather reasonable price point.

So why would I try to get out of this class? It sounds like fun, right? Well, the main purpose of the course was to provide the enrolled students with operational and concept development experience. I had been working in operations since the age of fourteen, and I did not feel that the additional experience I would gain from this one class would significantly affect my career as a foodservice and hospitality design professional. In my mind, this class seemed to be most beneficial for those who lacked the necessary operational experience or for those planning to open their own restaurant after graduation, neither of which seemed to be pertinent to me personally. Sure, one can always use more experience, but I had already selected hospitality design—not operations—as my area of concentration. I had hoped to use the TCAB time slot to enroll in some additional architecture and design classes. I had no plans to run a restaurant of my own, at least not anytime soon. Besides, I was already extremely frustrated that, due to scheduling and other course requirements, I was forced to wait until the second semester of my sophomore year to take my *first* design class. I did not want the school to control my academic destiny once again. This time, I was going to take matters into my own hands.

After getting dressed in layer after layer of clothing (I was, after all, a Florida boy in the cold), I put on my game face and made my way up the hill in the snow for a scheduled meeting with the registrar. I was determined to get out of this TCAB class! The first meeting with the registrar didn't go that well. She could not override the class requirement. During our conversation, she also shared that she had heard similar requests made before, but had never seen them fulfilled. If I was still interested in pursuing this effort, I would have to meet with the instructor, Dr. Christopher Muller, and make my request to him in person. This was not the best news, but there was still hope. I met with Dr. Muller and, as expected, my request to drop this class was turned down. Dr. Muller had told me that my request was not uncommon and that one semester, years before, he had allowed two students to drop the class for reasons similar to mine — operations was not their primary area of study. Dr. Muller then continued, indicating that in hindsight he had made the wrong decision by allowing those two students to drop his class, and he had promised himself never to allow the same mistake to happen again. Given his reasoning and committed position on this subject, and despite all of the valid arguments that I tried to present, it became painfully clear that Dr. Muller had no intention of changing his mind. I was stuck. I had lost the battle and eventually enrolled in the TCAB class. I enjoyed the semester and the experience, but I was still disappointed that I was unable to use my time for what I believed to be a more appropriate purpose — pursuing classes in design theory and application.

❖ ❖ ❖

Seven years after graduating from Cornell, I was living in Tampa, Florida, working for Louis Wohl & Sons/The General Group, my family's foodservice design and supply firm. I was preparing for a trip to Orlando to attend the annual Florida Restaurant Show when my wife brought the mail to me. Among the bills, flyers, and other solicitations was the latest edition of the Cornell Hotel School Bulletin, the school's alumni newsletter. As I was flipping through this particular issue, I came across an update on Dr. Muller, my former TCAB professor. He had left Cornell and moved to Orlando to accept a position at the University of Central Florida's Rosen College of Hospitality Management. I threw the bulletin in my briefcase as a reminder to track him down at the show, as there was usually a row where all of the state's hospitality programs were represented.

While at the show, during a lull in traffic from the attendees, I remembered that I wanted to stop by the UCF booth and leave a card for Dr. Muller. I didn't expect him to be there; I just wanted to leave a quick note to say hello, hoping that the representatives staffing the booth would be kind enough to pass on my contact information. I made my way through the Orlando Convention Center to the UCF booth and was pleasantly surprised to find that Dr. Muller was the one who happened to be staffing the booth. He was in the middle of speaking with someone else, and I patiently waited my turn, rehearsing a speech in my mind to help him remember just who I was. I only had Dr. Muller for the one class — TCAB — and I didn't expect him to remember me after teaching hundreds of students over the years at Cornell.

He finished his conversation and turned toward me, aware that I had been waiting for him to finish. I extended my hand and business card, prepared to remind him that I was a former student of his, when he caught me by surprise, initiating the conversation by asking, "What year did you graduate?" Without any new introduction, he remembered my face from the crowds that had previously graced his classroom.

"Excuse me?" I replied.

"What year did you graduate?" He continued, "I saw a lot of faces at Cornell, and I just can't remember what year you graduated."

"1996. To be honest, I am surprised that you remembered me at all. I wasn't a foodie, I was a design guy," I replied.

"I was close," he responded. "I would have guessed 1995. So how are you doing? What are you doing? Do you live here in Florida?"

I proceeded to update Dr. Muller on my activities since graduation, covering my time working for a foodservice design consulting firm in Colorado and moving to Florida to work as a designer in my family's firm. In return, Dr. Muller filled me in on his recent life changes, deciding to move to Orlando and accept a position at the University of Central Florida's Rosen College of Hospitality Management after numerous years as both a student and instructor at Cornell's School of Hotel Management. I always enjoyed Dr. Muller and his class, even though I originally didn't want to take the course. Dr. Muller really enjoyed what he was doing, and he helped those around him enjoy the subjects he taught as well. I remember that he had a sign in his office that hung unintentionally crooked and read "Learning Can Be Fun." I liked that, and I certainly agreed with that philosophy.

I had always been intrigued with the idea of teaching and liked Dr. Muller's style. As our conversation continued, I decided to offer to guest lecture on the topic of foodservice and hospitality design during one of his courses. In my typical style, I didn't make this offer once—I offered five or six times and would have continued to do so until he said yes. I have a habit of focusing on a goal and not letting go of that goal until I succeed or fail in its pursuit. Eventually, Dr. Muller agreed (or just grew tired of my more-than-obvious hints) and offered to let me guest lecture in his class. I must have performed adequately, as he invited me back for an encore performance the following semester.

After I guest lectured a few times, Dr. Muller came up with the idea that I should teach my own class on the subject of design entitled *Hospitality Facilities Planning and Design*. The students at UCF were enjoying the subject matter, and I was successful in keeping most of them awake — a feat that cannot be overlooked in a college classroom. Teaching had always interested me, but I thought I would pursue the opportunity much later in my career. A good instructor — knowledgeable, entertaining, inspirational, motivating, understanding, engaging, committed to a lifetime of teaching and *learning from* his or her students — always seems to have stories. No matter what the question posed by a student, there would be a story to answer that question. And although I did not have decades of experience, I did feel that I had compiled a significant number of stories during the course of my career, and I decided to give teaching a shot.

I began speaking with Dr. Muller on a more regular basis, and soon "Dr. Muller" became "Chris." Our relationship began to change from a teacher-student relationship to a peer-peer relationship. It wasn't long before many of my typical sarcastic remarks were directed at Chris — something I never would have done when he was my instructor. Don't get me wrong, I still held Chris in high regard. In fact, I had developed even more respect for him as we began to develop a closer friendship. He was supportive of my teaching efforts, offering general guidance when I was first starting out. I also enjoyed spending time chatting with him, because it was an extension of a lesson that started back in college. We would discuss theories and strategies on a variety of subjects. It was one-on-one instruction from the same source that, just a few years prior, required sizable tuition checks for comparable but more limited access. Now I had regular access to this source of information — and it was free! I viewed this as an amazing opportunity and tried to take advantage of each and every conversation, stopping in Chris's office after I was done teaching just to chat. I sensed, based on the nature and length of the conversations, that he respected my viewpoints and approaches, making the conversations even more beneficial to both parties.

Not long after accepting a position as an instructor at UCF, I attended a conference that featured a motivational guest speaker named Jeffrey Gitomer. Enjoyable to listen to, Jeffrey had numerous inspirational ideas. More than anything else, though, he pointed out the things that one could do, if motivated and committed, to further one's career. One of the concepts that Jeffrey proposed and actively practiced was publishing a column in an industry magazine to help increase awareness of his name and his company. In the middle of one of his lectures, he held up a page from a local business journal that was divided into two sections. Jeffrey's article was on the top half of the page, and a competitor's advertisement was on the bottom of that very same page. He held up the journal and pointed out that the advertiser had included his name, picture, and contact information in the ad. Then he paused for a long moment. Eventually Jeffrey continued, pointing out that the column he had published, located at the top of the same page, featured *his* name, *his* picture, and *his* contact information. Then he paused again. This time it was a longer pause to emphasize the point he was trying to make. "They paid me!" he proclaimed to an engaged audience. Not only was Jeffrey *being paid* for his work while the competitor was *paying* for the advertisement, but Jeffrey was on the top of the page! Well, I was hooked. It seemed to make perfect sense to me. Better yet, there was no reason that I couldn't use the same tactic. In fact, my position as an instructor at UCF lent credibility to this effort. I wasn't primarily interested in compensation for these columns, although I wouldn't have turned down the money; rather, I was realistic and more focused on personal and company exposure. One Friday night, after I returned home from the convention where I heard Jeffrey speak, I decided that if I were serious about authoring a column, I would have to develop a sample installment and a list of possible topics. This would prove not only to me, but also to potential host publications that I was serious and capable of publishing and continuing this column for a sustained length of time. So that is just what I did. I drafted a sample column entitled *The Secret to Foodservice Design: Follow the Flow of Food*. In addition to the sample column, my goal that evening was to develop a list of at least 12 potential topics for future columns, which, at a rate of one article per month, would account for a full year's worth of material. By the end of the evening, I had compiled a list of not 12, but 30 different topics, or two-and-a-half years' worth of articles. That was enough, I thought, to demonstrate to potential publishers that I was serious and capable of pulling this off.

I have come to learn that success is often based on both *who* you know and *what* you know. In an effort to try to get this column series in front of a few different publishers, I decided to ask Chris if he knew of anyone who might be interested. I explained to him what I was trying to do and why I was investing time in such an effort. Wanting to help, as he often does, Chris put me in contact with a couple of publishers. But while I was explaining this new goal that I just *had* to pursue, he decided to let me in on a little venture that he was feeling *he* had to pursue.

"I am getting another case of the flu—the 'I-want-to-open-a-restaurant' flu—again," he stated, ever so casually.

"Really?" I replied. "What kind of concept do you want to open?"

"Well, it is a gourmet pizza concept. Would you be willing to help me out?"

"Of course," I told him.

Better than just developing a relationship with my former professor, now I was going to help design *his* new restaurant concept. Considering all that he had done for me, I jumped at the chance to help. I had envisioned that my company would assist with the planning and procurement effort, but Chris had something else in mind.

At 10:44 one morning, coincidentally on my wife's birthday, Chris sent me an e-mail proposing the concept, strategy, and preliminary business model for this restaurant concept. I was intrigued. By that afternoon, all of the eventual restaurant development team members were already expressing interest in Chris's proposed project. This potential team represented the key disciplines and areas of expertise required to open a restaurant: concept development, growth/site selection, finance, culinary, operations, and design and construction. In fact, one e-mail, sent just hours after the original idea was officially proposed, contained preliminary financial models outlining food-cost percentages, anticipated revenues, the anticipated size of each store and number of seats, as well as a host of other pieces of data. This was fairly significant progress for a day's work. More importantly, it demonstrated to me that Chris was developing a team that seemed to know the difference between the *Restaurant Business* and the *Business of Restaurants*. This was, I concurred, a significant and important difference. It seemed like a good sign.

Chris and I began e-mailing one another on a more regular basis after that day, with the topic of our conversations shifting from philosophical in nature to practical, focused on this new restaurant concept he had proposed. In one of Chris's e-mails, he asked me about several matters that would typically be handled by the general contractor, not the foodservice design consultant or foodservice equipment supplier. The answers were clearly outside of my normal scope of work. I responded to Chris and explained this to him, stating that I wasn't really clear as to the role he pictured me playing in this effort. In fact, I was a little unsure as to how to raise the issue, so I buried it in an e-mail reply, hoping that it would not come across the wrong way. Well, that plan failed. Chris picked out that question, the one I tried to hide, and focused on it in his next e-mail. Chris knew all along what my role was going to be in this new restaurant venture, well before I knew. He responded strategically, asking me what I wanted to contribute to the development effort. I sat back and pondered this question, but not for long, before indicating my desire for a more involved role, even entertaining the possibility of an ownership interest. However, I feared my lack of available funds for investing in such a venture would be a hindrance. Chris countered, indicating that he was in search of knowledge, talent, and commitment—we would worry about the money later, as he stated that in his experience, money was never the problem. I was taken aback by this comment, as I thought money was *always* the problem. In fact, a number of industry sources maintained that the number one reason restaurants (or most small businesses, for that matter) fail is undercapitalization. To summarize, I was being offered the opportunity to be part of a sophisticated team that Chris was assembling, help develop a concept I found intriguing (we will discuss the concept in detail later), and obtain an ownership stake for pure sweat equity. No money? Where do I sign? If I were ever going to participate in the opening of a restaurant, this was, in fact, the right opportunity at the right time. For a venture of this nature to be successful, it would require a competent team, experience, commitment, trust, and passion.

Less than two weeks later, we had already found our first potential restaurant site, and we were drafting and negotiating a letter of intent for the landlord to hold the space. The process was moving quickly, but what did I have to lose? This was one heck of an opportunity—one that I couldn't comprehend missing. I knew that such an effort was going to take a lot of time and energy, and I had no plans to drop my day job—this would be in addition to my everyday responsibilities, which typically averaged 60 hours per week or more. I knew it would be tough—tough on me, and tough on my family. But after discussing it with my wife, we concurred that this opportunity was simply too good to pass up. I am not sure that my wife truly understood the level of commitment that would be required. In fact, I am not sure that I fully understood the implications of the decision I was about to make. If, however, the team was able to pull this off—create a new multi-unit restaurant concept—and be successful, it had the potential to significantly affect our lives. That was a risk I was willing to take.

THE STARTING LINEUP

When Chris approached me with the idea of creating a new restaurant, two questions immediately crossed my mind: 1) What was the concept (industry lingo for a description of a restaurant's complete set of characteristics)? and 2) Who else would be involved? We will address the concept in plenty of detail in the next chapter. For now, I want to focus on the team, because I found the group of individuals being assembled for this effort most appealing. We all had experience, either in the restaurant industry or in service segments that supported the restaurant industry, and most of us had both. Despite the lack of concept development experience, our collective résumés appeared to offer a wealth of expertise in virtually every critical area of the development process. After reviewing the credentials for each team member, I felt that our collective knowledge would allow us to make greater progress together than we could individually. In other words, the whole appeared to be greater than the sum of the parts. I also felt that it would be an invaluable learning experience.

In creating a restaurant, I believe six key disciplines or roles are required, with all other areas of focus falling under one of these primary categories: *Concept Development, Finance, Design and Construction, Growth/*

Site Selection, Operations, and *Culinary Arts.* Fortunately, through personal experience and contacts, Chris had identified who he felt was a qualified individual to fill each of these roles for this new development team. All of these potential team members were personal acquaintances of Chris—friends, colleagues, or former students from one stage of his life or another. I knew that we were pulling from seasoned veterans in each of these six key areas, and I was hopeful that the talent on our team would be able to intelligently and effectively capitalize on any opportunities or challenges that would arise. Many successful individuals share a common characteristic of surrounding themselves with other successful, talented, motivated people, and that was what I was hoping to do myself. If I were ever going to open a restaurant, this was the team with which I wanted to attempt such an effort. It is rare and difficult for an individual to possess exceptional skills in each of the six key areas, which made the team concept seem much more appealing in an industry that requires such a wide variety of skills and talents. I have tremendous respect for any successful entrepreneur in the restaurant industry that is capable of solely overseeing the development process from start to finish. Just for a moment, consider some of the skills required: financial analysis, forecasting and planning, negotiating, legal competence, customer relations, management, culinary talents, plan reading, construction management, and on and on! A team, of course, does not need to have all of the required areas of expertise represented internally. This talent can be acquired, hired, or sought through a number of different methods. The point I am trying to stress is that somehow, someway, an aspiring restaurant developer had better find access to such talent, as the ultimate success or failure of any new restaurant concept depends on it. Now, let's meet the team.

Chris: Our Father Figure

Dr. Christopher Muller, whom you have already met, was directly responsible for assembling this team. Not only did Chris initiate this restaurant concept, but it was his idea to put together a team of professionals to pursue a new multi-unit restaurant concept. While his official title was President and Chief Executive Officer, he was our father figure, for lack of a better term. He knew each of us individually from different eras of his past, and as a result, he often worked as a mediator, balancing the ideas and personalities as different opportunities and challenges arose. Chris was the only member of the team who had actually operated his own restaurant in the past. While his restaurant had some successes, in the end it did not meet the high expectations he had set, and it closed on the one-year anniversary of its opening. In Chris's estimation, the restaurant's closure was due in large part to his decision to take on more than he was trained to handle, forcing him to divide his time among various tasks. This is not a slight against Chris by any means. Rather, it is an important part of his history because it drove him to take a different path this time around.

Chris's past is quite varied. He ran a painting business. He was a wine sales representative. Shortly after our renewed relationship, he received tenure as a professor at UCF's hospitality school following a lengthy stint at Cornell's hotel school. In what little spare time he has, Chris consults for some of the industry's leading multi-unit restaurant companies, provides expert witness testimony for legal cases involving the restaurant industry, and is active in the European foodservice arena. Chris's variety of experience was certainly an asset to our organization. I jokingly asked him why he had so much trouble holding a job, but in reality I knew that he was simply an entrepreneur trained to seize the opportunities that he sees before him. Chris's contacts were perhaps even more important than some of his past experiences. The hospitality industry is, after all, a people business. Relationships in this industry are critical to success.

From the outset, Chris had identified the restaurant concept and the team members, which he referred to as the pieces of his puzzle. I remember that when Chris first approached me, he said he wasn't doing this for the money, but rather because he *had* to. This sounded great, and I understood where Chris was coming from, but do you really think that he would turn down any profits from the effort? I didn't think so either. Ultimately, Chris served as our guiding light. His job was to focus on big-picture items, strategies, relationships, positioning, and the general direction of the company. His personal relationship with each of the other team members helped him do just that. He sought advice on various topics from each individual and tried to balance the different perspectives in the best interest of the company. In fact, there were weeks when I probably talked with him as much as (or possibly even more than) I spoke with my wife. I could tell that Chris really enjoyed his role in the process. In addition, it was quite rewarding for him to look upon *his* team, the team that he had assembled personally, with a sense of satisfaction. He had the vision, he built it, he sold the idea to each of us, and he was preparing to watch his investment provide a return — or at least that was the hope.

Lee: Design and Construction

I was in charge of design, construction, and management of special projects for our company. I had accepted the official title of Executive Vice President, Design and Project Management by default, as I tend to find titles limiting and do not use them unless I am forced to do so. I grew up in the hospitality industry. From a very young age, I was always involved in my family's foodservice design and supply business. Started by my grandfather, the company — and subsequently the industry — was an integral part of my upbringing. I helped with inventory, cleaned the china and glassware in the showroom, and often accompanied my father on calls to customers. In fact, at the age of ten I was far more familiar with the back-door entrance to most of the local restaurants and hotels than with their main entrance. Perhaps my favorite time spent in my father's office, however, was in the design department. Even then, I was drawn to the art of creating new restaurants, hotels, clubs, hospitals, and other such foodservice facilities. I was mesmerized by the designers working at their drafting boards; I stood there and watched them for hours.

At the age of fourteen, the first summer when I was legally allowed to work, I informed my parents that I did not want to attend a summer camp, but instead planned to get a job and start earning my own money. I turned to the hospitality industry — it was what I knew. I applied for a job at Subway, but was turned down due to my age. Their insurance would not allow anyone younger than sixteen to work on the premises because of the danger associated with the slicer. After my first official rejection in the business world, I asked my other grandfather to drive me to an interview at TCBY. Fortunately, this yogurt store did not have any dangerous equipment, and I was hired. Every summer from that point forward, I worked in the hospitality industry. I worked in restaurants and hotels. I held positions in both the front-of-house and the back-of-house. I worked as a manager. I tried to soak up as much operational experience as I possibly could, as I knew it would be useful in my future endeavors — as a foodservice designer.

Following my four years at Cornell, where I specialized in hospitality design, I accepted a position with a well-respected foodservice and laundry design firm in Colorado. It was a terrific experience, and I learned a great deal during my time there. After a couple of years, however, the opportunities with Louis Wohl and Sons/The General Group, my family's firm, seemed to offer greater opportunities. My wife and I packed up and moved to Florida, where I soon found myself responsible for some very prestigious and challenging projects. I was also involved with some side ventures, including authoring a column on hospitality design and teaching the design course at UCF's hospitality school.

I, too, am an entrepreneur, and this restaurant venture was one of several that I was pursuing at the time. Although I possessed substantial experience in back-of-house design, I was hoping to broaden my horizons with this effort. I was extremely intrigued by other aspects of the design and construction process, and I viewed this restaurant project as an opportunity to grow both personally and professionally. During my years as a project manager on some very prestigious hospitality projects, I had taken an active role in parts of the design and construction process that were outside of the typical foodservice scope of work. As I noticed that many of my ideas in such situations were often well-received and adopted, I began to realize I had potential that, with some training, experience, or education, could lead to a new world of additional opportunities. Even in my role as a foodservice designer, I was already starting to gravitate in this direction, serving on occasion as the central point of coordination for some of the restaurant projects I was working on. It was a natural progression, as clients would often come to us before the architect looking for equipment and a layout for their restaurant. I would then contact an architect and contractor to assemble a team capable of taking the project from start to finish. After identifying the rest of the project team, I then began sketching the entire restaurant, including the walls, restrooms, dining spaces, seating layouts, service spaces, and other such components that were typically outside the traditional foodservice scope. This approach allowed us to address the integration of the space as a single entity.

My role as a foodservice design consultant, combined with my personal restaurant and hotel operations experience, helped me understand many of the intricacies associated with foodservice establishments. In my opinion, as well as in the opinion of many other well-respected designers, the design and layout of restaurants should first start with the heart of the operation—the kitchen—and then work out into the other areas. This is not to say the front-of-house and support areas are not important; on the contrary. But the kitchen and overall flow of the facility are the building blocks for any foodservice operation. Form follows function. This is an important concept, in fact the most important concept, in restaurant and hospitality design.

Jason: Finance

I remember meeting Jason shortly after I had agreed to hop on Chris's bandwagon. Jason was our Chief Financial Officer and Executive Vice President of Finance. Although he lived in Orlando and I lived in Tampa, it was pretty easy to set up a time to meet, as I was frequently in Orlando on business or to teach at UCF. Once we had each agreed to join this restaurant venture, there was a self-imposed rush for the entire team to meet one another in person. To that point, we had all relied upon Chris's judgment of character, hoping that the team would be as strong as he had perceived. It was time to see for ourselves. After teaching a class one afternoon, Jason, Chris, and I grabbed some lunch at a little restaurant in Chris's neighborhood, which was also conveniently located near the first potential restaurant site. This first get-to-know-you session lasted several hours, and Jason and I really hit it off. From that first meeting, we began debating various issues and sharing philosophies, long-term goals, and aspirations. In addition, each of our prime responsibilities was required early in the development process and, as such, Chris, Jason, and I quickly began to develop a solid working relationship. As was the case with Chris, I spoke with Jason on a regular basis, often several times a day. This was amazing, considering the fact that we were both committed to a common venture even before meeting one another. The initial meeting with Jason, however, made me feel quite comfortable with the decision I had made to join this team. If the rest of the team was as qualified and well prepared as he was, our chances for success would be pretty solid.

By day, Jason was a vice president with one of the largest restaurant and hospitality real estate investment trusts in the country. Specifically, he was involved with restaurant acquisitions. Prior to this role, Jason held various positions in investment banking and commercial lending, having analyzed, underwritten, negotiated, or worked out more than $2 billion worth of restaurant finance business at a relatively young age. With a degree in economics and finance, Jason also brought operational experience to the table. Throughout his operational tours of duty, he was fortunate enough to hold a variety of positions in both the front-of-house and back-of-house. Operational experience is always a plus, maybe even a must, when one is considering entering into the restaurant business — or should I say the *Business of Restaurants*? Restaurants are unique entities, and all potential owners should know how they operate from the inside out, even if operations is not the owner's primary scope of responsibility.

Now, you may be wondering how Jason and Chris knew each other. Chris was head of the Center for Multi-Unit Restaurant Management at UCF's hospitality school. As part of this effort, in May of each year Chris hosted two weeks of professional education seminars. Jason was enrolled in one of Chris's classes and they just hit it off. Later, Jason became affiliated with UCF's hospitality school as an advisory board member of the Center for Multi-Unit Restaurant Management. His lectures and research were shared with industry executives worldwide. Somewhat unusual for a numbers guy, Jason loved *the deal*. And because of his passion, he quickly assumed the role of lead negotiator for our team on items such as legal correspondence, leases, acquisitions, and the like. He had three modes of conversing: chatting, schmooze mode, and heavy schmooze mode (a term he often used to describe his own efforts). And while Jason brought a number of positive qualities to the table, perhaps his most valuable qualities were his patience, his ability to play devil's advocate, and his capability to remove emotion from any business decision. Opening a restaurant is very emotional, and Jason brought a sense of calm and a high level of expectation to the process, not to mention his belief in destiny. His constant advice to be patient was insightful and well-stated. In his mind, this restaurant development effort was destined to be successful, and nothing was going to stand in our way. Jason was a strong believer in fate, frequently assuring me that "If it is meant to be, it will happen." While I am not as strong a believer in fate, as I believe one has to make something happen for oneself, it was difficult to argue with him given the way this team developed and matured in such a short period of time.

Aaron: Operations

Aaron, like me, was a former student of Chris—he was an MBA student at UCF, although not in the hospitality program. He enrolled in one of Chris's classes out of pure interest. In his primary role for our emerging company, Aaron brought a wealth of operational credentials. Having served as a restaurant manager in Missouri and Georgia, Aaron's most valuable experience came as an area manager for a national restaurant chain's central Florida operations. In this role, Aaron was responsible for $10 million worth of annual sales and, more importantly, the numerous "unique" situations that arose as part of overseeing several multi-million dollar operations in the restaurant industry. Any experienced restaurant veteran will certainly understand that the employees in our industry often present non-traditional challenges for their managers and coworkers. This is just the nature of the beast. If you are not a restaurant industry veteran, take my word for it: those in the service profession live a lifestyle unlike many others. The hours are crazy. The schedules are inconsistent. Unless an employee has secured seniority, having worked his or her way up among the other employees after years of service, life is always at the mercy of the schedule.

As our Executive Vice President of Operations, Aaron's scope of responsibility included developing and implementing service standards, training, human resource policies, management policies, and other such operational matters. In the world of restaurants, operations is a general term that covers anything to do with overseeing the restaurant while it is running. Conveniently for our group, Aaron was not only an operations specialist, but a licensed commercial real estate agent as well. This was yet another advantage for our company, providing an inside track on potential restaurant sites—an important position given our hope and anticipation from Day One that we would be a multi-unit restaurant company. Aaron had access to sites and landlords through his real estate connections, and as a former resident of Orlando, he was familiar with our initial target market. He could travel around the city looking for potential sites, speaking with landlords and other commercial real estate agents, and then report his findings back to the group. More importantly, we were assured that we had an agent who had our best interests in mind. As if this combination of talents weren't enough, in the middle of our restaurant development project, Aaron decided that he wanted to attend law school. No complaints here—we can just add "lawyer" to the already-rich pool of in-house resources.

BRIAN: FOOD, PART I

At Cornell, Chris and Brian teamed up as my TCAB professors. Chris was my classroom and dining room instructor while Brian, Executive Chef at both Cornell's hotel school and the Statler Hotel at the time, was my TCAB chef. When Chris indicated that Brian was interested in assuming the role of corporate chef, a surreal feeling came over me. I was being asked to join my two TCAB professors to create a new restaurant concept, this time in the real world and not in the classroom. Yes, I said TCAB—the very class that I tried to drop in college. I could not help but think what a great opportunity this was, having paid for such access only a few years earlier. Chris and Brian go way back and have been personal friends for quite some time. You should also know that Brian and Chris were partners in their own restaurant years ago in the northeast, the one that closed its doors after just one year. But this time was going to be different. Chris was assembling his team and was focused on correcting the mistakes they had made the first time. Shortly after we initiated our effort, Brian made a trip to Orlando to meet some of the other team members, see some of the potential restaurant sites, and further discuss the development effort. Wanting to show Brian around, Chris provided a guided tour of the city, the sites, and some of the emerging concepts in the market, a hot bed for new concept development in the restaurant industry. What a great time that was—traveling around the city, observing, discussing, admiring, and critiquing various restaurant concepts with two of my former professors. How often does one have such an opportunity? Not often, I can assure you of that.

Early on, Brian took our initial input and developed a preliminary menu. It was one of the first tangible components of the restaurant that we could touch, feel, and wrap our arms around. In dramatic form, Chef Brian sent a memorable e-mail to properly prepare us for the menu we were about to read. I feel compelled to share it with you now, as it will give you some insight into the process, the excitement, and the emotion involved.

Remember, a menu is the sales tool that promotes your product. The shell of the property is part of the equation, but a much smaller part. One can have a palace, but with no substance to it, it's just mortar and brick. The menu is the communication between the customer and the sales team. You are left alone with it for a few sacred moments to determine what energy you will exchange for nourishment. It sets the tone, once the greeting has been shared. At this crucial encounter, expectations are set, the ancient process of trade begins, and the curtain opens. The dance of the second-oldest profession on the planet begins by looking at the "carte." The menu will be the personification of your dreams, the tally sheet for all who work for you. It will drive food costs, labor costs, the service style, ambience, the way you manage, and the ultimate success or failure of your operation. This, my dear friends, is what you have entrusted unto me. When it arrives, it should be gently reviewed, studied for its witty use of prose and cross-utilization of product. It unveils a sense of warmth and hospitality and an expectation similar to sex. Enjoy every second of the review. Then, after a few minutes of relaxing in the afterglow, enjoy the memory of it. Then, again, take a pencil in hand and drive it hard against the page, turning the offerings over and over in your mind, recreating what the chef has given you. Mold it in your own dream. Make it your love slave. The menu should arrive later today, so stock up on tissue, and have a cigarette before you call.

This is the type of enthusiasm that needs to be present for success in this business, although enthusiasm alone does not guarantee success. Brian's involvement early in the process was invaluable, as he offered substantial creative input that is evident even in the final generation of our menu. The timing of this effort was difficult for Brian, however, as his newlywed status and recent change in jobs left him little time to dedicate to the growing demands of our effort. Desiring to stay involved in spite of his lack of time, Brian offered to act as a culinary consultant to the group and resigned his position as corporate chef. As the old saying goes, with the closing of every door, another one opens.

DANIEL: FOOD, PART II

Chris reached back into his personal talent pool to fill the newly created vacancy in our team. Fortunately, Chris didn't have to reach far. In fact, he managed to keep his choice in the family — his brother-in-law Daniel, to be specific. Daniel was an accomplished executive chef with impressive credentials. His culinary experience and enthusiasm were evident from Day One. Even more importantly for our company, he excelled at breaking down and standardizing the recipes and ingredients. Furthermore, Daniel did not temper his creativity, quickly picking up on the style and objectives of our menu development process and offering welcomed suggestions and modifications. Having joined our group after its initial formation, Daniel was quite surprised by our collective talent and focus following his first participation in one of our weekly conference calls. He picked up right where Brian had left off, analyzing and formalizing recipes, focusing on suppliers and ingredients, and offering input based on his impressive culinary background. Trained at the Culinary Institute of America, he brought with him nearly 30 years of culinary experience in four-star and five-diamond hotels, restaurants, and upscale grocery venues. Prior to joining our effort, Daniel was the executive chef for the prepared foods department at the flagship store for Wegmans, one of the most progressive and forward-thinking grocery markets in the country. I had the good fortune of shopping at this particular grocery chain during my four years in Ithaca, New York. I can tell you that their presentation, quality, and marketing skills are among the best I have ever seen in the grocery store industry. They were offering home meal replacements, prepared foods, take-and-bake pizzas, and made-to-order sandwiches before most other grocery store chains in this country had even considered the concept. The combined input of Daniel and Brian was invaluable, with significant, positive effects on our company.

HAROLD: MAIN MONEY

For some time, Harold, a long-time friend of Chris from Ithaca, New York, had expressed his desire to invest in a restaurant development effort spearheaded by Chris. So, when this opportunity presented itself, Chris called Harold and asked if he was still interested. Harold was in!

Bottom line: We never could have launched the restaurant concept without Harold. True, he was our main financial backer, but he brought much more to the table as both an investor and an advisor with decades of hospitality experience. Fortunately for us, Harold had a desire to become involved and stay involved in the development of our company. With over 30 years of experience in the foodservice industry, much of which was in university dining, and a master's degree in Hospitality Management, he afforded us yet another well-educated, valuable perspective for our efforts. Several months into the development process, Harold was jokingly referred to as Charlie (as in Charlie's Angels) because at that point only Chris had met him in person. To the rest of us he was a strong, well-spoken voice on the other end of the phone, frequently offering advice on our "mission." Harold jumped at any opportunity to get involved and offer hands-on assistance. In one of his supporting roles, he traveled to Bellingham, Washington, for recipe and menu testing. In yet another example of his contributions, he and Chris attended a retailers' show, designed to match retailers with developers and landlords. Because this was early in our development process and well before any of our restaurants were open, the only thing that Harold and Chris had to pass out was a business card. This was the first introduction of our restaurant concept to the major players in the Orlando market. With Harold's assistance, the attendees were lined up three deep just to learn more about our new restaurant concept. This was no small feat, as several of the world's top restaurant companies were in attendance.

MARK: MORE MONEY

We had one additional investor, Mark, who was another friend of Chris. Mark had anticipated assuming a role as a passive investor. As time passed by, however, he became more involved with our efforts — especially at critical times. His input and involvement grew throughout the process, and he became another invaluable resource to the team. He was a developer and a landlord with years of practical business experience that was evident in every word he uttered. Mark had the ability to cut to the chase, avoiding any fancy speak. He frequently offered a fresh perspective, and his insights were always welcomed by the rest of the owners.

And there is our team: seven individuals with an impressive set of credentials and a common desire for calculated, controlled growth and success. As you can see, this was not your average group of guys who, over a beer one afternoon in late July, decided to open a restaurant. No, this was a carefully planned effort to create a new multi-unit restaurant entity that would hopefully be designed for success from the very start.

This was a group that was in the *Business of Restaurants*, and not the *Restaurant Business*.

❖ ❖ ❖

In college I took a course on entrepreneurship. One of the key lessons that my professor shared with our class repeatedly was "*choose your partners more carefully than you choose your spouse.*" This is good advice, but we weren't following it. We all shared one thing: trust. Based on our individual relationships with Chris, we had all trusted his judgment in assembling a qualified team. I am not saying that this was a good idea; in fact, it was downright risky and could have proven to be one of the worst decisions of my career. Who can look you in the eye, with a straight face, and advise you to invest money, sign personal guarantees, and put the future of your family's financial well-being on the line with a group of complete strangers? Answer: no one. This was just the method that we selected at the time, based on the opportunity before us. In fact, to this day it is surprising to me that it worked at all; not that we didn't have our fair share of problems — and some were significant, as you will learn.

We had optimists and pessimists. We had dreamers and realists. We had both long-term and short-term strategists. Quite often, these opposite qualities were expressed by the same people on different days, further demonstrating the unique capabilities of our team. As Jason once said, this was a polygamous marriage. And it was! Just imagine the occasional challenges that arise in a two-party marriage. Now try a seven-party partnership! Much like a marriage, this dynamic relationship has experienced ups and downs. For better or worse, in sickness and in health, until the end of our desired collaboration do we part. It required selfless attitude and constant focus on the ultimate goal of developing a successful organization. What made the risk worthwhile in my own mind was that I believed we all shared common values and objectives. This was a side venture for each of us, as we all held full-time positions and had no intention of leaving our day jobs to pursue this opportunity full time. This, too, was a characteristic of our efforts with its own set of pros and cons. We all had hopes and dreams of success, but deep down inside there was a love for the process of creating and opening a new restaurant concept. I am not saying that we would have been satisfied with failure, but if that undesirable notion became our reality, there would be a silver lining in that we all had spent time doing something that we loved. It was a unique set of qualities that our group shared. In the end, however, the element of trust cannot be overlooked. After all, we were sharing our personal financial statements, providing access to our tax returns, and discussing very personal issues among the team, keeping in mind that at the start of this process, we were all virtual strangers to one another.

This team did look good on paper, but we were unproven at this point. It was time for us to put our own team into action and see if we would be able to live up to our own expectations. Although we would not be able to determine the answer for some time to come, there were several key indications early in our process that success was at least possible. Despite our areas of focus, each team member showed an interest in the others' scopes of work. Chris challenged me on some of my early designs, I challenged Brian and Daniel on the menu, and Aaron challenged Jason on the financial projections. This was not a sign of disrespect, although other teams might have perceived such challenges as questioning one's knowledge or capabilities. On the contrary, it was a sign that we were all focused on the success of this effort. We wanted to make sure that we were considering every angle and point of view possible, and setting up a company that could truly benefit from the in-house knowledge we possessed.

It wasn't just the team's knowledge and experience that would prove to be an invaluable asset, but also our collective access to information. Each of us held positions in fields that were tangential to the restaurant industry — supporting roles that afforded us valuable data. For instance, Chris often consulted for many large restaurant companies. Through his consulting and educational efforts, he received regular exposure to various theories and concepts utilized by these trend-setting companies. He gained insight into their corporate structure, ownership models, views on potential areas of growth, and strategies, just to name a few valuable pieces of information. This information, of course, came in handy during our own strategic planning process, enabling our management team to pick and choose from the various policies of others to develop a strategy that best fit our concept and objectives. Jason was in a similar position, given his involvement in financial dealings having to do with bankruptcies, workouts, acquisitions, and other such transactions. With his direct involvement in these activities, Jason learned a great deal about what *not* to do, and we formulated our company's plan around this advice. We wanted our company to be attractive for sale from Day One, recognizing that the development and sale of this restaurant concept was one possible strategy. As such, Jason provided us with a number of financial ratios that would have to be met in order to make our company attractive to a potential buyer. These ratios helped us determine our construction budget, viable lease rates, required tenant improvement dollars from a landlord, and other such targets. In essence, these ratios drove many of our key decisions early in the development process. There was nothing illegal or dishonest about this, as we would never violate the trust or rights of privacy of our clients. It was advantageous for our newly formed company, however, to have such experiences to consider as we were making our own decisions.

The team's combined skill set allowed us to more objectively evaluate opportunities and challenges. To demonstrate this benefit, let's take a look at our site evaluation processes. Many first-time restaurant developers might select a site without properly evaluating available data. Sure, there are demographic reports and research that an aspiring restaurant owner *could* access, but I can tell you from years of experience that this does not occur as often as it should. In fact, many first-time restaurant developers with whom I have worked do not understand the process enough to even know what information they need or where to get it. While financial projections might be considered in an independent restaurateur's decision, what are such projections based on? Table turns? Check averages? Food cost percentages? Again, from past experience I can tell you that few first-time restaurateurs take the time to compile such data. Given our resources, the site selection process in our group would be executed in a more formal manner. Aaron, through his access as a real estate agent, would find a site and simultaneously report on the demographic information for the area. We would obtain a floor plan of the potential space from a developer, and I would begin sketching to see how our concept would fit in the space. Though one can use an average per-square-foot rule to try to determine the number of seats a space can accommodate, general formulas such as these do a poor job of considering site-specific characteristics such as the shape of the space, the number and location of doors, stairways, or columns. With a preliminary layout in hand, I would relay the actual number of seats to the team, and an accurate financial projection would be developed. Nothing was guaranteed, but you can see that our systematic methods led to more accurate information and, thus, more accurate decisions—or so we hoped.

As a design professional, I often recommend to restaurateurs that it is well worth their money to pay for a preliminary sketch before committing to a lease for a space. Too often I am faced with a client who has already signed a lease and only then finds out that the space will not work for the layout or concept that they had in mind. Visualization is an acquired skill for many. As a result, the preliminary planning efforts executed by these first-time restaurant developers often are inaccurate and lead to false expectations. For instance, I spoke with a gentleman who felt he had planned out his restaurant accurately. Once I began questioning some of his assumptions and reviewing his sketches, however, I found that he had made some erroneous assumptions and critical design mistakes. His bathrooms were too small to comply with local codes and did not contain the necessary aisles around the restrooms. Much of the equipment that he had sketched was to the wrong dimension, allowing him to depict a layout that would not work in reality. His walkways were only two feet wide. There were many such errors, which gave him a false sense of security, and thus the confidence to sign the lease, as he was *sure* that the space would support the design that he had created. He was wrong, and it was a costly mistake.

The members of our team also had a collective desire to fix the failures we were all forced to deal with in our daily professions. This was our opportunity to do it the *right* way, at least from our perspective. Jason was frequently involved in financial workouts of companies that had made critical mistakes in their preliminary financial planning. With his experience, he wanted to make sure that we avoided such costly errors in our own venture from Day One. Similarly, I was frequently hired to remedy the failures of a previous designer or help a restaurateur make a space work that was insufficient in the first place. During the course of his interaction with numerous emerging concepts, Chris had seen drastic errors by companies that understood neither the marketplace nor their position within that marketplace. Our team had a wealth of first-hand experience from watching former clients demonstrate what *not* to do, which was essential in helping us determine what we *should* do. We wanted to benefit from these valuable lessons and use them to the advantage of our newly formed company.

While each of us had known Chris individually, we needed to

establish open lines of communication among ourselves so that we could begin making progress and getting to know one another better. As I have said, this was a marriage—an arranged marriage, for that matter—and the same need to become better acquainted with the partners existed. We began with group e-mails, but as the issues became more complex and required more discussion, we knew that we would have to find an alternative method of communication that was both practical and affordable. We were very sensitive about the use of our precious capital and did not want to spend any money unnecessarily. The importance of these conversations was supported by the fact that most of us resided in different cities and states. At the beginning of the process, I lived in Tampa, Aaron lived in South Florida, Daniel and Mark resided in upstate New York, and Harold's main residence was in Pennsylvania. Only Chris and Jason actually lived in Orlando, the market we identified for our first restaurant. We were all over the place, which you would think would be an obstacle to our success. Knowing that we needed to overcome the geographical barrier, early on we established a weekly phone call, held on Sunday nights. Everyone called in from their respective locations and we would address any issues that were pertinent to our stage in the development process. Even when there weren't any pressing issues, the habit of speaking with one another at least once a week was positive for unity within our group.

There was another upside to this team: future opportunities. We had all entered this venture with the hope that we would try to grow the concept to between five and ten stores in the Orlando area, and then re-evaluate our position. If we were able to achieve these goals, we would then determine whether it was time to sell the concept or hire professional managers to run and grow the concept even further. We had already talked about the possibility of creating additional concepts. It makes sense to diversify and have the capability to offer clients a portfolio of restaurant concepts. We already had a second concept in mind before we ever opened the first restaurant. Besides, it was the concept creation part that we truly loved. We were, however, smart enough to stay focused on this first concept and not get distracted or spread ourselves too thin.

So there you have it. Hopefully I have been able to demonstrate the unique qualities of this team. We could only hope that our collective experience and knowledge would give us a leg up on the average first-time restaurant developer. With our team in place, it was time to begin our journey.

3

GRASPING THE CONCEPT

During each semester that I taught my class at UCF, I would ask my students to define the term *concept* for me, as it relates to restaurants. It is a common term used liberally throughout the industry, but it is often used in differing contexts. In a nutshell, I personally define *concept* as everything that defines what the restaurant is to its customers, staff, community, and investors. It includes the menu, décor, imagery, logo, marketing strategy, unique service styles, financial philosophies, and so much more. By the time we opened our doors for business, I was in love with *our* restaurant concept. This wasn't always the case. When we first started discussing the concept of our restaurant, it did not sound to me as though the differentiation was strong enough from some existing restaurants, which was unacceptable in my mind. Given the composition of our team, my expectations were quite high. I wanted to participate in the development of a unique, distinctive restaurant that would separate itself from the competition and offer our patrons an option like no other. As the concept evolved over time, the differentiation from existing restaurant companies became evident.

When Chris originally assembled the team, he did so with a strong inclination of the type and style of restaurant that he wanted to open.

There will be more on the ownership structure in the next chapter. For now, the focus is on the restaurant concept itself. I remember talking with Chris in the halls at UCF when he first began to share his vision, which was inspired by a restaurant on the other side of the Atlantic. During a trip to England, Chris visited a restaurant chain called Pizza Express that offered a number of high-end gourmet pizzas, not unlike a California Pizza Kitchen here in the United States. However, the menu mix was quite different and featured a European slant. A similar concept in the Orlando marketplace would offer local clientele a fresh alternative. As we would eventually learn through the evolution of our concept, Pizza Express's menu was not our only inspiration. Rather, there were other key features of the English restaurant chain that we believed would fair well in our marketplace. First was the affordability of the dining experience. Chris and his wife were able to go out to a nice dinner and order a full meal that included an appetizer, gourmet pizza, dessert, and a glass of wine, without breaking the bank. The entire experience was affordable. The average check for this European-style pizzeria was the equivalent of around $15 per person. Due to the level of service, the atmosphere, and a variety of other factors, the experience felt like it was worth much more. The end result was a true sense of value. This soon became one of our key descriptors for the restaurant concept we were developing—we would seek to offer a $30 experience at a $15 price tag. It was similar to the advertising campaign used by Target: expect more, pay less. We wanted each and every customer to feel as though they were receiving tremendous value.

This idea of an affordable experience was particularly interesting to me. As the parent of a two-and-a-half-year-old at the time, my wife and I had a difficult time going out to dinner and a movie for less than $100. This did not equate to an elaborate evening on the town, but by the time you added up the dinner ($45–$50, including tip), the movie ($15), and the babysitter ($35), it became quite an expensive evening. The $45–$50 range is easy to reach at almost any casual restaurant. After tossing more than $100 at an evening, my wife and I just didn't have the sense that we had received much for our money by the time the evening was over. Our new restaurant would address this lack of perceived value in two ways. First, we would offer quality menu entrées in the $10–$12 price range for dinner, with selected items priced even lower. This way, if a couple wanted to enjoy an evening out but did not want to spend $20–$25 on an a la carte entrée, they would have a less expensive alternative. Second, regardless of the price point of entrée chosen, we would offer an atmosphere, ambiance, and style of service that, at a minimum, would provide the customer with a sense of value. Our concept included an open kitchen, staff interaction, creative interior design, and live music. Such an ambiance is typically not available at an establishment with entrées available for $10 on a Saturday evening.

The second aspect that we designed our concept around was the profitability associated with the pizza product. You have already heard me discuss at length the difference between those in the *Restaurant Business* and those in the *Business of Restaurants*. This was a key component of developing a profitable new restaurant concept. After all, we were in this to make money. Pizza is clearly an American favorite. It is also a fairly inexpensive product to make, with cheese being the most expensive ingredient. While the average food cost for a restaurant can run in the neighborhood of 30 percent, meaning that the combined cost of the food accounted for 30 percent of the total cost of revenue, the average food cost for pizza was much lower, in the 15 percent range. Furthermore, we would be riding the coattails of one of the industry's greatest pioneers, Wolfgang Puck. Wolfgang Puck was one of the first to experiment with and offer high-quality, gourmet ingredients on pizza. California Pizza Kitchen took this concept to the next step, fueling widespread acceptance of this type of cuisine, even making it available in the frozen section of your local grocery store. Believe it or not, the inclusion of gourmet ingredients on these pizzas can actually help lower the food cost, as less cheese is required on the pizzas. This did not equate to a reduction in the quality or quantity of the ingredients. Rather, the inclusion of too much cheese on these gourmet-style pies would overwhelm the palate and drown out the flavors that were being offered. In essence, it was a win-win scenario. The customer received better ingredients and a unique taste, and it was less expensive to produce this type of menu item.

A third influence from Chris's dining experience at Pizza Express was the need for this concept to be a small, neighborhood location, situated "among the rooftops." These restaurants needed to be in or near the neighborhoods where people lived. The concept was designed to be the local neighborhood favorite. We wanted to be the restaurant of choice two to three times a week, not once a month, and our pricing-value ratio was designed to help us achieve that goal. Consider the original strategy of California Pizza Kitchen. They focused almost exclusively on restaurants in malls and high-traffic areas. This was not where we wanted to be.

Interestingly enough, during our development process, California Pizza Kitchen announced an initiative, modifying their site-selection strategy for new stores. They began locating some restaurants closer to the neighborhoods where their customers lived.

As the evolution of our concept continued, we began to realize that the focus on pizza was, perhaps, too limiting. While we were quite pleased with the low food-cost model and potential profitability associated with selling gourmet pizzas, such a limited menu did not offer us the unique market position and mix of menu offerings that we were after. In fact, the original name that we selected for the restaurant, Pizza Bistro, sounded limiting as well. Looking at the logistics of producing the food in our restaurant, we knew that we would require a stone-hearth oven to produce the type of product that we wanted. Through our conversations, we then began to discuss other menu items that could be cooked in this oven while maintaining the desired food-cost percentage — or at least close to it. After thorough research, we were able to identify several such items and justify them in our cost structure.

The natural evolution of our restaurant was in full swing, and we were emerging as an oven-based concept, not just a pizza place. Everything that we produced, aside from the cold items, would be produced in the oven and in front of the guest. In addition, we would not be an Italian restaurant, but rather a European-influenced bistro offering menu items with heritage from various parts of Europe. It was unique, it was fresh, and it was a concept we felt the general public would embrace. We would be able to limit the amount of equipment required to produce the food, reducing the cost of the opening equipment package and increasing our potential profitability.

The original name that we selected, Pizza Bistro, would soon be modified as well, and 'Za-Bistro! would emerge as our name of choice. One evening in the Muller household, Chris proposed that the family order pizza for dinner. But Chris, using some of his dated terminology, insisted that he wanted "za" for dinner. Back when Chris was a youngster in college, "za" was short for pizza — as if pizza were a lengthy word that required abbreviating. Nevertheless, Chris's choice of words was quickly picked up by his oldest daughter.

> "That's it, Dad!" she exclaimed. "That's the name of the restaurant. It's 'Za-Bistro!"

And so the name of our restaurant concept became official—'Za-Bistro! Our new name not only retained its connection to the original, Pizza Bistro, and the roots of our concept, but it also seemed to offer a different perception to potential customers. This was confirmed in the initial market research that we conducted. Leveraging the bistro nomenclature was indicative of the menu varieties that we would offer, and the 'Za portion of the name supported the European influence while also referencing the abbreviation for pizza. The punctuation was added intentionally to provide a sense of movement and excitement as an integral part of the name. The apostrophe, hyphen, and exclamation point were part of our imaging and branding efforts.

Given the objectives and nature of our restaurant, we determined that it was a perfect fit for the emerging town centers that were being built throughout Orlando. These town centers, developed as part of the traditional neighborhood design movement, feature lively interaction among the buildings, people, and sidewalks. As an associate member of the American Institute of Architects, I was fortunate to attend a lecture by (and actually meet) Leon Krier, a recognized father of neo-urbanism. His lecture clearly defined the objectives of these town centers. This may get a bit philosophical for a minute or two, so bear with me, as I believe that the theory is important to fully understanding our rationale for targeting these emerging town center developments.

The physical design of our cities has a great deal to do with the way that we live our lives. With a few exceptions, most of the growth in America over the past several decades has included an emerging downtown area as a center for business activity and the expansion of suburbs for homes and residences around this core. In such a scenario, the elimination of height restrictions on buildings resulted in the construction of skyscrapers and other tall structures in downtown areas. Subsequently, the value of this real estate rose rapidly. As a result of this increased property value, downtown residents and numerous businesses required to support everyday life, such as grocery stores and pharmacies, were quickly pushed out of these urban areas, as they could not afford the cost of living or conducting business. The net result was growth in the suburbs, where housing and other life essentials were more affordable, leading to the subsequent death of the downtown area outside of typical business hours. For decades, many downtown areas in medium-sized and small cities have remained quiet during the weekends and weeknights. Businesses and activities that support everyday life have emerged within suburbia, following the migration of the population.

Now consider the development style in much of Europe, which is quite different. The average European city is typically not more than five or six stories in height, with fewer tall buildings. As a result, there is an evenly distributed combination of residential and retail entities throughout all areas of the city. Primarily due to the physical configuration and development of the city, one is able to live, work, and shop in the local neighborhood without having to travel very far. Daily needs can be supported within the immediate vicinity. Residences, offices, and retail venues are mixed within the same proximity. This example leads to an entirely different lifestyle. One can stop by the market on the way home each and every night, as opposed to hopping in the car and driving to the grocery store once a week, as is often the way of life in American suburbia. Parents can send their child downstairs for some milk or eggs. Yes, this type of environment exists in some of the big cities in the Unites States, but that is the exception and not the rule. As Leon Krier so eloquently and clearly displayed in his presentation, the common method of growth throughout the United States is unnatural. We spend our lives commuting back and forth in our cars, from home to work and then work to home. This dependency on cars affects our quality of life, the design of our cities, our political objectives, and even the contents of our food. Consider for a moment how much time and money we as a society spend on commuting to and from work. Look at the cost of owning a car—the cost of purchasing or leasing your automobile, the cost of repairs and maintenance, the cost of gas, the cost of insurance; all for an asset that depreciates in value. Do you have two cars? Do you really want to have two cars, or are you forced to have two cars just to support the lifestyle resulting from the design of our cities?

Leon Krier showed a slide in his presentation of a man and a woman. The next slide showed a satirical, clearly ridiculous set of options for the growth of their family. The first picture depicted the man, the woman, and two children. The second picture illustrated the man and the woman at twice their normal size. The male and female subjects appeared to have been over-inflated with air and were abnormally huge. What Mr. Krier was trying to demonstrate was the fact that growth in our cities should be comparable to growth in nature—new objects are created in proportion to the original objects. He was illustrating that the growth of the family occurs by the addition of new, proportional family members and not by the *enlargement* of the original family members. When considering the growth of our cityscapes, Mr. Krier was advocating proportional growth, while simultaneously demonstrating how unnatural and destructive our blueprints for growth in the United States have been to our way of life. The lifestyle provided by the European city model has become more appealing to Americans in recent years.

With the objective of establishing new neighborhoods featuring a mix of residences, office spaces, and retail establishments, numerous sections of Orlando initiated the development of town centers. The lifestyle offered by these town centers paralleled the way of life that results from European city design, while offering amenities to which Americans have become accustomed. Given the nature of our concept, the menu, the style of service, and our objectives, we felt as though these town centers were a perfect match for 'Za-Bistro!, and we began targeting them for potential locations for our restaurant throughout the city. The neighborhood feel, activity throughout the day, and increased foot traffic were just what we felt we needed to be successful. There were several of these town centers under development in the Orlando area, and we began reaching out to them.

Richard Melman, the world-renowned restaurant developer, has used a successful approach in the development of many of his restaurants. He creates a storyline—a real storyline—comparable to what might be developed for a movie. The reason that this technique is so helpful is that it ensures authenticity and offers a constant guide that can be used in making the numerous decisions required during the concept development process. To be most helpful, the storyline must be developed in extraordinary detail. Actual characters, locations, events, and feelings must all be reflected in the story to give it real personality. Once developed, the story can then be used as a barometer for decisions that must be made. Say, for instance, that a center-city location becomes available in the middle of a high-income area. However, the concept as defined in the storyline requires a waterfront location, and the site that has become available is surrounded by buildings and pavement. A decision must be made, realizing that a variance could lead to many decisions straying from the original concept. The same would hold true for selections of interior finishes. It could be a chair, light fixture, or bathroom sink that was deemed to be attractive or a good value. Yet, once again, if the elements do not complement the storyline, they can begin to deteriorate the validity of the concept.

I would like to tell you that we implemented this technique and developed a detailed storyline as I have just described, but, in all honesty, we did not. What we did do was identify customer profiles that we planned to target, and develop a concept description that we felt would meet our customers' needs. From the outset, we had determined that we wanted to be female friendly. Women are often the key decision-makers in a group, with their male counterparts abiding by the decisions that are made. Our logic was simple: if the women liked us, the men would follow. We wanted to be family friendly too, but we would not be featuring happy meals or a slide for the kids to play on. Kids were welcome, but they were expected to behave like grownups for the night. Our menu structure and culinary offerings were designed to provide our guests with the opportunity to make of the experience what they desired, in size, number of courses, and price. It was conceivable that one party could have an average check of $11, with a $7 wrap and a $4 glass of wine, while an adjacent party could easily have an average check of $40 or more, depending on their appetizer, entrée, wine, and dessert selections. The idea was that our guests could custom tailor the experience to their time, palate, and budget. The dessert menu and dessert wine list also offered the potential for the concept to become a late-night, after-movie destination. Regardless of the menu items selected, the environment would support a sophisticated experience without a pretentious, stuffy atmosphere.

Listed below are various excerpts from an early version of our business plan that described our concept.

The 'Za-Bistro! concept is a casual, upscale, sophisticated, neighborhood, family-friendly café bistro serving gourmet dishes cooked in an open-flame, stone-hearth oven and set in an exposition kitchen. Menu items will include European-style hand-tossed pizzas, bistro specialties, fresh salads, oven sandwiches, baked dishes, and extravagant desserts, complemented by a full wine list by the glass, craft beers, and specialty coffees and teas.

The target market consists of locals within a 1.5- to 3-mile trade area of new "neo-urban" town centers, or perhaps a 10-minute drive, targeting ages 25–60. The environment will be comfortable and inviting for single diners, couples, and families with kids at dinner, but geared more specifically toward couples later in the evening who are looking for a sophisticated but casual experience offering beer and wine only in order to avoid a "bar" feel. We will have two-piece live jazz and adult contemporary musical entertainment on Fridays and Saturdays, with an opportunity for local musical talent consistent with the ambiance and theme during the rest of the week. With value as one of our core competencies, we will offer full table service, with main entrées in the $10–$12 price range per person for dinner, and $8 for lunch. Operating hours will be Sun-Thurs, 11 a.m.–10 p.m.; Fri-Sat, 11 a.m.–Midnight.

Our ideal restaurant seats 120, with additional outside seating under canvas umbrellas being very desirable. Our designs will be hip but not too pretentious or funky.

Using existing market concepts, 'Za-Bistro! will have a thoughtful, original menu available within a warm, inviting atmosphere that will feature an open kitchen area and a prominent open-flame, stone-hearth oven. No bar seating will be available, but "counter seating" will offer guests the opportunity to watch and interact with our culinary team as they produce the sultry menu items for which we will be known.

Key words for the concept: European/Mediterranean, Neighborhood, Sophisticated but Casual, Jazz, Exposition Kitchen featuring an Open-Flame Oven, Bistro, Pizza, Wine

As a European-bistro concept, the focal point of 'Za-Bistro! is an open-flame oven and display kitchen, which is fully visible throughout the dining room. This central area will feature a dining counter, allowing for open interaction between the culinary staff and patrons.

The primary colors of the logo, and the restaurant, will be a burgundy and reflex (bright) blue, with neutral tones for secondary coloring throughout the space. Research on the psychology of colors in restaurants conducted by the University of Michigan has determined that the maroon will offer a calm environment, while the blue, a cool color, will stir some excitement. The blue will be used as an accent throughout the restaurant: walls, lighting fixtures, tabletop presentation, etc.

The dining room will be comprised of multiple, smaller dining sections to offer the intimacy of a European-style bistro. Half walls with risers and headers will be used to divide these sections, resulting in a feeling of separate spaces, while maintaining most sightlines throughout the restaurant's front-of-house.

As the idea and concept of this new restaurant began to take shape, we started to survey the landscape to determine whether there was a demand for such a concept, and if so, how it would fit within the current marketplace. While our team was passionate about our desire to open a restaurant, we did not want to open just *any* restaurant. Rather, we wanted to carve out our niche and make a name for ourselves. We wanted to push the envelope. We wanted to be original. In the end, we wanted to create something that was fresh and new, not a "me too." This was an opportunity for the academic world to meet the real world. What a fantastic case study! But in order to benefit fully from this case study, we would have to implement a collection of our personal theories and beliefs. These were the same philosophies that we believed separated us from the crowd of other first-time restaurateurs.

We anticipated that in order to achieve this objective, we would likely have to include both the development of our own original ideas and modifications and adaptations to existing practices. In fact, some of the most successful companies in our business have been able to modify the customers' perceptions in order to achieve their desired position within the marketplace. Outback, for instance, is a steakhouse—not that different from numerous other casual steakhouse restaurants. However, the Australian theme, spicy flavor profiles, and original menu items helped Outback separate its concept from the rest of the pack, and ultimately played an important role in its eventual success. Perhaps an even better example is Starbucks, whose success has been well documented. Think for a minute about Maxwell House or Folgers, both of whom dominated the coffee market long before Starbucks was ever created. Either one of these companies had the infrastructure and resources to squash Starbucks when the company was in its infancy. What they didn't have was an understanding of the market and their place within that market. Maxwell House and Folgers sell their product for a fraction of what Starbucks charges, and never capitalized on the retail opportunities. What these companies failed to realize is that Starbucks' customers aren't just buying coffee; they are buying image, status, and an experience. They are paying $4 for a cup of coffee because they like the ambiance and aroma in the store. They like ordering a *venti* instead of a large. They want the choice of selecting from a variety of quality roasted beans and creative yet authentic flavors. Starbucks, like Outback, studied the market and developed a method to package and present their products in a way that their core customer base could not resist. That, too, was our objective but on a smaller, more modest scale. These establishments were not the first to sell steaks or coffee, but they were able to re-invent the way that steaks and coffees were sold, with their unique spin on the products. Now we did not expect to be the next Outback or Starbucks, but we did hope to utilize elements of their strategies and approaches to increase the likelihood of success for our own new restaurant concept.

In the late 1990s and early 2000s, there was the birth of the fast-casual market segment. Led by such concepts as Panera Bread and Chipotle, this was an entire market segment that surveyed the existing marketplace and found a way to bring its products to market with great success because these concepts, too, understood their customers. The fast-casual market segment has successfully responded to the needs and wants of the American public, delivering quality food fast (not fast food) in a desirable environment at reasonable prices. Panera Bread, for example, offers fresh sandwiches on bread baked in the store, soups, and salads, with a single meal typically costing $6–$7. Likewise, Chipotle offers burritos made fresh in front of you with quality ingredients in the same price range. (These burritos are not only tasty, but they are also huge! I have literally stood one on end before—just because I could.) True to the core values of the fast-casual market segment, Chipotle takes pride in the use of corrugated metal, wood, and artwork in their stores to offer a trendy yet inviting ambiance. Compare these concepts, and all that they offer, to some of the early, traditional fast-food chains. With all of their success, the fast-food pioneers are not known for their quality ingredients. Furthermore, their ambiance and service were developed for efficiency, not necessarily for customer satisfaction. For example, the bright colors and hard seats are specifically chosen to discourage patrons from lingering too long. Conversely, Panera Bread and Chipotle have created environments that are inviting, and as a result draw customers to their establishments. True, the average price of a meal at a traditional fast-food restaurant may be a dollar or two less, but the American public has shown that they are willing to pay a little bit more for what they perceive to be an upgraded product in an upgraded environment. The fast-casual market segment has been successful in finding the sweet spot in the price-product relationship. Their products are priced higher than the quick-service segment of the foodservice industry because they are offering a better overall experience. However, the prices are not high enough to drive away customers or compete with the casual-dining segment. The cost difference is one that the customer base is willing to absorb. Like the fast-casual market segment, we were looking for a niche — a void — that we could fill within the existing marketplace's landscape.

Early on, we received confirmation from a variety of different sources that our concept was in fact filling a specific niche. Perhaps the simplest form of feedback we received came from general conversations about our concept, where we described the product that we would offer, the ambiance in which it would be offered, and the anticipated price point. Although not scientifically controlled, the responses we received were extremely positive, especially from members of our target market segments. Furthermore, a number of articles from industry periodicals also confirmed that we were on the right track. This initial feedback was extremely encouraging to our group.

To describe our concept in another way, we were taking California Pizza Kitchen, removing the California portion, replacing it with a European flavor, expanding the entrée portion of the menu, and offering our products in a warm, inviting dining environment, featuring a display kitchen, an open-flame oven, a desirable but affordable selection of beer and wine, and live entertainment — all while focusing on the local community and our support of the local community's efforts. Although this description is not as sexy as the one presented earlier (not to mention the fact that it is a run-on sentence that would likely make my elementary school grammar teachers cringe), it is fairly accurate. Like some of the companies mentioned before, we were attempting to repackage some existing attributes of current restaurants and present them in a new way. Having a clear understanding of our concept and the niche within the marketplace that we wanted to fill helped us make decisions that were right for us, even though they may not have been right for other restaurants.

As a hospitality design professional, I have had the opportunity to meet with countless restaurateurs, and I can tell you that each and every one of them hopes to open several restaurants. I have yet to meet a restaurateur that wanted to open just one. My first meeting with a client, almost predictably, starts out with "We are going to have 15 of these real soon," despite the fact that the first restaurant has yet to open. In reality, some of these individuals never even get their first restaurant open. I, of course, have learned to nod my head in agreement when I hear such aggressive expansion goals, while knowing that the chances of that goal coming to fruition are quite slim. It is time now for me to be hypocritical, however, and tell you that from Day One we planned on 'Za-Bistro! being a multi-unit concept. Trust me, I would cringe as I allowed myself to even think such thoughts, let alone share those thoughts with other people. I could just sense that the other person partaking in the conversation (and assuming my typical role) was thinking, *Yeah, sure pal! Why don't you get the first one open and then we will talk.* After all, this is how I would have reacted. But the fact of the matter is that we were planning to open a certain number of stores within the central Florida market within an established time frame. The key difference is that we were focusing equally on the first store and the long-term goals, not allowing one to distract us from the other. Chris, as you will recall, was the head of UCF's Center for Multi-Unit Restaurant Concepts — he specialized in chain restaurants.

The growth of our concept, however, would be controlled. Even before we had a restaurant open, we had interest in franchising rights. Despite the enticement of such funds at an early stage in our growth as a company, we opted to say no. The franchising structure would have been in conflict with our ownership model, and it would have resulted in growth outside of the central Florida market that would have been difficult to control. Instead, we wanted to focus on the growth of 'Za-Bistro! within the central Florida market first, before potentially growing outside of the region, so that we could better manage costs and operational performance as the company grew. We wanted to keep things close to the vest early on, and then grow on our terms, when the right opportunities presented themselves. Besides, central Florida had been proven as a successful region for the development and introduction of new restaurant concepts. With companies such as Darden (Red Lobster, Olive Garden, Bahama Breeze, Smoky Bones Barbeque & Grill, and Seasons 52) and Outback (Outback Steakhouse, Carabba's Italian Grill, Fleming's Prime Steakhouse & Wine Bar, Lee Roy Selmons, Roy's, as well as other concepts) headquartered in central Florida, we felt that the demographics were right for testing the viability of our concept.

This focus on multi-unit expansion, without neglecting the attention required by the first restaurant, influenced some of the early decisions that we made. Perhaps the best example of this was the development of our logo. Just two weeks after the first e-mail about the *possibility* of opening a restaurant, Chris and I were already discussing hiring a graphic designer to help us develop our company logo. The firm that assisted us with our logo design was hired just a few weeks later after the restaurant name was finalized. Given my focus on design and Chris's focus on brand management in the classroom and through his private consulting efforts, we set out to create our logo and, more importantly, our identity. At Cornell I was taught that the dining experience started in the restaurant's parking lot. The lesson here was that the experience before the experience would influence the guest's impression of the meal, the environment, the service, and their overall satisfaction. While the premise of this lesson is correct, I must disagree with its specifics. The experience starts long before the guest pulls into the parking lot—it starts with the brand identity and imagery that are often shared well before the patron decides to get in a car and head toward that parking lot. In reality, the guest's expectations begin during the initial presentation of the restaurant, whether via word-of-mouth or a more formal form of advertising. Ever present in this initial advertising campaign is the logo! The logo communicates a multitude of messages on both conscious and subconscious levels through shapes, colors, contrast, relationships, and style. The logo should tell the customer who and what you are. That was the task set before Chris and me as we set out to develop our own logo.

The logo must reflect the essence of the brand. The components of brand identification for any restaurant include a half dozen, give or take, *things* that are holy to the concept. These are sacred components that help identify the restaurant brand regardless of the context in which it is presented. The Cheesecake Factory, for example, has a separate dessert station at the entrance, an open kitchen, an extremely large menu, oversized portions, and upscale décor. Panera Bread has fresh bread stored on racks, sandwiches made to order, a defined paint palate, and specific fonts that are used in all types of communication with the customer. In order to demonstrate that this concept of creating and defining a brand applies to all business types, consider The Home Depot. What would The Home Depot be without the orange exterior, warehouse-style shelving systems, their trademark black font on orange cards to indicate pricing, and their mascot who is featured in all of their advertising? How about UPS? They have taken a color—brown—and turned it into an essential portion of their brand. In fact, in some of their advertisements "brown" and "UPS" are completely interchangeable. We would have to develop the same type of imagery and brand identification for 'Za-Bistro!

In reviewing successful logo designs from other companies, it was clear that there was a separate class of logos that conveyed a message on both a conscious and subconscious level. These were more than just good-looking logos — they served a purpose, and served that purpose well. The use of an *entity* in place of a letter or punctuation mark in the company's name is one successful method in helping to reach this higher echelon of logo design. Chili's Bar & Grill, for example, uses an actual chili in its logo. In some instances, the chili replaces an apostrophe, and other times it replaces the entire word "chili." The use of the chili in the logo subtly supports the name and message of the Chili's brand without being overbearing. It is a great example of successful logo design. When Federal Express set out to update their logo, they utilized a couple of interesting tactics. First, they adopted the name that the general public had given them and officially changed the logo on all of their packages and trucks from Federal Express to FedEx.

Another intriguing part of this change was the actual design of this FedEx logo. If you study the wording style carefully, you will notice that the void between the letters "E" and "x" create an arrow. The design and marketing team must have worked very hard to include this arrow, an international symbol for movement, which is a core piece of FedEx's business function. Yet again, the message is present but subtle — not overpowering. Then there is the Nike "swoosh" logo — a masterpiece in logo design. So simple yet so effective. Its shape relates to movement, activity, training (increase in performance), style, and so much more. The "swoosh" is a symbol that is instantly identified with the company it represents, while invoking certain emotional responses from those who come in contact with it or who go so far as to proudly (and voluntarily) purchase clothing featuring the company logo. By definition, this is successful logo design. Now it was our turn.

Although we lacked the talent for creative drawing, Chris and I both had very specific ideas as to what we wanted the logo to accomplish. We also realized, however, that we needed to keep an open mind so as not to prematurely rule out any possible options. The development of a logo is a creative process, and we needed to explore every option and possibility. We hired a company that advertised over the Web and in several business magazines. I had reviewed some of their previous work, posted online in photo galleries, and felt that they were qualified to assist us with the development of our logo. The company was located in Canada, and we communicated primarily by e-mail. Believe it or not, only a few phone conversations were made during the entire process. A number of logo-development packages were offered by this company, with key differences being the number of revisions and designs presented. We opted for a package that included an unlimited number of revisions until we were satisfied. This package turned out to be a *very* wise investment, as in the end, we rejected between 40 and 50 different logo variations before selecting our final design. We began by filling out a survey to provide the designer with an overview of our concept so that he could best represent our brand through the design of the logo. In an effort to keep an open mind, we suggested that the first batch of logos come from the designer without any input from us. We received six logos — none of which we liked. Several of the logos presented in the first batch included oil jugs, olive branches, and other references to Italian or Greek cuisine. This was not desirable, as we were not an Italian or Greek restaurant. We were a European bistro, and, despite the inclusion of various menu items influenced from these two countries, we needed to express through our brand image that this European-bistro concept represented cuisine from a number of different countries. We did not want to allow our restaurant concept, despite a menu mix that was skewed heavily toward pizza, to be pigeonholed as an Italian restaurant, and the logo was a great place to squash this stereotype from the very beginning.

One of the logos featured a font that was more appropriate for a 1950s diner, while another featured a bundle of seemingly recently harvested wheat. There was only one logo from the first batch that we even remotely considered for the second round of development, but we still were not satisfied with any of the initial options. Given the disparity between the brand image presented by the first batch of logos and the brand image that we desired, I opted to step in and give our designer a bit more direction with regard to our concept and expectations. I indicated that two items holy to our concept should somehow be included in the logo — wine and the open-flame, stone-hearth oven. In addition, it was at this time that we shared the desired colors for the concept — burgundy and blue. The burgundy served a dual purpose, representing the wine, a critical part of our concept, and offering feelings of warmth as a member of the earth-tone palate. The blue was specifically chosen for excitement and highlights or accents throughout the actual restaurant facility, but also served double duty as a subliminal connection to the color of a hot flame. This blue was eventually used in a variety of lighting fixtures, colored glass, and tabletop accessories, which would allow an opportunity for us to bring the logo to life and create consistency between the graphic image and the physical environment. And, to be quite honest, I just love the color blue; nothing too scientific about it. That is part of the fun in creating something that is your own — you don't always have to have a reason.

The next batch of logos that we received was much better than the first. With the minimal input that I offered, the improvement was substantial. There were a number of different styles of flames and wineglasses, as well as a variety of shades of blue and burgundy. The font from the one logo that we considered worth pursuing from the first batch was used in several of the proposed designs, while the remaining logos depicted a variety of font styles. This was a giant step in the right direction, as compared to the first selection, but we still were not in love with any of the logos.

At this time, I decided to jump in and offer more specific detail regarding my vision of the logo. There was one particular wineglass that accurately represented the style and feel of our concept. However, none of the flames, in my opinion, fit our personality. I have a personal affection for the use of graphic objects within an actual logo design to replace a word or letter. In studying our logo, I realized that the "i" in bistro was fairly central and could be easily replaced with an object—the wineglass! So in an episode of kindergarten regression one Saturday afternoon, I pulled out my son's scissors for a cut-and-paste work session. I proceeded to cut out the wineglass that I liked and then pasted it on one of the logos from the second batch, right over the "i" in bistro. The shape of the wineglass included a straight stem, so it was easy to recognize that the wineglass served the dual role of icon and letter. Pleased with this new direction, I also noticed that the wineglass added some height and balance to the logo, creating a pyramid shape—a shape that was symmetrical, strong, and even. Now, I had to find a flame that I liked, as none of the flame shapes we received were close to what I had in mind. Given my artistic shortcomings for free-hand drawing, I began searching the Web for a flame that was closer to what I had in mind. After a brief search, I found something close. So, I grabbed my son's box of crayons and started to trace the image, modifying it slightly, and using different shades of blue and burgundy to see which I liked better. The flame was then placed behind the wineglass, as if to represent the oven in the background. I taped this whole thing together, scanned it into the computer, and then e-mailed it to our designer. We spent some time experimenting with fonts, color placement, pantone color selections, and shadows. Soon we had yet another batch of logos to choose from, but the variations were subtle. We were getting closer.

In the end, with dozens of versions of the logo developed, our decision to select the logo-development package that allowed for unlimited revisions proved to be a wise choice. We never felt any pressure or limitations during the logo-development process, and we were able to make sure that we got it just right. The logo says so much, and it needed to be perfect. The final design allowed for an added bonus—a secondary, graphics-only logo. Although it was intentional, it was not until the design work was completed that we realized the true potential of this decision. The wineglass, centered with the flame behind it, was a great icon that could be used to more subtly indicate our presence and convey our brand image. We had hoped that, one day, patrons would be able to see this wineglass and flame and instantly recognize it as our logo. This secondary logo was a tremendous asset. We really had developed two logos for the effort of one, and we could use the graphic logo with or without the wording. The result was everything that I had hoped for and a little more. Okay, so I spent a lot of time talking about the development of a logo—why bother? The answer is simple: Because the logo is the catalyst for the restaurant's image, the advertising, the design of the dining environment, and the brand.

Once we had the logo completed, we knew that we needed to protect our rights to use the logo and, more importantly, prevent others from using it. We invested the money in the early stages to legally protect the logo, filing the appropriate paperwork with our lawyers. We were forced to get a little creative at one point due to one of the requirements for trademark protection. The law stated that we could only file for the necessary protection within a couple of weeks of opening for business. We were, quite frankly, months away from opening the first restaurant, not weeks. Faced with a challenge, Chris put on his thinking cap and proposed that we advertise as a catering company, an active business, to allow immediate protection. We had no intention of actually taking any catering jobs. In fact, the running joke was that as we passed out the sample catering menus, we would let each potential customer know that whatever date they had in mind, we were already booked. A missed revenue opportunity? Perhaps. But it was far more important to focus on the primary task at hand. The logo was now protected, and could be used in our promotional efforts for the new 'Za-Bistro! concept. To this day, I believe that the development and use of our logo in the early stages was one of our greatest successes. It provided an aura of professionalism for our team and helped us appear much larger and more established than we actually were at the time. This perception, in turn, was a tremendous asset to us in negotiations and general business dealings at the outset of our venture.

I will continue to emphasize that our team was focused on the *Business of Restaurants*. This included the model that was required to ensure financial success, profitability, and long-term stability. We were highly focused on the financial component of the concept in order to ensure that it was economically viable. In fact, some of our preliminary projections were contained in one of Chris's first e-mails proposing the development effort. Here is how he envisioned the equations early on:

100 seats, 2500 SF, $15 average check for lunch and dinner. Assuming that the restaurant would turn twice daily during the week, that would result in daily revenue of $3000. Turning the restaurant three-and-a-half times on Friday and Saturday would bump the daily revenue up to $5250, resulting in average weekly revenue of $25,500 and annualized revenue of just over $1.3 million. If we were to feature pizzas at $8–$10 each, most with limited mozzarella (70% of the cost of a U.S. pizza is the cheese) but with high "value added" toppings such as salmon, shrimp, field mushrooms, grilled vegetables, smoked cheese slices, and the like, we should be able to keep a food cost around 15%. Labor should remain under 35%. At the projected revenue of more than $1 million per store, a conservative 15% net return would equate to $150,000 annually. The ownership model would likely be structured so that the parent company would maintain 51%, the market/area partner would receive 10% ownership, the store-level operating partner would receive 25%, 10% would be applied toward interest payments, and 4% would be split and used as incentives for the staff and management. A higher net should be possible, as these estimates are conservative in nature. For the first two years, debt would be paid back with interest only with a three-month grace period. Principal would be paid back at the end of three years or after profitability, whichever comes first.

While the eventual model strayed somewhat from this early description, and the specifics were adjusted to match the realistic requirements and opportunities that we faced, the core concept of our financial objectives was well summarized in this early e-mail. As a comparison, the Pizza Express model in England, according to Chris, featured the following approximate cost structure: Food, 28 percent; Labor, 28 percent; Property Costs, 14 percent; Utilities, 10 percent; and Profit, 20 percent.

The organization and structure of the company continued to evolve. We had reached a point, however, where we needed to organize many of our random thoughts. We soon developed a formalized business plan, which began with a quote that we borrowed from a cookbook written by Patricia Wells in 1989, entitled *Bistro Cooking*. We felt it accurately described our ideals. It went something like this:.

The world, I am sure, will never agree upon the exact origins of the word "bistro"…Whatever its origins, everyone agrees that whether it's a café, a small unpretentious restaurant, or simply a place to enjoy a glass of wine and a simple yet hearty sandwich, a bistro is a place for good times with friends.

Our business plan included several components intended to relay our concept to potential landlords and business partners. It featured the concept description and identification. It featured our target markets, as well as our reasoning for pursuing the identified demographics and methods for attracting them to the restaurant. The business plan went on to include information about our Web site, detailed biographies on the team members, and a sample menu. We also went so far as to include information on potential sites that we had already targeted, including demographic information and maps identifying local competitors and complementary restaurant concepts. Furthermore, we included sample conceptual floor plans for those possible sites; another advantage of having such capabilities in-house. The package was fairly detailed given our stage in the development process, but in its detail afforded others accurate insight into our concept and our philosophies. We opted not to include specific financial projections within this document, but rather provide them on an as-needed basis when appropriate. Ideally, we wanted potential landlords and additional investors first to fall in love with the team and the concept—then we would discuss the specifics as required. With the 'Za-Bistro! concept better defined, we were ready to move forward and take this restaurant development effort to the next level.

4

OWNING A PIECE OF THE PIE

The basic groundwork for the ownership model had been addressed in some of our earliest e-mails and conversations, but had not been completely defined. Generally speaking, our intention was to establish a parent company, or holding company, that would serve as an umbrella organization and own a majority stake in each of the individual restaurants, keeping in mind that our ultimate goal was to create a multi-unit restaurant organization. Each restaurant would be set up as an individual corporation, beneath the corporate umbrella. This would allow for flexibility in growing the concept, allowing us to tailor the ownership structures at the individual store level to best suit the local market and specific scenario. Needless to say, there were a tremendous number of details that needed to be tied down in order to achieve this desired goal, and miles to go before we would finalize the structure. The ownership models needed to be developed at both the holding-company level and at the store level. First, let's take a look at the holding company.

Shortly after Chris had assembled the team, we were faced with the task of developing an ownership model. Keep in mind that, at the time, the team members really didn't know one another all that well, and making a proposal for ownership can be tricky among a team with as many players as we had. No one wanted to appear too greedy, but at the same time, none of the pioneering members of this emerging organization wanted to miss out on what we believed was an opportunity to make a buck or two. There was a fine line that had to be traversed. Chris had asked all of us to make a proposal for the holding company's ownership structure, but this request went unanswered for a few weeks mainly because no one was anxious to make the first move. Somebody had to move first, and I figured why not me? I had developed a proposal, including excerpts from the team's earlier discussions, which allocated 20 percent of the company for venture capitalist ownership and the remaining 80 percent would be divided among Chris, Jason, Aaron, Brian (later replaced by Daniel), and me. This initial proposal was drafted before Harold and Mark entered the picture as investors. Chris clearly needed to have a significant percentage of the remaining shares as our President and CEO. I had proposed that he receive 35 percent of the remaining 80 percent of the company, which equated to 28 percent of the holding company. The chef's amount was to be approximately 5 percent of the remaining 80 percent (or 4 percent of the overall company). The corporate chef's ownership percentage was lower, as it was not anticipated that the ongoing requirements would be that significant once the concept was up and running. The remaining share of the company was to be divided among Aaron, Jason, and me.

When Chris and I first had our discussion, I explained that I was high on energy and low on cash for the venture. With a reassuring "money is never the problem" from Chris, it was understood that I was planning to invest only sweat equity. In other words, I was going to trade labor and knowledge for a certain percentage of the company, but I had not anticipated investing any cash. It was during the discussions with our legal counsel that we learned this arrangement, while desirable and agreed upon in theory among the team, was not going to provide each partner with the desired level of ownership. Our legal counselors informed us that sweat equity alone would not equate to the ownership model that we had anticipated. There were legal and tax implications cited by our lawyers. More specifically, there was an actual ratio that we would be forced to use to determine the value of the sweat equity offered in relation to the value of actual dollars offered; it was not a one-for-one exchange. The sweat-equity value was subject to a one-to-five ratio that, in the end, resulted in an actual value worth 20 percent of the anticipated sweat equity value. We soon realized that it would require a combination of both cash and sweat equity to achieve our desired structure.

What resulted next was something a bit unexpected. Chris had offered up some initial seed money to fund our early activities. This was an investment that he had planned to make in the concept anyway. He had also begun conversations to solicit additional funds that would be needed for the company's development and growth from his long-time friends, Harold and Mark. Jason, Aaron, and I had originally anticipated utilizing our sweat-equity contributions to secure an ownership stake. One of Chris's earlier e-mails indicated he wanted each of the original team members to obtain a piece of ownership based on their expertise. However, after realizing that the sweat-equity-only approach would offer only limited opportunity for ownership in the company, the game changed. What ensued was a bidding war of sorts for the remaining percentage of the company. We had received some additional advice from our legal counsel that forced us to shy away from outside investors at the store level in the early restaurants. This investment format, discussed more extensively later in the chapter, was used by many other successful restaurant companies. The fear in our case, however, was that there might be too many cooks in the kitchen (to use a pun that is both pertinent and industry related), which could potentially complicate the early growing pains we were sure to experience. Furthermore, Jason had grown confident that we could raise enough money internally among the group and then secure a loan from the Small Business Administration (SBA) for the remaining amount, equaling a total that would cover our development costs for the first store. As a result, Jason had committed to investing actual funds into the parent company in addition to offering his efforts and expertise, and Aaron soon followed. I then had a discussion with Chris in which it became readily apparent that I, too, would have to invest cash in the business or face losing a significant portion of the ownership percentage I had anticipated receiving. I reached into my personal rainy-day fund to come up with the needed cash. There was some see-sawing in the amounts that would be required, as the three of us jockeyed for ownership percentages based on a formula that would reflect actual cash contributed as well as services provided. This round of capital contributions offered initial funds for the company's establishment. Furthermore, it was encouraging to see a desire to contribute *more* funds to maintain a desirable stake in the effort; an effort that we all felt confident would be successful. This energy soon led to the investment of funds from Harold and Mark and resulted in the following ownership structure, which considered both cash and services, in accordance with legal requirements. At this time, Brian was still slated for the executive chef's role in the organization, and Daniel had not yet been brought on board.:

'Za-Bistro! Restaurant Holdings, Inc. Ownership Allocations

	Percentage of Ownership	
Chris	25%	
Jason	20%	
Lee	15.5%	
Aaron	15.5%	
Brian	2%	
		78%
Harold	20%	
Mark	2%	
		22%
Totals		**100%**

With the factual aspect of our early efforts to formalize the ownership structure now documented, it is important to look at the emotional side for a second. As I have stated before, opening a restaurant—or any business, for that matter—is truly an emotional experience. The founding owners are pouring heart, soul, and available capital into something that they believe will provide a return on the investment that is being made. Is the return guaranteed? Of course not. But if a return on the investment was not perceived as probable, the investment would not happen in the first place. For me, in this stage of the process, the world looked pretty good. As was the case with my partners, I saw significant upside potential for this venture. The team, the concept, the available funding—so many things seemed to be falling into place. A healthy dose of perceived immunity is required for any entrepreneur in order for a new venture to make it off the ground. Otherwise, it is too easy to find reasons that the plan will not work, and the innovation process then grinds to a halt. Too much optimism and a loss of perspective on reality, however, can be detrimental as well. There would have to be a balance. Did we strike that balance? Were we too optimistic? Were we not optimistic enough? Only time would tell.

As the ownership structure was coming into focus, it was at that time—for the first time—we, as a group, began defining what services would be provided by each partner. Harold and Mark were pure financial investors, as they provided cash contributions but did not have any official requirements to provide services in exchange for ownership. We began looking at the actual responsibilities that each of us would have, and I drafted a list of anticipated responsibilities. This was a first attempt by a group of individuals who had never done this before. In hindsight, it is remarkable to consider all that was *not* covered in the following descriptions. Here is what we came up with.:

Chris, President and CEO: Chris, as CEO, will be in charge of overseeing the interests of the organization and will be responsible for coordination within the ownership team. These terms are deliberately vague, as the many needs of the organization are undetermined at this time and are likely to change as the organization grows and evolves. Specific responsibilities of the CEO will include:
  1. Coordination and communication with the Ownership Team.
  2. Coordination with and supervision of the Managing Partners.
  3. Review and management of financial statements.
  4. Review and management of operational costs.
  5. Development and implementation of operational standards.
  6. Coordination with purveyors.
  7. Menu development and implementation.
  8. Advertising and promotion efforts.

 Jason, Treasurer and CFO:Jason, as CFO, will be responsible for overseeing the financial health of the organization. Specific responsibilities will include:
  1. Review and management of financial statements.
  2. Management of the organization's funds and investments.
  3. Review of all leasing agreements and management contracts.

 Lee, Secretary and VP Design and Construction:Lee's responsibilities will include:
  1. Coordination of the overall design effort, including election of and coordination with the design team members.
  2. Coordination of the overall construction effort, including acting as the owners' representative throughout the construction process.

3. *Oversee purchasing and procurement of all furniture, fixtures, and equipment.*

Aaron, VP Operations and Development:*Aaron's responsibilities will include:*
1. *Development and implementation of operational standards. This should be coordinated with the CEO.*
2. *Site evaluation and selection.*
3. *Coordination with management and leasing companies.*

Brian, Executive Chef:*Brian's responsibilities will include:*
1. *Menu development and implementation.*

There was another interesting twist to the proposal that I had developed as part of this exercise to document responsibility and accountability for those members of the team who were contributing sweat equity. My initial draft included a requirement for a minimum level of participation and performance from each team member who was contributing specific services to the company, as outlined above. The objective that I had was to include in the partnership agreement a method with which to hold one another accountable for our stated responsibilities. I was considering a formula whereby a certain percentage of the "earned" shares would be guaranteed based on the contribution of funds, but ultimately, performance of the services that were considered as part of the ownership structure would have to be completed in a satisfactory manner in order to gain the full proposed ownership percentage. Without allowing the idea to become too convoluted, my goal was to make sure that the commitments each of us had made for services were upheld and performed to the best of our ability. This would help ensure that the company and its constituents would not suffer due to the lack of performance from one or more members of the team. If sub-par performance were to occur, the full *potential* ownership level would not be realized by the partner falling short of his responsibilities. Unfortunately, the legal ramifications and lack of a clear way to measure performance standards, given the varying scopes of the services being provided, made the proposal a bit difficult to enforce. My proposal soon faded and never made it into the shareholders' agreement. In hindsight, this was a *real* mistake.

One additional consideration in the structure of the organization that is important to note was the salary schedule slated for the ownership team, or the lack thereof. There were no salaries. This entire effort was strictly an investment for the long term. None of the owners would be drawing a salary in exchange for the financial or sweat equity contributions that were to be made. Any returns for the investors would come as a result of a sale of the concept, in whole or in part. Thus, neither the corporate- nor unit-level models would be burdened with additional financial commitments.

Perhaps the most common reason for failure of any new business venture is *undercapitalization* — a lack of sufficient funding that forces the business to focus on cash flow and paying bills as opposed to growth and building for the long term. I took an entrepreneurship class in college. In that class, my instructor shared with us this lesson: *You pay your bills with cash, not with profits.* Take a brief moment and re-read this very important lesson. What he was impressing upon us through these words of wisdom was that although you may be able to show a profit for the year, that does not mean that you will be profitable during every part of the year. And regardless of your profitability in any particular month, the rent, utility bills, insurance, and other such financial commitments must be met. This is the pitfall that many new companies fall into — a lack of financial planning and reserves, which leads to a cash-flow crisis. Fortunately, we were aware of this common pitfall on the front end, and we worked diligently to avoid it. Through our internal fundraising efforts and contributions by the partnership, we had secured nearly $600,000 in preparation of opening our first restaurants. It was our plan to apply this capital toward our 25 percent contribution for each of the first three stores, leveraging the remaining 75 percent of the required capital through loans from the SBA. Jason, savvy in planning such leveraged arrangements for many of his clients, was confident that this approach would allow us to maximize the use of our capital — a very precious resource that we had accumulated.

With the structure for the holding company set, there was the matter of establishing the ownership structure at the store level for each restaurant. This task received a significant amount of attention during our initial planning stages, as this was one area of our organization where we planned to differentiate ourselves from some of our competitors. We were fortunate in that we had a wealth of information on the various methods for establishing ownership models used by other restaurant companies, due in large part to our access to influential industry members and hard-to-access sources of industry data. At the time, there was a movement throughout the industry to provide store managers with a piece of ownership in the restaurants that they were overseeing. A common term used for this new breed of managers was *Managing Partner*, or a manager who was also a partial owner. When the restaurant is managed by someone other than the majority owner(s), both the owners of the restaurant and the managing partner benefit from this structure. Our philosophy was articulated this way by Chris:

> *Ideally, the managing partner and between four and ten local, limited partners would contribute to the cash and equity in each store. Corporate contributions would be leveraged to maximize returns. The three primary objectives with this model are 1) provide up to a 25% ownership at the store level to the managing partner in an effort to provide an attractive salary, 2) use the 51% corporate ownership in each store to help fund future growth, and 3) return positive cash flows to the investors.*

These were, no doubt, noble objectives. We had hoped to create opportunity and wealth not only for the ownership team, but for those who were set to partake in our growth and development, whether in an active or passive role. Due to the roles of the executive team (namely, full-time commitments to other employers), we were fully aware that we were going to require a managing partner at the store level who we could trust and rely on—one who would act as an owner, in the true sense of the word. It was our belief that the only way to encourage a manager to act as an owner was to provide actual ownership. We certainly did not pioneer this concept; it has been used by numerous leading restaurant companies, including Outback, P.F. Chang's China Bistro, and many other national chains. In fact, due to the volume and ownership position, many Outback managers are making well into six figures annually, albeit on a much larger volume than we had anticipated for our stores. Once again, this was a demonstration of the shift from the *Restaurant Business* to the *Business of Restaurants*. A manager who is also a part owner is more conscious of and concerned with the financial performance of the restaurant because every dollar earned potentially impacts the managing partner's earnings. Further, as the salary increases for the managing partner, the return for the corporate entity and any investors also rises. This is exactly what we were striving for; a win-win scenario. We were in a position where we *wanted* to pay our management more money, because with every extra dollar our managers earn, we earn more as well. One key component to this structure, however, is—figuratively and literally—a buy-in from the managing partner. As part of the plan, the managing partner was required to invest capital and buy in to the restaurant. More important than the cash that it would provide for working capital at the store level, this outlay of funds by the managing partner would solidify his or her ownership at the store level. Simply stated, there is greater appreciation for something that must be earned or purchased than for something that is provided free of charge. Easy come, easy go. Also, a manager who had physically invested in the store and who had an ownership interest would be less likely to blow up and storm out on a Saturday night, quitting on the spot. It would promote stability among the management team, which we had hoped would translate to stability among the staff. After all, turnover rates in the restaurant industry of 100 or 150 percent annually are not uncommon. Listed below is an excerpt from our original managing partner plan, articulating some of these points with greater detail.

> *During the past decade, leading restaurant companies have created new unit management ownership models. Like Outback Steakhouse, Ruby Tuesday, and P.F. Chang's China Bistro, 'Za-Bistro! will utilize a Managing Partner Program offering the General Managers and certain key employees an ownership interest in the individual restaurant. Low General Manager turnover is a key component to holding employee turnover down, which in turn promotes overall stability in the restaurant. Studies have shown that as turnover falls, profitability at the restaurant level increases dramatically, training expenses fall, theft falls, and the productivity of the staff increases. In order to achieve low turnover, progressive restaurant chains have been offering their General Managers an equity interest in the restaurant operations in return for a cash payment of approximately $10,000 to $25,000. The General Manager would receive a five- to ten-year contract with a bonus structure based on their ownership. As part of that contract, the GM usually has a put option (the ability to force the corporation to purchase back the shares) to the corporation based on a multiple of cash flow (less debt) exercisable at the end of the contract, and the corporation in turn has a call option based on a similar valuation.*

The General Managers of 'Za-Bistro! will be offered the following equity investment after attaining 12 months of employment and satisfaction of a set of criteria designed to identify the best and brightest General Managers in the industry:

For a $20,000 cash investment into the LLC operating unit, the General Manager will receive the title Bistro Managing Partner ("BMP"), as well as:

a) A five-year employment contract for a base salary of $52,000 and a 30% share of the free cash flow after tax, debt service, and capital expenditures, all based on the unit's annual performance. For example, at $1,144,000 of sales, the BMP is currently projected to receive total compensation of $52,000 plus $19,000 in bonus dividends payable semi-annually, or a total of $71,000 (6.21% of sales). At $1,500,000, the BMP is projected to receive total compensation of $95,000 (6.33% of sales). Other subjective performance criteria will have to be satisfied in addition to attaining budgetary goals, and operating losses will carry forward against payouts.

b) A full suite of strong medical and dental coverage, long-term disability coverage, term life insurance of $200,000, a cell phone, and a Blackberry, Palm, or similar PDA.

c) Upon achieving and sustaining unit sales of $1,400,000/yr. or more, the BMP will receive a brand-new leased Dodge Durango SUV or similar vehicle to drive for the remainder of his/her contract.

d) Upon the sale of the restaurant or the holding company, the BMP will participate in the enterprise valuation of the unit and receive 10% of the net enterprise value (after debt) associated with the sale of the unit, payable over a two-year period. For example, based on EBITDA (Earnings Before Interest, Taxes, Depreciation, and Amortization) of $200,000, an assumed purchase price multiple of 6.5X EBITDA, and outstanding unit level debt of $300,000, the BMP would receive $100,000, paid in quarterly payments over a two-year period.

At the end of the five-year contract, the BMP will be given the option of:

a) Receiving his/her original $20,000 investment plus a return of 20% on the investment over the five years (20% over 5 years = $33,919 *plus the $20,000 original investment = $53,919) payable over two years thereafter, or*

b) *Signing up for another five-year contract, in order to receive upon expiration of the contract, the greater of a 25% return on the original $20,000 investment, or 3X the average annual EBITDA less the then-current debt, times a 10% "equity" interest, payable over a three-year period.*

The larger bonus payouts described above will be subordinated to any debt service and subject to loan covenant compliance. The agreement will be structured to be pro-employer/HoldCo in order to protect the company in the event of termination or early breaking of the contract.

No doubt, the plan was aggressive; however, we were strong believers that the commitment at the unit level was not only critical to our success, but would be a key component of our competitive advantage in the marketplace. We were planning to be a neighborhood restaurant, "among the rooftops," and this managing partner was going to be the face that our local guests would see on a regular basis.

Although it did not end up as part of our arrangement, the concept of having between four and ten local partners was something that we still planned to pursue in the future. As with the managing partner, the benefits of having these local partners superseded the benefits of the capital that they would be providing—although the money would be helpful. How often have you heard of successful professionals, often with a résumé of accomplishments in fields other than the foodservice industry, wanting to open a restaurant? In fact, you may even be a member of that group. There is rarely a burning desire to open a car wash, a bowling alley, or an art gallery—but restaurants seem to have a powerful appeal. Personally, I believe that it stems from the basic role that restaurants play in the social interaction of society. Restaurants offer more than just a meal; they also offer a sense of community, a sense of belonging. Restaurants are often used as a gathering place to exchange ideas and emotions. To own a restaurant is to be at the center of this communal activity. No, it is even better—it is the ability to *host* this community interaction. And while the appeal is intoxicating to many, the realities of what it takes to open and run a restaurant are often a mystery to these same individuals. This calls to mind the old adage that states the best way to make $1 million in the restaurant business is to start with $2 million.

That is what was so appealing about the inclusion of local, limited partners. It offered these professionals the opportunity of restaurant ownership without all of the headaches that often come with overseeing day-to-day operations. Many of these successful professionals who seek to open a new restaurant are more focused on the ability to invite friends and family to their social meetinghouse than they are on the demands of the *Business of Restaurants*. A limited partnership offers the upside benefits without the need for daily involvement. It was our intention to offer, and in fact encourage, the limited partners to use the restaurant for meetings, events, and special gatherings. We were planning to set up a system for signing privileges that would simply allow the limited partners to put such events on their tab. These amounts would be deducted from the financial distributions to be issued as part of the return on their investment.

From the restaurant's perspective, the real cost of these dividends would only be the cost of the food, as no other additional expenses would be incurred. In other words, we would not have to pay any more for utilities, rent, or labor—all of these costs will have already been committed. If our food costs were to average 30 percent, the dividends issued to the limited partners through food credits, or signing privileges, would be 30 cents on the dollar. Not a bad deal. It creates a win-win scenario for the restaurant and the limited partner. And there is yet another added benefit to this concept: the marketing. With a series of local professionals touting *their* restaurant, the word-of-mouth advertising would only help to increase customer counts. It was also assumed that any professional desiring to invest in a restaurant would likely be involved in social circles that included members of our target market. The restaurant's name would be dropped in conversation at business and social gatherings, supporting the viral marketing plan that we hoped to employ. Imagine this group of limited partners acting as marketing crusaders, helping to advertise our restaurant. It was a tremendous opportunity and would likely increase traffic, profitability, and the return on the limited partner's investment. Now, we were certainly not the initial creators of this format—it had been used successfully by others in the past—but the advantages to both the limited partner and the restaurant organization on the local and global levels were clear. The restaurant would offer anticipated returns at a reduced rate, and the limited partners would receive signing privileges that would help the restaurant's financial performance. While our original ownership breakdown at the unit level was to have included 51 percent for the holding company, 25 percent for the managing partner, 20 percent for local investors, and 4 percent for incentives and discretionary uses, the 20 percent allocated for the limited partners would be retained as part of the corporate holdings, at least for the first store or two, based on the legal advice of our attorneys. A formal solicitation for limited partners would have required the compilation and distribution of a document package that was compliant with the Securities and Exchange Commission (SEC). The estimated cost of this effort, over $20,000, did not seem like the best use of our available funds at the time. And while not the original model, it was understood that retaining the additional 20 percent could potentially offer a higher percentage of profits that would be retained by the holding company and used for future growth. Ultimately, we chose not to pursue local, limited partners initially.

With the conceptual structure of the organization now defined, it was time to move to the next step and formalize the creation of the company — or more correctly stated, companies. Not only would we have to incorporate, but we also would have to draft and agree upon a shareholders' agreement between the ownership partners. After much discussion, and with input from our accountants and attorneys, we finally agreed to structure the organization whereby 'Za-Bistro! Restaurant Holdings, Inc., the holding company, would be an S Corporation, often referred to as a "Sub-S," and the individual restaurants would each be established as a freestanding limited liability corporation, or an LLC. The individual LLCs help to shield the parent company from additional liability, just as the name suggests. For instance, if an employee or guest is injured at a particular restaurant, only that specific location — a separate business from the other sister restaurants that share the same name and menu — will be liable for results from the incident, not the parent company. Though a plaintiff would not be prevented from pursuing the parent company, the likelihood for a successful judgment is significantly reduced when separate LLCs are utilized. This setup can also help protect a company's assets from lawsuits involving allegations that are frequently made against restaurant owners, ranging from sexual harassment to the spilling of coffee that was too hot. The ownership will want to keep minimal cash and assets at the store level to help minimize risk. To achieve maximum protection, there are a number of practices that the organization must abide by, such as maintaining separate bank accounts for each entity to ensure that each LLC is truly separate. As with most business decisions, there are no guarantees. However, implementing these types of precautions from the outset will help provide the company with greater protection. It is important to consult both legal and accounting professionals to devise a plan for your specific situation. The time and money invested in this research are most certainly worthwhile.

The shareholders' agreement is the sole document that defines the relationship among all of the owning partners. To say that it is important would be a gross understatement. Lawyers spend a great deal of time addressing the "what if" scenarios that may or may not ever occur, and that is what this document attempts to define—many of the "what if" scenarios before they have an opportunity to present themselves. Ours was not a simple arrangement. There were numerous partners, some with significant personal wealth, and this single document had to define our commitments to—and protection from—one another. Despite the goodwill that may be shown in the early stages of a venture such as this one, any reputable legal team will have the experience to know that not every story has a happy ending. It is the legal team's responsibility to bring objectivity to the equation and ask questions of the partners that the partners might not have previously considered or wanted to address. The lawyers need to ask the tough questions up front, even though some of the questions may trigger an emotional response. There is one shot, and one shot only, to develop the shareholders' agreement. Through his employer, Jason had a relationship with one of the largest and most prestigious law firms in the city of Orlando. Aside from his personal experience with their performance, the law firm's list of restaurant clients was quite impressive, including some of the largest restaurant companies in the industry. It was important to find a law firm that was familiar with the specifics of our industry and our objectives. A firm experienced in dealing with restaurants would likely offer insight related to matters we had not even considered, based on their past experience. Of greater relevance, however, was their representation of a successful, regional, multi-unit restaurant company. This particular restaurant group appeared to have a number of similarities to ours, and we were confident that the law firm we had chosen would be able to parlay their experience with this particular company, as well as others in their portfolio, to our benefit. The ownership model utilized by this regional chain, including the concept of a managing partner at the unit level, had similarities to the model that we had outlined. In the end, we felt that it was a sound decision—and an important one. When we hire an individual or organization to help with a discipline that is not contained internally within our organization, that individual or organization becomes, in essence, an extension of our organization. They become part of our team, with significant influence over eventual decisions.

It is not my intention to bore you with every minute detail of our shareholders' agreement, but I do want to highlight some key concepts and points that were included in the final draft. Just as important, there were elements of our discussions that we did not include, which in hindsight should have been incorporated. The agreement, once completed, would define the obligations of each partner to the corporation and the other partners. There were components of the agreement, some of the "what if" scenarios, that seemed to have little or no chance of ever materializing. What can I say? It was not the first time—nor would it be the last time—that we would be wrong. Call it a bit of foreshadowing if you want.

In its final arrangement, as defined in our shareholders' agreement, the ownership structure at the corporate level looked like this:

The Corporation currently has ninety-nine thousand, nine hundred ninety (99,990) issued and outstanding shares of common stock which are held as follows:

Name of Shareholder	*Number of Shares*
Chris, President and CEO	*25,000*
Jason, Treasurer and CFO	*20,000*
Harold, Investing Partner	*19,990*
Lee, Secretary and VP Design and Construction	*15,500*
Aaron, VP Operations and Development	*15,500*
Daniel, Executive Chef	*2,000*
Mark, Investing Partner	*2,000*
Totals	*99,990*

For the most part, these amounts match the earlier allocation schedule, with a few notable modifications. The first is that Daniel was now reflected in the ownership model, receiving 2 percent of the company for his contributions as the corporate chef, taking over for Brian. Daniel did not make a cash contribution. Mark's percentage was based strictly on cash contribution, and no services—just the opposite of Daniel. Finally, Harold had received 19,990 shares for his capital contributions. This distinction, just below the 20 percent mark, is significant. Given that Harold had already contributed a significant amount of capital to this effort, his desire—and rightly so—was to limit further personal liability. Thus, the requirement by the SBA and others, such as landlords and certain creditors, to have any member of the team with a 20 percent ownership stake or greater in the company offer a personal guarantee was considered early in the process. This is what stipulated Harold's slight decrease in ownership, just below the 20 percent threshold.

The shareholders' agreement went on to define EBITDA (earnings before interest, taxes, depreciation, and amortization), used as the basis for some of the valuation formulas. Because of its use in other parts of the document, this definition, too, was important. The definition was phrased as follows:

> "EBITDA" means, with respect to any given time period, the net income of the Corporation plus the Corporation's share of the net income of its subsidiaries, calculated in accordance with generally accepted accounting principles, consistently applied, and before application of any deductions or increases to such net income in respect of amounts paid or accrued or received during such time period for (a) income taxes, (b) interest expense on indebtedness for money borrowed, purchase money indebtedness or other obligations, (c) depreciation, (d) amortization of intangibles or other assets, (e) gains or losses on the sale of assets not in the ordinary course of business, (f) interest income, and (g) extraordinary items under generally accepted accounting principles. For purposes of this Agreement, EBITDA will be calculated by the Corporation's independent certified public accounting firm and such determination will be final and binding on all interested parties and other Persons.

Prior to the drafting of our shareholders' agreement, Chris had relayed to us a story about three partners in a small, independent restaurant. The three men had known each other for quite some time, and the restaurant was a modest success. Unfortunately, one of the three men passed away prematurely. The deceased partner's will stated that all assets would be transferred to his surviving wife, including his shares of the restaurant. The two remaining partners, in a gesture of goodwill towards their ex-partner's widow, decided to let her retain the shares without having to uphold any of her former husband's responsibilities. In essence, she would be able to retain the revenue stream without any obligations for services owed to the restaurant. The gesture was much appreciated by the woman in her time of need. Eventually, as time passed, the woman remarried. Once her husband realized that she had retained the ownership in the restaurant, he determined that this would be a viable career move for him, and he decided to take an active role in his new wife's former husband's restaurant company. There he was, a complete stranger to the other two partners, showing up and introducing himself as an equal one-third partner. The two remaining partners, due to their absence of any language prohibiting or restricting such a scenario, had no choice but to accept their new partner. Whether this turned out to be a beneficial addition to the team or not is not the point of sharing this story. Rather, place yourself in the shoes of one of the two original partners. Imagine for a moment a complete stranger showing up and introducing himself or herself as your new partner. Now imagine that there is nothing you can do about it. This is, quite obviously, an undesirable scenario. Our agreement tried to prevent a comparable event by including language that stated, "No Shareholder may, during his life or upon his death, transfer all or any portion of his Stock or any right or interest therein, whether voluntarily or by operation of law, to any Person, other than to the personal representative of his estate upon his death." Additionally, any transfers of stock would have to be approved by the board of directors, providing yet another method to restrict and monitor those who would become part of the organization. This concept was consistent throughout the agreement, with specifically defined scenarios. From a desire of a shareholder to simply sell or transfer stock to the redemption of shares upon the death of one of the shareholders, we identified and agreed upon the protocols on the front end.

In an effort to further prevent the scenario whereby an uninvited "guest" would appear on our doorstep as a self-proclaimed partner, we also included in our agreement the capability, though not necessarily the obligation, for the company to purchase life insurance policies on key members of the organization. The company, if such a policy were acquired, would be the beneficiary. Our objective here was to provide a benefits package to the spouse or surviving family members indirectly while focusing on the protection of the corporation at the same time. The desire of the two surviving partners in the earlier scenario to concern themselves with the well-being of their deceased partner's family was noble and certainly respected by our organization. The eventual outcome, however, was not. In the event of the death of one of our shareholders, a life insurance policy held by the corporation could provide a payout to the corporation. This payout would then be used to purchase the outstanding shares from the shareholder's estate, based on the pre-defined valuation formula. In the end, a policy held by the company would offer compensation to the estate of the deceased shareholder through the purchase of these shares. The family would receive money, and the company would retrieve the outstanding shares, keeping in mind that the transfer of any stock would have to be approved by the board. In this format, both sides would be protected.

This then raised a key issue that is addressed throughout the shareholders' agreement: the purchase price. How would a purchase price be determined? Most agreements will contain some type of formula, whether static or variable, for determining the value of each share. A static formula would include the value of the shares as a fixed amount and dictate in the agreement, fairly clearly, the purchase price of the stock. Static formulas typically have to be updated on a regular basis. The other option includes some variable measure, or collection of variable measures, for determining the value so that the net worth of the shares of stock is relevant to the value of the company at any given point in time. The static formula would not reflect any increases or decreases in value based on performance. It was clear that the variable formula offered a more realistic financial assessment for the outstanding shares. Following is another excerpt from our agreement that defined the methodology for determining the purchase price for any outstanding shares of stock:

> *Offered Shares will be the lesser of the following: (i) the purchase price offered by the proposed purchaser(s), or (ii) the fair market value of the Offered Shares. For purposes of this Section 2, the fair market value of the Offered Shares is hereby agreed to be an amount equal to the fair market value of the Corporation, divided by the Outstanding Shares on*

the effective date of the Offer Notice, times the number of the Offered Shares. If the Corporation has had one (1) or more operating subsidiaries for at least three (3) full Fiscal Years, then, for purposes of this Article III, the fair market value of the Corporation will be an amount equal to the average annual EBITDA of the Corporation for its last three (3) full Fiscal Years multiplied by the number three (3) less all liabilities of the Corporation and its subsidiaries. If the Corporation has not had one (1) or more operating subsidiaries for at least three (3) full Fiscal Years, then, for purposes of this Article III, the fair market value of the Corporation will be an amount equal to the EBITDA of the Corporation for the immediately preceding twelve (12) full calendar months multiplied by the number three (3) less all liabilities of the Corporation and its subsidiaries. The fair market value of the Corporation shall be determined by the Corporation's outside certified public accounting firm in accordance with generally accepted accounting principles, and, absent manifest error, such determination will be final and binding on all interested parties and other Persons.

Noticeably absent from our shareholders' agreement was a definition of responsibilities and accountability for the services to which each member of the organization was committed, investment-only partners excluded. These were services that had been promised by several of the partners in exchange for ownership. There was a responsibility to provide these services, and the organization would be counting on each individual and their respective areas of expertise. In the event that one of the members did not perform as expected or required by the corporation, the agreement included no provision for holding this member accountable. While I had raised the issue during our initial conversations of ownership and valuation, it was excluded from the final shareholders' agreement. This was a mistake. The responsibilities did not have to be static — we could have included provisions for updating responsibilities as the need arose. These responsibilities could have been defined in a separate schedule, referenced by the agreement. There were a number of options that could have been utilized. In the end, however, the accountability component was absent from our agreement.

There are a number of legal issues that can significantly influence one's business in the early stages, and it is important to secure reputable counsel. I cannot express this point enough — the time spent to address the "what if" scenarios is necessary and wise. As you will learn, some of our "what ifs" unexpectedly turned into "just dids."

5

So, What's on the Menu?

Ah, the menu. A central part of the dining experience. What? *Central* part? Not the *entire* experience? Well, no. For those of you who contend that restaurants are "all about the food," which is an argument that I hear quite frequently, I must respectfully disagree. A restaurant's cuisine no doubt plays a critical role in the overall experience—one that will vary depending upon the restaurant's concept, price point, and targeted quality level. However, there are a number of successful foodservice establishments that have what I consider to be pretty miserable food. Nevertheless, the parking lots in front of these establishments are full at 2 p.m. on a Wednesday all year long. These patrons, I assure you, are not there for a profound culinary experience. What guests seek in a restaurant is an overall experience, of which the food is one component. With all of that said, we *really* wanted our food to knock the socks off of our guests. We wanted to distance ourselves from the mainstream segment that featured bland, "safe" food—much of which was prepackaged and mass-produced, and whose culinary creators were clearly not focused on delivering a savory experience for the taste buds of their patrons. This was our goal, despite the fact that our price point placed us in the same category as most of the casual dinner houses. Our food was going to be succulent. It would be bold, with strong flavors, and just a little daring, yet feature enough recognizable ingredients to woo the average diner into a slightly more adventurous dining experience. Remember that this entire concept, this whole effort, had been spawned with one bite from Chris into a gourmet pizza in England. That pizza featured fresh spinach, crumbled bleu cheese, and walnuts, drizzled with extra virgin olive oil. The inception of our restaurant was based in the culinary arena. In order to provide our proverbial $30 experience for $15, we would have to offer food that supported the $30 experience claim, yet balance the ingredients used to maintain a desirable food cost.

Just a few weeks after we had decided to pursue the idea of creating a new restaurant concept, our first menu was already beginning to take shape. This early version included items such as Fresh Fire-Roasted Asparagus and the BaZitro Pizza (soy, ginger, garlic shrimp with green scallions, peppers, broccoli, and wasabi drizzle). We knew that this initial assembly of culinary offerings was a diamond in the rough, and by no means the final menu mix that would be offered on opening day. Perhaps our biggest challenge, in my mind at least, would be shaking the reputation as an Italian restaurant simply because we offered pizza. We had been describing the restaurant as a European bistro since its inception, in an effort to convey that we would offer a menu reflecting influences from a variety of European cuisines, although not tied to any one cuisine exclusively. Hints from Greek, English, French, Mediterranean, and other fare could be unearthed in various parts of the menu as a component of a dish or as a dominant method of preparation. In case this sounds a little too ambiguous, let me offer you a specific example: demi-glace. Demi-glace is a brown stock that is reduced to produce a thick, concentrated, flavorful, mouth-watering sauce that can be added to another recipe. The flavoring is quite powerful, salty, and hints of its meaty influence within any dish to which it is added. This one ingredient, a mere component of a larger offering, was distinct from the mainstream American cuisine offered at many of the popular full-service, casual restaurants. It was a strong flavor. It had body, and it had depth. Many of the offerings within the full-service, casual dining segment were quite bland in contrast. Our target market, we felt, was ready to be reintroduced to a stronger, more savory flavor profile. The simple addition of a demi-glace reduction changed the entire taste and aroma of several of our dishes. It was just fantastic.

Here is a quick look at our very first menu:

❖ ❖ ❖ THE ANTE ❖ ❖ ❖

Zoup de Pistou
A hearty blend of vegetables and beans, served with
a variety of toppings, grated cheese, pesto, tomatoes,
caramelized garlic & flat bread.

Bruschetta for All
For one, two, or four, grilled breads with crocks of spreads
and dips, spinach & artichokes, white beans and mint,
Portabella tapenade, herbed eggplant, fresh
tomato and basil.

Fire-Roasted Shrimp
Scampi served in a basket-shaped flat bread
with lemon aioli.

Baked Knots
Pull-apart dough knots with herb and roasted garlic oil.

Fresh-Roasted Azparagus
Balsamic vinegar marinated with Parmesan and herb butter.

❖ ❖ ❖ SALADS ❖ ❖ ❖

Zaesar Zalad
Roasted herb croutons, creamy Zaesar dressing.
Add: Chicken, Shrimp, or Sausage.

Mozzarella & Tomato
Classic style, great taste with black olives, basil dressing.

Mixed Fresh Greens
Crisp and delicious with 'Za-Bistro! Dressing.

Bowtie Pasta Prima 'Za-Bistro!
Chilled pasta bows tossed with fresh vegetables, tarragon,
oregano, and tomatoes.

❖ ❖ ❖ PASTA & PANINI ❖ ❖ ❖

Ziti For 'Za-Kidso
Baked with meat-a-ballz in Grandmother's tomato sauce, and
garlic sticks, or just sauce, or just butter, or just cheese . . .

Tortellini 'Zalinda
Ricotta-filled pasta tossed with caramelized onions,
roasted peppers, spicy sausage, capers, olives, and herbs.

Panini Pollini
Oven-toasted Parmesan chicken breast, provolone & roasted
vegetables on herbed flat bread.

Oven Ravioli St. Michael
Smoked salmon, dill, onions, capers, asparagus,
chopped eggs, and lemon dressing.

Scampi Sandi
Garlic shrimp, three cheeses, sliced tomato, herb mayo
on herbed panini bread.

Portobello Panini
Fire-roasted Portabella mushroom slices, caramelized onions
and melted cheese on oven-toasted flat bread.

❖ ❖ ❖ Piz'Za ❖ ❖ ❖

Fresh baked in our Brick Oven, our 10" pizza serves one or two; our 16" serves a group.
Step up and see how we make 'em.

'Za-Plain
Mozzarella, tomato sauce, olive oil, on fresh square dough.

St. Germain
Fresh spinach, peas, artichokes, olives, and goat cheese.

Mellow Portobello
Oven-roasted Portabella 'shrooms, caramelized onions and marjoram.

Marco's Pollo
Cilantro lime chicken and chipotle aioli, chopped tomato, scallion, and Jack cheese.

The BaZitro
Soy, ginger, garlic shrimp, green onion, peppers, broccoli & wasabi drizzle.

'Za's Margherita Mode
Roma tomato slices, mozzarella rounds, fresh basil.

Upper East Zide
Smoked salmon, asparagus, herbed goat cheese, dill oil & capers.

Bistro Saucizon!
Spiced sausage, roasted tomato, fresh mozzarella and peppers.

Grilled Vegetable Provenzale
Eggplant, zucchini, yellow squash, caramelized onion, capers, olives and three cheeses.

Chicken Caesar Salad
Warm cheese crust topped with creamy Caesar salad and Parmesan.

Big Mama Za Za's Crazy Calzone
Three cheeses, fire-roasted vegetables, 'Za Zausage, and 'Bella mushrooms, bursting at the seams.

❖ ❖ ❖ THE SWEETS ❖ ❖ ❖

Carmelized Sweet Apple Dough
Mascarpone cheese mousse.

Chocolate Espresso Torta
Chocolate and coffee cake caramel sauce.

Roasted Strawberry Shortcake Pizza
Whip Cream.

Handmade Gelato
Vanilla, Chocolate Chip, Hazelnut Blackberry, Lemon.
with strawberries
with almond biscotti
with triple chocolate fudge sauce
with all of the above and more

❖ ❖ ❖

This first menu, which barely resembled the menu that we eventually presented to our guests on opening night, initiated a number of philosophical conversations regarding not only the menu, but also our target customer, our financial goals, approaches to marketing, and so much more. The first pass at this menu was too heavily influenced by Italian fare and did not depict what we felt was a European bistro, with influences from all different parts of the region. There were other issues that we needed to tackle as a group. Should a salad be included with an entrée? How many appetizers should we offer? Should we offer fried foods, and would it set a tone? Would we offer anything as a giveaway when people first sat down at the table? Should the pizzas be offered in family-style large pies or in individual sizes only? Should we have a full bar, or beer and wine only? Would we deliver? What would the staff and payroll structure be like? Should we have a kids' menu? Would we be using linen or paper napkins? Was there the potential to offer ready-to-go or take-and-bake items for the home? The questions, quite literally, were endless. The sheer number of decisions that needed to be made was quite amazing, but this was the fun part. This was the creation of the concept. Though the discussions were centered on the menu, we were making decisions that would shape the entire personality of the concept and reach much further than just the culinary component

One other aspect of the menu that we considered was its longevity — and not for any one specific entrée, but rather for the style of offering. We wanted a menu that would be able to withstand the various dietary fads that have a tendency to sweep the nation. It was our desire to offer a healthful menu, featuring fresh ingredients and balanced nutrition that would appeal to a large number of dietary categories and preferences. In 2002, before it was popular or legislation had been passed that would require the disclosure of trans fats, we discussed offering foods prepared without any partially hydrogenated oils. It was part of our concept, it was who we were. Even by just discussing the subject, we were demonstrating that as a neighborhood restaurant we cared for our local community and viewed our customers as extended family. We wanted to promote a healthful lifestyle without sacrificing quality or flavor. We had also discussed providing selections for individuals who were observing diets such as vegetarian, lactose-free, Weight Watchers, heart healthy, and protein heavy. Again, this was before the major influence of low-carb diets. And while we sought to offer such culinary options, we wanted to present these items as part of the mainstream menu, not as an alternative to the regular menu. We wanted entrées that appealed to these specialty diets to be integrated throughout the menu and available to all. With the advantage of hindsight, I can tell you that our strategy worked in many ways. We were referred to as a great vegetarian restaurant in one local review after our opening, despite the fact that we were not a vegetarian restaurant. A similar discussion about our restaurant in another local publication touted our low-carb menu. We did not have a low-carb menu. It was proof that our original concept had been implemented successfully.

While we had envisioned that gourmet pizzas would account for a large part of our menu mix, the desire for more entrées increased among the group. We conducted informal market research with our families, friends, colleagues, and members of our target market, and found that most felt the offering of several entrées, aside from pizzas, would be beneficial and help to complement the menu's product mix. Soon, this desire to add entrées to the menu gained even greater support internally, and what was once a 75 to 25 percent ratio of pizzas to entrées soon became a 55 to 45 percent ratio of the same products. Was this evolution a refinement of the concept, or were we straying from our initial vision? These are questions that every restaurant developer must ask continuously during the course of the concept development process. In our case, we felt that the addition of these entrées was consistent with our theme and business model. As you will notice, the original menu featured a number of pasta dishes. This was a source of much discussion. Not just from the perspective of the potential onslaught of low-carb diets that appeared to be on the horizon at the time, but also from an operations and design standpoint. The pasta, if featured on the menu, would significantly affect the way that food would have to be produced, and thus influence the design of the food preparation areas. It was our objective, which we stated early on, to feature a display kitchen with our stone-hearth oven as the only working piece of cooking equipment in full view of the dining room. Although it was possible to produce the pasta ahead of time, plate it, and then re-heat it in the oven, we were concerned about the limitations this method of preparation would present and the quality of product that we would be able to offer consistently. In essence, we would be limited to crock-style cuisines. Also, the addition of pasta would only further promote an association as an "Italian" restaurant, a connotation we were working diligently to avoid.

There was yet another discussion, this one primarily between me and Chris, that continued for months: ice cream. Chris was insistent upon the fact that we would need to offer at least one ice cream for dessert. I, on the other hand, was not convinced and pointed out that it was not sensible to invest thousands of dollars in equipment, construction, and utilities for one menu item. I felt that we could offer an attractive array of desserts without having ice cream. My focus on eliminating the need for an ice cream freezer demonstrated one potential way for us to reduce the cost on the front end. Perhaps this is a bit odd coming from a guy of my background who grew up in the restaurant equipment sales business, but in my professional experience I have always tried to look at the equipment package from the owner's perspective. Our firm acts as an owner's protagonist, keeping their long-term best interests in mind. It just so happened that in this instance, I was the owner. In hindsight, though, Chris was right on this issue. We eventually included an ice cream freezer, and the sales from ice cream more than made up for the initial investment and operational costs incurred. In reviewing this issue, I want to demonstrate not only the types of issues that will arise for discussion, but the logic that must be used to evaluate each and every opportunity.

Yet another emotional debate among the partners was the concept of offering Starbucks coffee at 'Za-Bistro! This was a topic that I was extremely passionate about, and I refused to back off my position—you have to pick your battles. I refused to allow it, fearing that the inclusion of the Starbucks logo and product in our restaurant would dilute our own brand. Starbucks, at that point, was already available in gas stations and every corner grocery store. Would a European bistro serve such a product? No way! If 'Za-Bistro! were to be known as a European-style bistro, we simply could not afford to dilute our image from the outset by allowing a widely accessible product such as Starbucks coffee to be offered. It was not consistent with our image or our concept. I won that one; we never did offer Starbucks coffee, but an authentic European brand instead.

As these conversations continued, the menu began to take shape. During the course of this process, we also saw the changing of the guard in the culinary ranks of our corporation, with Daniel taking over the menu from Brian. The transition was seamless. While Chris and Brian had initiated the menu development effort, it was Daniel who truly took ownership of the culinary realm of our concept and formalized the menu. He took the menu we had, which was in a constant state of flux, and developed recipes and specifications so that they could be executed with consistency. He experimented. He tweaked. He explored alternative ingredients, preparation methods, and presentation techniques.

Once Daniel had progressed to a point where he was comfortable with a majority of the menu, we decided that it was time to take a trip to Wood Stone, the manufacturer of the oven that we would be using as the basis for our restaurant concept. Though we will talk about the restaurant's equipment layout and design in far greater detail in a later chapter, it is important to take a moment now and at least address the heart and culinary spirit of our operation. Wood Stone, located in Bellingham, Washington, is a leading manufacturer of stone-hearth ovens. These ovens are often referred to as "pizza" or "wood-burning" ovens. The use of such nomenclature highlights the misunderstanding that is typically associated with this category of equipment. First, these ovens can be used for a great deal more than just pizza, as we were determined to prove. Second, very often they are not actually burning any wood, but rather operate exclusively on gas. Extensive testing at Wood Stone's facility determined that the actual wood burning, though providing an appealing aroma outside of the restaurant, imparted little flavor on the food. It sounds hard to believe, but in a taste test of two products side by side—one cooked in a wood-burning oven and one in a gas oven without any wood used in the cooking process—the products revealed no discernable difference in taste.

There is something very primal and very romantic about cooking in a stone-hearth oven. It offered the ability to cook using a method similar to those that had been used for thousands of years. This oven was to be the centerpiece of our restaurant concept, both figuratively and literally. Wood Stone had long contested that the oven could do more than just cook pizzas, which was its most dominant use in commercial foodservice applications. In our preliminary discussions with the factory, we had come to the conclusion that our menu would push the oven as far, if not farther, than it had ever been pushed before with respect to menu diversity.

We had reached a critical stage in our development process, and it was time to fly to Washington and utilize the test kitchen at Wood Stone's factory to bring our menu to life. This was quite a significant step, as it would be the first physical contact that we would have with the restaurant, our first tangible 'Za-Bistro! experience. When discussing a restaurant in general conversation, one question that always comes up is, "How was the food?" In all honesty, despite the amount of planning that had already been invested in 'Za-Bistro!, we still had no idea how the food would taste.

Daniel had chosen to fly out a day ahead of us in order to check that all of the proper ingredients were available and to do some prep work. Harold was able to meet Daniel in Washington a day early as well. Frank, Wood Stone's corporate chef, worked diligently to prepare for our arrival, and he was ready with a number of suggestions ranging from the utilization of specific ingredients to recommended facilities planning and layout configurations for the oven and its adjacent areas. Chris and I arrived a day later.

Daniel and Harold used the extra day to prepare all of the *mis en place*, or base ingredients, that we would be using for our test recipes. We all worked diligently ahead of time before the Wood Stone trip, looking at different menu options, service styles, facility layouts, and the like. However, there is only so much that you can do ahead of time. It was an exciting time.

We started bright and early, the day after Chris and I arrived, for a full day in the factory's test kitchen. Wood Stone had a 7-foot round oven, similar to the one that we were planning to utilize, fired up and ready to go. We also moved around some of the portable tables in the test kitchen to simulate the counter locations and clearances reflected in our original design. Frank started the morning by cooking frittatas in the oven. This was a deliberate selection, as he wanted to show the versatility of the oven's capabilities. Over breakfast, Daniel had shared some of his thoughts and early lessons learned from the previous day's preparation. One of the tapenades would be eliminated from the menu. While it was quite tasty and had a wonderful presentation, the time required to prepare the mixture was simply too great. Our focus on controlling labor from the outset, one of the largest costs in operating a restaurant, would force us to eliminate or replace this particular menu item. The food, in addition to being appealing and tasteful, must also be profitable.

Numerous chains, including California Pizza Kitchen, had proven that Wood Stone's ovens could perform well in the production of gourmet pizzas and pizza-style products. And though our menu featured a selection of such entrées, we wanted to focus on the non-pizza products first to see how well the oven could support their production. By this time, the 'Za-Bistro! menu had evolved to include fresh fish fillets, beef dishes, escargot, fire-roasted asparagus, and a host of other non-pizza dishes that did not have an extensive track record with this piece of equipment. As such, we needed to determine how best to produce these items in the oven and whether the product would meet our desired standards. The entire morning was dedicated to some of these specialty items. The spinach and artichoke dip that we tested was literally the best I had ever tasted, no exaggeration. It tasted fresh and had an even distribution of flavors. We tested our recipes for Beef Bourguignon, Fire-Roasted Shrimp, and Roasted Duck. The duck, believe it or not, came in a vacuum-sealed package and had already been cooked, then chilled for storage. We used this duck product as a base for our recipe, added our own seasonings in the form of a rub, and then tested it in the oven. The end result was nothing short of spectacular. Once

again, the oven's impact on the food was tremendous. The flavors were vivid, lively, and complete. The base duck product cost a little more than $3. The additional cost of the spiced rub, sides, and labor would allow us to sell this entrée for $13.95 all day long, which would support our desire to offer the $30 experience we sought at half that price. In the end, the non-pizza products performed amicably in the oven, which led us to believe that we were on to something with this 'Za-Bistro! concept.

Our testing of various menu items and cooking methods continued throughout the day. But with our group, of course, we had to use a sophisticated approach—even to test recipes. Take the pizzas, for example. We separated our testing efforts into dough and sauce. First, we tried three dough products, all with the same sauce, which served as the control element of the experiment. Two of the doughs were purchased from different food purveyors and the third was made fresh on site. The third, the fresh dough, was a clear favorite of the group and won the competition hands down. Once the dough was identified, three different sauces were tested. One was pre-made while the other two were made from scratch in the Wood Stone test kitchen. The winner, amazingly (or perhaps not so amazingly), was the simplest of the three: crushed tomatoes cooked in the oven with a little bit of salt and pepper. That was it. The resulting sauce was simply fantastic and was once again a clear winner among the three options. The results from our "battle of the sauces" made me an even stronger believer that the cooking methods utilized with this oven, a combination of radiant heat and conducted heat, had a direct effect on the food and truly enhanced the flavor profiles and colors of the products we were cooking. Referring back to the spinach and artichoke dip, the flavors in this popular dish, which is featured on numerous menus across the country, were unlike anything that I had tasted before. The flavors truly blended and melded together to create a savory delight that was well balanced in its different culinary elements, including texture and mouth feel. It was a home run as an item. It came out of the oven bubbling around the perimeter of the dish, clearly conveying that the item had been prepared fresh. In another very memorable example of the oven's performance, we were in the process of roasting garlic in the clove. When this is done properly, the garlic cloves turn to a soft paste and can be spread on bread just like butter. In this particular instance, the clove was not completely covered, and one of the cloves literally jumped right out of the head of garlic! The oven was also used to execute different cooking techniques such as braising, roasting, and searing. The beef that came out of the oven was tender. The salmon was flavorful — crispy on the outside and moist on the inside.

Our test results would affect more than just the food itself, they would impact the facility's layout, the cooking equipment required to execute the menu, and the operational systems needed to produce the food properly and consistently. Subsequently, the results would also influence our business model, and thus influence both startup and ongoing operational costs. These were significant decisions.

Prior to our visit, we had arranged for a focus group to be held with the staff at Wood Stone, as we were in search of quality feedback. In preparation for this focus group, we spent the late morning and lunch hour preparing various items that we sought to offer as part of our menu selection. Now that we had the opportunity to taste the food and develop our own opinions, we wanted to solicit the candid

opinions of others. Keep in mind that, by this time, the menu had changed a bit from its original form — an anticipated evolution. Though similar in some areas, the differences were significant in concept and preparation. Daniel had standardized much of the original menu, making adaptations and adjustment as necessary, so that

the menu could be executed by the operations team.

The menu's evolution was driven and influenced by a number of key issues, several of which involved some significant and often heated discussions among the team members. Given the number of owners and our collective experience, it was not surprising that we did not always see eye to eye as a group from the outset, which was healthy in my opinion. Groupthink can be a dangerous scenario, depriving the development process of the necessary challenges and questioning that help to improve the end result. Evolution of the menu during the development process is natural, even expected.

Continuing to look at the menu from a business perspective, the cross-utilization of product was much greater in the revised menu. For those not familiar with this term, cross-utilization in the restaurant industry refers to the use of a single ingredient in a number of different dishes, which ultimately saves both labor and food costs. Looking at our menu, for instance, the dough that was used for the Fire Bread was the same dough that was used for the pizza. Other ingredients such as the olives, certain cheeses, and various main entrée proteins were used throughout the menu on appetizers and main courses. Through this method of cross-utilization, preparation time may be spent on the one ingredient, and then that ingredient can be incorporated into a number of different dishes. From a financial perspective, this spreads out the preparation cost over all items using the ingredient, resulting in a lower labor cost to produce the items. Cross-utilization of ingredients also results in a lower number of ingredients in inventory, which in turn leads to better pricing due to volume of use and lower spoilage rates. Remember, this is the *Business of Restaurants*.

Our menu was distinct not only in the menu items offered and their preparation, but in the end product that was served—specifically the portion size. Portion sizes in many restaurants throughout the United States are grossly oversized. This trend is evident in almost every market segment. Consider the fact that as a nation, we have been trained to "super size" our meals for an extra 99 cents. Several national chains, from the quick-service market segment to the casual-dining market segment, are guilty of abnormally large portion sizes. Many of their entrées are *enormous*, and should not be finished in a single sitting, as the calorie, fat, and sodium contents far surpass the allowances recommended. If one takes the time to truly evaluate these offerings, it will quickly become evident that the portions, while oversized, include a significant amount of cheap filler ingredients or side dishes to enhance the perception of food quantity. Items such as potatoes and soda, which are inexpensive and high-margin items to begin with, are increased while the protein quantities remain the same and are even reduced in certain instances.

Part of our desire to offer a healthful menu at 'Za-Bistro! not only included the menu items and ingredients, but the portion sizes as well. The portion sizes we planned to offer were not small, but rather appropriate in size. The culinary offerings did not include low-cost fillers. We also felt that a correction of the average portion size in restaurants throughout the country was on the horizon, and we would be ahead of the curve. However, I can tell you, based on experience from some of my other entrepreneurial efforts, that being slightly ahead of the curve is not always easy. Not to say that our desire to offer appropriate portion sizes was revolutionary, but I must admit that I was concerned there could be a backlash from patrons who would be comparing us to some of the restaurant concepts that seemingly cared less about their patrons' health and more about eye appeal and value. Conversely, we did not want to be perceived as an expensive gourmet concept that offered undersized portions, overselling the *quality* of the ingredients in each entrée.

Following all of the changes and discussions among the team members, here is what our menu looked like as we were preparing to move forward with the first restaurant. In comparing this version of the menu to the original one from earlier in the chapter, you will notice the decreased role that gourmet pizzas played and the increased role that the entrées played.

❖ ❖ ❖ ZTARTERS ❖ ❖ ❖
Great stuff to start a meal, or mix and match to make a meal . . .

Daily Zoup
A different hot or cold soup each day of the week.

Bread Spreads & Dip
Fire bread with spinach and artichoke dip, black olive tapenade, and fresh tomato and basil bruschetta.

Oven-Fired Shrimp
Spicy jumbo shrimp with fire bread and lemon aioli.

Baked Z'zzzz
Pull-apart dough Z'z with Parmesan cheese and our fresh-roasted tomato dipping sauce.

'Za-Best Stuff on a Plate
Roasted vegetables, warm goat cheese, marinated fresh
mozzarella, kalamata olives, fire bread,
and tarragon dijonaise.

Fire-Roasted Azparagus
Drizzled with balsamic vinegar, virgin olive oil,
and shaved asiago.

Que 'Za Dilla
Cilantro lime chicken, peppers, jack cheese, scallions
sour cream, and chipotle sauce.

Mussels Cataplana
Green lip mussels roasted in their own savory saffron
and fire-roasted tomato broth.

Mozzarella & Tomato
Roasted tomato salad with fresh mozzarella cheese and black
olives, drizzled with a fruity balsamic dressing, greens, and
burgundy roasted garlic cloves.

Warm Brie Roast
Chunks of brie cheese with tomato, herbs, roasted garlic,
diced olives, and fire bread.

❖ ❖ ❖ 'ZA-NDWICHES ❖ ❖ ❖
Some hot, some cold . . .

Oven-Roasted Vegetable Baguette
Fresh-roasted vegetables with pesto and mozzarella cheese.

Cilantro Lime Chicken Ciabbatta
Cilantro lime chicken, tomatoes, scallions, chipotle sauce,
and Monterey jack cheese.

Oven-Fired Shrimp Wrap
Spicy jumbo shrimp, spinach, scallions, lemon aioli,
and mozzarella.

'Za-Bistro! Baguette
Parma proscuitto, pesto mayonnaise, fresh mozzarella,
and field greens.

Mac's Meatball Grinder
Jumbo meatballs, mozzarella, and sauce on an oven-toasted sub roll.

❖ ❖ ❖ BISTRO ZPECIALTIES ❖ ❖ ❖
Served with 'Za- Bistro! roasted vegetables and potatoes.
Add a bistro 'Zalad

'Za-Bistro! Chicken Tarragon
Oven-roasted breast braised in tarragon demi-glace,
roasted mushrooms, and pearl onions.

Oven-Roasted Mahi
With spinach and Portabella mushrooms.

Beef Bourguignon
Beef chunks braised tender with red wine, mushrooms,
and pearl onions, bubbling hot from our oven.

'Za-Gratin
Shrimp and scallops in a creamy Parmesan garlic sauce.

Oven-Seared Salmon
Succulent balsamic-roasted salmon with
'Za-Bistro! seasoning blend.

Salmon de Provence
Oven-roasted with olives, artichokes, tomato, and garlic.

Oven-Braized Beef Short Ribz
Slow-roasted and braised in a rich red wine sauce.

❖ ❖ ❖ 'ZA-LADS AND OTHER GOOD ZTUFF ❖ ❖ ❖
Fresh, delightful, complicated, and simple

'Za-easar 'Za-lad
Long-leaf Romaine lettuce, roasted herb croutons, and shaved
Asiago with creamy 'Za-easar dressing;
a house specialty.

Mixed Fresh Greens
Fresh field greens and bruschetta topping with 'Za-Bistro!
Parmesan peppercorn dressing.

Spinach Prima 'Za-Bistro!
Chilled fresh spinach tossed with provolone, strawberries,
mushrooms, and sweet mustard dressing.

Bleu & You
Bleu cheese, curly endive, and roasted walnuts with
a balsamic dressing.

(add Oven-Fired Shrimps, Cilantro Lime Chicken, or Balsamic Roasted Salmon to any above salad)

Port 'Za Bella
Roasted Portabella mushroom topped with roasted
vegetable salad and mozzarella and bleu cheese,
field greens, virgin olive oil, and balsamic vinaigrette.

Bistro Salad Brunch, Anytime
Smoked salmon, roasted potatoes, asparagus, red onion
and olives with fresh greens and
sweet mustard dressing served with a baked "Z."

❖ ❖ ❖ PIZ'ZA ❖ ❖ ❖
Fresh baked in our stone-hearth oven, our pizza serves one or two. Step up and see how we make 'em!

'Za-Plain
Mozzarella, tomato sauce, olive oil, on a fresh dough,
add pepperoni if you choose.

Mellow Portobello
Oven-roasted Portabella mushrooms, caramelized onion,
and smoked mozzarella.

Marco's Pollo
Cilantro lime chicken, chipotle aioli, tomato, scallions,
and jack cheese.

'Za Margherita Mode
Roma tomato slices, mozzarella, and fresh basil.

Upper East Zide
Smoked salmon, asparagus, herbed goat cheese,
dill oil, and capers.

Bistro Saucizon!
Spicy andouille sausage, roasted tomato,
fresh mozzarella, and peppers.

Gouda 'Nuff
Spicy buffalo chicken, bleu cheese sauce, red onion, and smoked Gouda cheese.

❖ ❖ ❖ SWEETS ❖ ❖ ❖
Confections, pastries, & sweets: freshly prepared for dessert, for an
afternoon break, or just to indulge that urge for a treat.

Crème Brûlée
Tasty cups of vanilla or milk chocolate custard
and caramelized sugar.

Lee'z Key Lime
Creamy, sweet, and tangy with macadamia gingersnap crust,
whipped cream and raspberry sauce.

Fresh Fruits and Berries
Berries, oranges, and bananas with Grand Marnier
and whipped cream.

'Za- Chocolate Brownie
Dark chocolate brownie wedge, vanilla bean ice cream,
roasted walnuts, and chocolate ganache.

Lombardi's Favorite
Your choice of any three of the above desserts.

Chocolate Espresso Indulgence
Chocolate ganache with almonds, espresso Crème Anglaise, and caramel sauce.

❖ ❖ ❖

Getting back to the Wood Stone focus group, we were very specific in our request for the composition of this tasting team. We wanted women! Lots of women! There is a reason for this. As discussed earlier, next to children, women are the most influential demographic in deciding where to eat in any group—family, friends, or just a couple. Because of this position that women hold, they possess something very powerful—the veto vote. That is to say that, because their sole opinion holds a great deal of weight, a woman's desire *not* to dine at a particular location can influence the eventual outcome of a group's "where-to-eat" dilemma. Thus, we call this the veto vote because a single opinion can veto the potential dining venue for the entire group. What about a man's opinion? Well, there is *some* influence there as well, but it is typically not as strong. Now, we must look at the power that women have over the where-to-eat decision-making process from an entirely different angle. Just as women are likely to veto a dining location from contention, they are equally likely to champion the selection of another location that they do like. If women like it, and the choices for other party members are adequate, they can drive the party toward a particular dining establishment, rather than away from it. And so, the reason we spent so much time making sure that our concept was female friendly is quite evident. This is not sexist, but rather a demographic observation identified and utilized by our team.

For our taste test at the factory, we strategically laid out almost all of the menu items on the table and provided the focus group with an opportunity to sample the dishes that we had prepared. Overall, the comments that we received on the food were encouraging—very encouraging, in fact. There were some questions and differing opinions regarding the portion sizes that were presented. We had some requests to produce several of the featured dishes without adding any additional fats (for example, olive oil). Other input reflected the personal and dietary preferences of various focus group participants, which was to be expected. Even with our relatively small test group, sometimes the input from the participants was conflicting. At other times, comments were consistent and in strong support of our effort and direction. Perhaps the most memorable feedback we received was in the form of the focus group's facial expressions after we revealed the pricing structure of the menu. We were very careful to allow them to taste the food first, and then tell us what they would expect to pay for such a meal in a restaurant of the nature that we described. The unanimous decision from the group was that our menu items would likely range in price from $19 to $25 per entrée. Once this opinion was unanimously affirmed around the room, we revealed our actual pricing structure, which would feature an average check of about $15. They were floored! The expressions and shock were priceless and probably the most influential moment of the entire trip for me. It was concrete confirmation of our concept and the entire development process with which we were involved. Here are a few of the actual comments that we received:

"One of the best things about the presentation of the entrées was the healthy manner in which they were prepared. The shrimp and salmon were among my favorites, full of flavor without the added fat. The variety was great and truly everything sampled was wonderful. The concept for a reasonably priced lunch spot coupled with family-friendly meals for a dinner out should do very well. I wish we had one of your restaurants in Bellingham!"

"I was impressed with the variety of food choices at a reasonable price; very family friendly."

"I think your demonstration (food) was one of the most dynamic I have been involved in. Your food represents simple, straightforward cooking in front of an open flame, ending in exceptional presentations and flavors for

your guests. I strongly believe you are at the heart of the onrushing kitchen revolution of 'fresh, simply seasoned food.' Congratulations."

"My favorite and most memorable was the saucy beef dish. Plenty of bold flavor. My only advice is to not be timid about flavor, and you've done that well."

"Everything I tasted was outstanding. The simplicity of ingredients made for a bold but not overpowering taste. This should appeal to a broad base of family and female customers while maintaining the male segment. Presentation was outstanding, simple but catchy. It doesn't need to be complicated; the product spoke volumes by itself."

In addition to these wonderful comments, one of the key members of the Wood Stone team leaned over to Frank, their corporate chef, and

whispered into his ear that the food we had prepared was simply the best she had ever tasted by any group in the Wood Stone test kitchen. This was a significant statement, as Wood Stone averages two to three visits to their test kitchen every week. The most flattering part about this comment was that it was not meant for my ears—it was an accidental eavesdrop of a true sentiment being shared among colleagues. We had pushed this piece of equipment further than anyone before us. We pushed it where the factory thought it could go, but had not found a restaurant group that was brave enough to try it.

The Wood Stone trip was a valuable experience. But upon our return to central Florida, there were a number of conceptual issues that the team still needed to hash out. The first of these issues was the kids' menu. Should there be a kids' menu? This was quite an emotional issue for the group, and the discussion continued right through the opening of the restaurant, flip-flopping back and forth several times. Some members of the team had young children, and some did not. Regardless, we tried to look at this matter from a purely business viewpoint, from the perspective of our target customers. One of the fears that was raised regarding a special children's menu was the crowd that it would attract—young, loud kids. Would it be appropriate for the concept, the customer base that we were targeting, and the atmosphere that we were working diligently to create? There were plenty of restaurant concepts that did not have a kids' menu, but instead offered items that kids might like, at full price. Where did the unwritten rule—that kids' menus needed to be priced less than the main menu—come from? Panera Bread, for example, does not have a children's menu, but they do have peanut butter and jelly, which is available to anyone who would like to purchase the sandwich. They have bagels, sandwiches, and soups that appeal to children as well, though they are not specifically designed to do so. Their kids' menu is integrated into the overall menu, with no separation. Other restaurant concepts that are quite successful in attracting a loyal, regular crowd, however, do have separate kids' menus. Think of many of the major multi-unit concepts—Chili's, Bennigan's, TGI Friday's, and the like. It was a tough decision, and I am not sure that there was really a *right* answer. In the end, we chose to go without a special kids' menu. The logic behind this decision was that we had certain items that already appealed to children. We wanted the restaurant to be a place that parents could take their kids and feel comfortable, but we did not necessarily want to target kids for the fear that doing so could drive away some of the key customers in our target market group.

Another hot topic among the group was the decision to offer beer and wine or a full liquor bar. In Florida, as in many other states, there are different licenses that are required depending on the alcoholic beverages that are offered to the guests. A beer and wine license is typically much less expensive and easier to acquire than a liquor license. Access to a liquor license of any kind will vary greatly by region and local jurisdiction. In some areas, all a restaurateur needs to do is simply apply for the license and pay the fees, and then a liquor license will be issued. In other jurisdictions, however, there are a limited number of alcohol licenses available. In these locations, a liquor license becomes a limited resource and is much harder to come by. Lotteries or bidding by restaurateurs desiring to add alcohol service may be the only way to obtain a liquor license in these locales. There are a number of factors to consider when making this decision. A full bar will, of course, require a much higher initial and ongoing investment. From the bar equipment and inventory to the staffing and insurance, costs for a full bar are much higher than one that simply offers beer and wine only. The upside is that a full bar offers revenue potential that a beer and wine bar simply cannot match. When a patron is willing to spend $10 on a martini with dinner, the additional revenue will have a positive affect on both the average check and the overall gross revenue and net profit.

A beer and wine license requires far less infrastructure as it relates to the equipment and physical inventory, and the cost of the license is typically lower. With the ability to limit upfront and ongoing expenses, and still allow patrons to purchase a bottle of wine that might be $30 or more, the beer and wine license also offered significant upside potential. Ultimately, we decided to go with a beer and wine license only—not a full bar. The cost, infrastructure, available space, and original concept description all led us to this particular decision.

Finally, there was the discussion regarding the day parts, or meal opportunity periods, that would be supported. Lunch and dinner were a given, but the decision whether or not to offer breakfast required further discussion. Personally, I had always felt that this particular restaurant concept lent itself quite well to Sunday brunch. However, the group struggled to reach a consensus as to what should be done regarding breakfast during the other days of the week. Some argued that we should offer counter service for breakfast. Some took exception to this desire, arguing that this was not the original intention of the concept. This decision would have a significant affect on the operations model as well as the physical facility itself. We opened with no breakfast at all, and eventually introduced the Sunday brunch meal period once the staff was prepared and properly trained to execute the alternate menu. The breakfast function, we determined, would be site-specific. The restaurant *could* offer a breakfast menu, if we determined that the business model would justify such an option in the local market.

With these major decisions out of the way, the menu was really taking shape, and our menu testing allowed us to move forward with more confidence. We had finally tasted the food. Now when people asked, "How's the food?" we would be able to respond sincerely and say, "Fantastic!"

6

Out of Site, Out of Mind

"There is more than one way to skin a cat," as the saying goes. Well, the same holds true for restaurant development. There are three primary elements in the creation of a new restaurant: the *concept*, the *site*, and the *market*. Restaurant development has to begin somewhere, but fortunately there is no one formula that must be followed. The process can start with any one of the three elements, or any combination of the three. A restaurateur may have defined the concept but is in need of a physical location in order to open this new place of business. On the other hand, an aspiring restaurant developer may have access to a location in a neighborhood with a wealthy, retired population, but may not be sure exactly what kind of restaurant to open. A concept is required. There is also the possibility that a particular market segment, with a particular need, may have been identified, but both a concept and a location are needed in order to capitalize on the opportunity that has been unearthed. Any of these methods are acceptable means by which to start the development process.

In our case, we began with the concept, which was discussed at length in Chapter 3. Remember that the concept is everything that defines what the restaurant is to its customers, staff, community, and investors. We started with the menu, the logo, the design and ambiance—all of the items discussed to this point. Our target market was fairly well defined, though we would not be completely sure of this until we actually opened the doors of our first restaurant. What we were in need of was a site. I never realized just how hard it would be to secure a restaurant location. As you will soon learn, the delays, negotiations, economy, and general business environment, as well as numerous other factors, significantly hindered our ability to locate and finalize our first deal.

While it is possible to secure a site first and then determine what the concept and market will be, I am not sure that it is the most desirable approach. Some may thrive given such an opportunity, but concept development under the gun does not typically yield the best results. Should new construction be considered in lieu of an existing space? It is certainly a strong possibility, but consider for a moment the potential for a delay. What impact would that have on the restaurateur's livelihood? Is the restaurant going to be the soul source of income or not? How about looking at an existing site location, whether previously occupied or brand new? These are all valid questions that we would have to address.

Orlando is well known for its tourism and influx of visitors. Business in the tourist areas of the city can fluctuate a great deal, however, based on seasonality. We made the decision early on that we did not want to be near the tourist corridor, but instead we wanted to be "among the rooftops"—near the houses and the neighborhoods where residents could frequent 'Za-Bistro! year-round. The seasonality in the tourist corridor of Orlando would pose too great a risk, we thought, especially for the first restaurant. In our very first discussions, we talked about leasing a 1,500-square-foot space, which is the size of a typical storefront in a suburban strip mall—20 feet wide by 75 feet long. This estimation was made, however, before our concept was fully defined. We quickly determined that a space of this size would simply be too small to house the concept that was emerging. The space that we would require would have to be somewhere between 3,000 and 4,000 square feet. This would be quite a bit larger than most of the single storefront spaces, but smaller than many of the casual-dining chains that can reach upwards of 6,000 square feet or more. A space in our range would typically break down as follows: 35 to 40 percent for the kitchen and back-of-house, 6 to 9 percent for the restrooms, and the remainder for the dining room and other public or support areas. The percentages will vary based on the size of the space, because certain elements will remain stagnant in actual size, thereby increasing or decreasing their percentage of the overall space. The bathrooms, for example, need to be a certain size to meet accessibility codes and comply with the number of stalls that are required. Assume that these restrooms are 300 square feet. In a space that is 3,000 square feet, the bathrooms would comprise 10 percent of the total space. In a space that is 4,000 square feet, however, these same restrooms would only account for 7.5 percent of the total space. The increased seating capacity in the larger restaurant would not reach the next threshold requiring an increase in the number of restroom stalls. As you can see, a discussion strictly based on percentages of the total square footage can often be misleading. This same logic would hold true for some of the other key areas of the facility, directly affecting their percentage of the total space.

The location is the hardest thing about a restaurant to change once the restaurant has been opened. The menu, staff, décor, marketing, signage—virtually every other component of an existing restaurant is easier to change than the location, stressing the importance of selecting the right site. Numerous issues need to be considered when selecting a restaurant location—some that are pretty straightforward, as well as some that are less intuitive. In the world of site selection, there are "A" sites, "B" sites, and "C" sites—anything less than a "C" site is probably not worth considering. The "A" sites are usually more expensive because they are in locations where the natural traffic and demand generators are located. A movie theater, for instance, is a natural traffic generator as patrons are always flocking to the movies, often looking for a place to eat either before or after their show. Grocery stores, large big-box retailers, and community shopping areas, whether a traditional indoor mall or a more modern outdoor complex, are also natural traffic generators. Restaurant sites near these types of businesses are typically more expensive but receive more exposure. The "B" sites may have some demand generators near them, but do not generate nearly the amount of traffic that is experienced at the "A" sites. They may be harder to access or located within an emerging neighborhood—one that is not as desirable *right now* as an "A" site. A "C" site will have even more drawbacks. The asking price for rent on each of these location types should vary based on the type of location—"A" sites are more expensive than "B" sites, and "B" sites are more expensive than "C" sites. Throughout my hospitality education, I was taught that the three most important factors in a restaurant's success are location, location, and location. Whether one completely agrees with this statement or not, it has been demonstrated time and again that the location of a restaurant can have a significant impact on its success.

When considering a potential site, access and visibility must be evaluated. Can you see the restaurant from the road? Can you see it from all directions, from each approach? Can you get to it easily? I have seen plenty of restaurant sites that are clearly visible from main roads or highways, but accessing them is difficult. There is the potential to lose customers who become frustrated during the search for access to a restaurant, despite the fact that they can see it clearly. Parking is closely tied to these site characteristics as well. Is there sufficient parking? If not, potential customers will choose the path of least resistance, in many cases, and may not be willing to park three blocks away just to have dinner at a particular restaurant. Factors like these can drive customers away and negatively influence the restaurant's chance for success.

Evaluate the site's condition. How much work is required to convert or create the space so that it can house a particular concept? What physical obstructions or limitations are there? For instance, can a hood be added anywhere that is deemed desirable, or are there restrictions due to the building's configuration that may not permit utilization of the layout that is most efficient? Are there columns, electrical panels, grease traps, or other permanent obstructions that may limit potential design solutions? Some of the issues might not be as intuitive, requiring further research. For instance, is the potential leased space in a flood zone? Will any of the site conditions drive up your insurance rates? Are there any outstanding liens on the site or judgments involving the property being considered? What is the landlord's track record? There are an infinite number of issues to consider.

A building's complete set of characteristics, which are often overlooked during initial evaluations, can significantly impact the build-out of the space. Consider for a minute two identical restaurant spaces, both on the ground floor: one is in a single-story building and the other is in a four-story building. Even with the same shape, same layout, same equipment, and same finishes, these two identical projects will have drastically different cost structures. The additional costs required for the multi-story building will include longer and more complex refrigeration line runs for remote compressors, as well as more expensive ductwork for the exhaust hoods and HVAC (heating, ventilation, and air-conditioning) equipment. The multi-story space may also require soundproofing, fire-system sprinklers, and a whole host of costs that may not be as extensive or even required in a single-story or freestanding space. Simply put, the multi-story space would be much more expensive to build out, a fact to be carefully considered when identifying potential restaurant locations.

There are also the intangibles to consider. If the desired space is an existing restaurant, what kind of restaurant was it before? What kind of business volume was the restaurant generating? Has there been more than one restaurant previously located in this space? What were *their* customer counts and revenues? Some spaces become "haunted" in the restaurant business. They bounce from one concept to another, turning over every so often. The question needs to be asked: Why does that occur? Was there something wrong with the concept(s)? Was there something wrong with the site itself? The local market? In order to find these answers, the potential restaurateur must dig deep. The standard demographics offered by developers and local real estate brokers simply do not offer sufficient detail. The valuable information is in the places that one would not intuitively look. The restaurant developer should ask local businesses, both restaurants and non-restaurants, what the business environment has been like for the past several years. Try to identify trends. Attend parent-teacher association meetings to get a feel for the local clientele—what their needs and wants are and what their personalities are like. Volunteer with some of the local charity organizations to gain the opportunity to speak with some of the activists in the community (not to mention help the organization of your choice in the process). Working overtime and turning over such stones will reveal the most valuable information about a site. It is important to be creative in gathering information if you are truly to evaluate a site's potential for success.

The local competition is also a consideration, for obvious reasons. Are there any concepts like the one being planned that already exist in the local market? How are they doing? Are there concepts that are different but may fall into the same category? If so, how are *they* doing? It is equally important to note who these competitors are and whether they compete with or complement your proposed concept. There is a natural tendency to want to avoid having too many other restaurants within a short distance for fear that these restaurants will reduce the new establishment's fair share of the marketplace. In some cases, where the restaurant concepts are similar, that can be a legitimate concern. However, a collection of restaurants in proximity to one another can be helpful as well, provided they are complementary. In other words, if there are two restaurants that have the same target market but one is a Mediterranean restaurant while the other offers Asian fare, they can actually help one another in a number of different ways. If lines are long at one restaurant, the second restaurant would be able to accommodate the overflow of guests who might not wish to wait. Also, multiple restaurants that share the same demographic will help train the local market to frequent the location on a regular basis, driving traffic to the area. It would help form a habit in the customer's routine. I am sure that you can think of several restaurants located adjacent to one another somewhere in or near your hometown that are always busy. It is the same principle.

In our planning efforts, we developed a quick list of site characteristics that we felt were important in order for 'Za-Bistro! to be successful.

'Za-Bistro! Minimum Site Guidelines

1. *High-visibility end cap and freestanding locations between approximately 3,000 square feet and 4,000 square feet.*

2. *Located no more than 100 feet from the main road serving the center.*

3. *Minimum frontage of 60 to 75 feet.*

4. *High concentration of daytime population. Prefer daytime population of 20,000 or greater in a one-mile radius.*

5. *Residential population of 40,000 in a one-mile radius.*

6. *Median household incomes in the top 20% for the Metropolitan Statistical Area (MSA).*

7. *Per capita income greater than $40,000.*

8. *Strong co-tenancy consisting of Town Center-type location, or grocery, movie theater (eight-plex or greater), daily needs, and/or lifestyle centers.*

9. *Minimum of 40,000 vehicles per day along the main frontage.*

10. *In-line locations will be considered if they meet the above criteria and are not more than 50 feet from the road.*

11. *Maximum signage as allowed by code with ability to secure tenant panel shopping center signage and/or individual monument sign.*

12. *The ability to incorporate patios, awnings, and umbrellas adjacent to the premises.*

The last item in the list above, the concept of outside seating, is particularly interesting. When looking for a location, it is important to ask if space is available outside of the leased premises for support of the restaurant operation. This space may be used for anything from seating to housing the walk-in cooler/freezer. The reason for this is that the space outside the envelope of the building is typically free of charge and does not count toward the rent amount. We will cover more on this subject in greater detail in the following chapter on leases.

Perhaps the most important (and often most difficult) consideration when looking for a restaurant location is to look at the opportunity from a purely logical and business-minded perspective. This is, after all, the *Business of Restaurants*. It is very difficult, but the emotions must be controlled. Although we as a team were aware of this little piece of wisdom, I am embarrassed to say that we did not always abide by our own logic, as you will see. Much like buying a home, it is easy to get caught up in the sense of urgency that many of the professionals involved in the process have a tendency to create. These same professionals make their living from commissions and do not get a dime if a potential tenant does not sign on the dotted line and commit to a lease or purchase. Once the deal is signed, however, the landlord will simply be looking for the monthly payments that are due. A broker, if involved, will move on to the next deal. In the case of a purchase, the seller will move toward activities they find more important as well. It is up to the business owner to ensure that the business can be sustained profitably in the potential location. Also, keep in mind that there is *always* another site. Always! Restaurateurs cannot afford to become so focused on any one location that other opportunities are not fully evaluated. Do not try too hard to convince yourself or others that any one site is the "only" option, or the "single best" location available.

Our efforts to secure a site focused on leasing a space from a landlord. In the case of 'Za-Bistro!, we had an unproven concept and limited funding, so constructing a building from the ground up was an unrealistic option for us. Rarely will a first-time restaurateur have the need or capability to build a new restaurant from scratch, including the exterior shell. As you read our story, you will see that many of the issues with which we had to contend are relevant to both new freestanding and leased restaurant spaces. When it comes to leased premises, there are two main categories: existing and new construction. Fortunately, from an educational perspective, we dealt extensively with both existing and new construction sites in our efforts.

When Chris originally approached me with the idea of starting what would eventually evolve into the 'Za-Bistro! concept, one of my first questions was about the location. As with many other aspects of this process, Chris was one step ahead and had already identified a location: a town center development that was just a couple of miles from his house in Sumner Springs, a northeast suburb of Orlando, Florida. I must admit that I knew how important the location was, and I had some reservations about participating in the site selection. While I had a gut feeling on some of the issues, I had little personal experience with site selection and tended to lean on others who possessed greater expertise in the area. That was part of the reason that we established this team in the first place.

The Sumner Springs site was located on the corner of two major roads in a commercial town center development. This center would feature a mixture of other restaurants, some office space, and basic necessities for the local community, including natural traffic generators such as a grocery store, bank, salon, and movie rental store. The town center would be surrounded by both existing and new home developments. The actual space we identified was 3,500 square feet, which was within our stated requirements, and located adjacent to the most prominent corner in the entire development. Visibility would be clear as all traffic approached the town center from the closest major highway. The space was on an end cap and had plenty of room for outside dining. On the negative side, the space contained three sides of glass, which posed a logistical problem regarding the design of the restaurant. Because of the town center influence and the development's design style, there really was no back side of the space. The restaurant had to appear as a storefront from both the street and the parking lot, which were on opposite sides.

The third side of exposed glass faced an open courtyard where the outside dining area would be located. Further complicating the matter, the city required a minimum clearance from all windows to any walls or permanent structures. Restaurants have many areas and functions that simply should not be in view of the guest, and the three sides of glass would have put some of them in view of the guests and passersby on the street. Does anyone really want to see an employee scraping

Sumner Springs Conceptual Plan

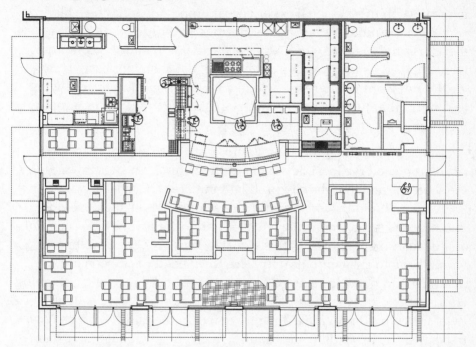

food, banging plates, tossing flatware, spraying off soiled dishes and glasses, and generally creating an unappetizing mess? Most patrons would answer with a resounding "No!" That is why the three sides of glass made this space a challenge—but not an impossible challenge. We would have to make some accommodations, and consider their costs. In the end, how would the required modifications influence the function or feel of the space?

The local area was not yet well developed. There was a decent amount of housing in the area, but limited commercial or retail development. Though it is a bit risky to enter a market in such an early stage of its lifecycle, there can be some significant rewards as well. My wife and I decided to buy a home in an expanding area of the Tampa market called New Tampa, located just north of the city, when we first relocated to Florida. The area was booming, and there were tons of houses under construction in the area, but very little retail. The retail establishments that were there were packed with customers all the time, as there were so few other options. Within the next few years, commercial and retail businesses began to pop out of the ground at an incredible pace. Restaurants, a 24-screen movie theater, numerous grocery stores, home improvement stores, big-box retailers; you name it. With this personal experience in mind, the lack of developed commercial entities in the Sumner Springs area didn't really bother me. Chris and his wife were extremely active in their local community, which helped us keep a pulse on the potential customer base. Though we did not want to cater strictly to the local community, we did want to confirm that the concept we were developing would in fact appeal to the local population. If not, it was the wrong site.

In one of our first official moves to bring this concept to fruition, Chris contacted the local developer of the Sumner Springs town center. We soon learned that the city itself had initiated the master planning process and hired the town center's developer. Often, the developer that purchases the land is the one that undertakes the master planning and development efforts. In this scenario, however, the developer would have to answer to the city. This town center had been under planning and development for several years, and the detailed planning efforts were clearly evident. The integration of retail and residential dwellings would provide a downtown feel in the middle of a heavily treed area full of wildlife and mature, thick Florida foliage. The main street would be lined with parallel parking spaces, sidewalks, trees, and steps leading into the local businesses and homes. The buildings themselves were to include detailed architectural elements in an effort to combat the simpler, economic design approach that has been adopted by many national retailers for cost efficiency. Though more cost effective, these less intricate designs do not necessarily enhance the structure's visual appeal. The guidelines set forth by the city for design and construction within the town center were incredibly complex, with the intended purpose of creating architectural interest at every corner. As an example, the local grocery store was required to create a faux façade along the entire rear side of the store within the town center that included recessed entrances, awnings, display windows, and a number of other features that would attract the attention of any passerby. Keep in mind that this was the *back* of the facility, and we were told these design treatments cost hundreds of thousands of dollars. In this particular case, the grocery store happened to be part of the largest chain in Florida. Their compliance and willingness to spend additional funds over and above their typical build-out costs on a faux storefront was a clear indicator that this company believed strongly in the neighborhood.

In Chris's initial conversation with the developer of this town center, he expressed our desire to begin discussions regarding a lease for the space we had identified. The two of them discussed the restaurant concept, the team, and our collective credentials, as well as Chris's involvement in the local community. The first conversation went well, as most do. Remember that a developer's key objective is to lease space. In reality, we were a restaurant startup — a business of which many developers are naturally skeptical due to the perceived high failure rates of restaurants. Nevertheless, the developer appeared enthusiastic, and he requested a meeting with our team. Chris, Jason, Aaron, and I all met on site with the developer just a week or so after Chris had first contacted him. While Chris and Jason lived locally in Orlando, I drove over from Tampa (about 100 miles, one way) and Aaron came up from South Florida, which was an even longer drive. Chris had forwarded to me the directions from Tampa, which would also serve as a test of sorts — if I could find the site, then our customers should be able to do the same. Well, I did find the site fairly easily, but I also passed through a lot of green space and undeveloped land on the way.

The four of us met just outside of the construction trailer in a field of dirt, earth-moving equipment, and construction debris. The ground had been scraped and prepared for the start of construction, with wooden pins placed strategically and plastic fluorescent orange flags flapping in the breeze. Each pin indicated a corner of one of the buildings that was to be erected on the site. The underground sewer system was in the process of being installed, evidenced by the large cement cylinders that were stacked on site. We stood outside and gathered our thoughts before this first meeting. We anticipated that we were about to take the first official step on our journey, somewhat similar to the gun (or buzzer these days) that goes off at the start of a race. We entered the trailer and introduced our entire team to the developer's representative. The president of the development firm was due in later that afternoon for a presentation to the city regarding the town center's progress. Our conversation with the field representative seemed to be quite positive. We discussed topics such as the design of the interior space, utility requirements and coordination in relation to our anticipated build-out, our target market, marketing strategies, financing, construction timelines, and a host of other issues that were of interest to the developer. Several restaurant spaces were to be included within the town center, and they were vital to the long-term viability of the development. Restaurants, after all, are community centers for social interaction. The types of restaurants that were to be included within the town center were important to both the developer and the city.

Following our initial conversation with the developer's local representative, who seemed impressed with our concept and team, we met briefly with the president of the development company. We had a very similar conversation with him, but focused more on specific details. It was, in fact, the beginning of our negotiation process, as the local representative had expressed his support of our concept and desire to lease a space within the town center to 'Za-Bistro! By the end of the afternoon, the developer indicated that he would be sending us a letter of intent for our consideration. A letter of intent, often referred to as an LOI, is a letter summarizing the key points that will be included in the lease. It is, in essence, the first formal step in the negotiation between a potential tenant and a landlord. Typically, the LOI is non-binding, meaning that it legally does not obligate either party to the terms of the agreement. What, then, is the purpose of such a document? Look at it this way: The agreement between a tenant and landlord is not unlike a marriage in many respects. If we were to use the analogy of a couple on their first date, talk of marriage only hours after meeting would be premature. Instead, if all is going well after the first few dates and both parties want the relationship to move forward, there is a discussion of exclusivity. The LOI is similar in its intended nature. It is a discussion of the major terms that will be included in the lease, laid out for both parties to agree upon. If either party has a problem with the terms, the differences should be discussed and remedied at this stage if possible. Also, because the LOI is not legally binding, it is an opportunity for both tenant and landlord to save money, carrying out negotiations without the direct involvement of legal counsel. If the two sides are unable to come to mutually agreeable terms, then there is no reason to draw up a lease or involve legal counsel. If, on the other hand, an agreement on key issues can be reached in an LOI, then the negotiations may continue, and a lease can be drafted. A lease is much more detailed than an LOI. A typical LOI may be just 3 to 5 pages long, whereas a full lease can be 80 pages or more. Lease negotiations must be handled with extreme care, as the lease has a significant effect on the long-term financial performance of a new restaurant. The lease can greatly impact the potential for success or failure. This is serious business. Do not underestimate the importance of the terms contained within an LOI, and the lease that follows. The contents of a lease will be discussed in greater detail in the next chapter.

Based on our conversations with the Sumner Springs town center developer, and our desire to show continued support for his efforts, the four of us — Chris, Jason, Aaron and I — decided to attend the city meeting that was called that evening to address the status of the town center development. The meeting included a presentation by the developer on the progress of the design and construction effort. There were detailed discussions regarding individual buildings within the town center with answers and clarifications provided by the developer's architect who had flown in for this presentation, bringing with him a host of renderings, plans, and drawings. The architect came prepared for the questions that might be asked. It was clear that the developer had been through this process before, as he entered the meeting armed and ready for any questions that might surface. It was also evident that the community, both city officials and concerned residents, were quite involved in the development process of the town center. They demonstrated intricate knowledge of the architectural plans and were determined to remain involved from concept to fruition. As we sat through the presentation, our initial confidence in the project and the local market seemed to be justified more and more with the comments and questions raised by numerous concerned citizens. To our genuine surprise, several questions surfaced during the open forum regarding the restaurants in the town center. Concerned area residents wanted to know what restaurants the developer had been speaking with and what the proposed timeline was for their construction and opening. There were no such questions posed for the general retail spaces — just the restaurants. Once again, it demonstrated the central role that restaurant life would play in this town center, as well as the pent-up demand that existed for such an option within the local community. The developer, fresh from our meeting and clearly thinking of the conversations we had only hours earlier, indicated that he had been speaking with one restaurant group in particular. He then began to describe our concept to those in attendance. What a moment — to watch someone else explain your concept for the first time to your potential customer base and then wait for the reaction. With eyes wide open, all sitting in a row, the four of us began turning and looking at one another and then anxiously awaited a response from the audience as the developer continued to regurgitate most of what we had shared with him earlier that afternoon. As he finished his dissertation on the 'Za-Bistro! concept, the crowd began to turn and chatter with one another in a frenzy of excitement and acceptance of what they had just heard. It was an overwhelmingly supportive initial reception. The remaining questions quickly turned to the subject of the construction timeline, with multiple inquiries as to when the restaurants would be opening. Aside from feeling confident about the decisions that we had made to date, by attending that city meeting we quickly realized that our concept would not only be welcomed by the local community, but our negotiating position with the developer had just improved. There he stood, in front of the entire city council and a large group of local residents, describing our concept in every detail. How would he be able to stand up in a later meeting and declare that the restaurant concept he had so eloquently described, and which was welcomed by all in attendance, would not be participating in the town center? From such a positive community response, we confirmed that demand existed for a concept like the one that we had developed. The demand also provided leverage in terms of dealing with the local municipality during the development and construction phase.

It was not long before we used this political card to our advantage. In a choreographed move with the landlord during the negotiation phase, we drafted a letter stating that the impact fees were simply too high for our budget and might cause us to look for alternative sites in lieu of the Sumner Springs location. Impact fees are required by local municipalities during new construction. These fees cover the costs for the infrastructure required to support new growth. Sewer lines, utility lines, roads, and other such services must be provided and funded by local government entities to support new development. Impact fees help offset the cost to local taxpayers, with the developer and tenants sharing in the cost for new infrastructure. It is common for the developer to cover the impact fees for basic retail operations. In the case of restaurants, however, there are typically additional impact fees over and above the standard retail amount. This additional assessment is due to the burden that restaurants place on the sewer system, the additional utilities that they require over and above a standard retail shop, and the increased street traffic that they tend to generate. It is important to realize that these impact fees generally apply only to new developments, and not to existing spaces. It is a significant additional cost of which many first-time restaurant developers are unaware. In the case of the Sumner Springs site, the total impact fees were nearly $56,000, with about 40 percent of that amount due from the landlord for basic retail and the remaining 60 percent due from the restaurant tenant. Our letter, which was submitted to the developer, was quickly forwarded to the city council for review and consideration. The impact of the presentation at the earlier city meeting that our team had attended was soon clear. Our letter stated that the impact fees were simply too great and could not be absorbed in our business model, and it explained that the impact fees might cause us to pass on the site and look elsewhere. In consideration of our letter, the local municipality decided to waive the impact fees for our location. This was a significant potential savings for both the developer and us, and the first tangible lesson in what would become a recurring theme: *everything is negotiable*.

With the capital that we had raised internally, we planned to use a portion of our war chest for each site and utilize an SBA loan to fund the remaining amounts required for development. Based on the amount of money we had available, and in consideration of our strategy, we anticipated that we would be able to open a minimum of two restaurants with our initial capital. If all went well, it was possible that we could leverage the same funds for three stores. We then believed that the profit from each store would be re-invested into the development of future locations, as you may recall that none of the team members had anticipated drawing a salary from this effort. We continued looking for additional locations even while the Sumner Springs negotiations progressed. It was not long before we found our second opportunity — a new development that was to be constructed just a couple of miles from downtown Orlando, on the site of an old naval base. Harbor Commons was the genuine image of the *Traditional Neighborhood Design* concept, or TND for short, which had been growing in popularity. This design concept sought a return to a more traditional community by promoting the type of interaction that was prevalent in the pre- and post-World War II days. As suburbia has evolved, heavily influenced by the economic drivers and priorities of suburban home developers, some of the characteristics of the more traditional communities have fallen by the wayside. The TND concept sought to re-create those characteristics by design, though somewhat artificially, in order to help communities regain certain qualities of life that were once commonplace but have now vacated daily life. Stereotypical suburban residents do not walk to the store for a half-gallon of milk. They do not walk to dinner. Rather, these aspects of life are ever-present in cities, but not in suburbia, due primarily to the physical design of the neighborhoods. Suburbia does, however, offer some clear advantages over high-rise city living. Whether it is the additional space, independent yards, or community activities, some characteristics of suburban neighborhoods remain desirable. The real appeal of the TND concept is that it seeks to combine the best of both worlds. TND communities feature a mix of housing styles—full manor homes, smaller town homes, and city-style apartments. Furthermore, these TND communities offer an integration of living, working, and recreation spaces for a better quality of life. Aside from the different home styles that exist, office space, shopping, restaurants, parks, and courtyards are all integrated into the community's design.

This was the case in Harbor Commons. The development's design featured multi-million dollar homes integrated with town homes, city homes, and rental apartments. The garage doors, garbage, and automobile access ways were concealed on service streets, so the front façades of the homes could face the main streets or adjacent parks. The development included lakes for recreation and fishing, as well as freestanding office buildings. The jewel in the crown of this development was clearly the village center. Stretching four or five blocks, the village center was to feature the true integration of retail and residential space. At three stories in height, the first floor was dedicated to retail space, while the upper floors included apartments and office spaces. In an effort to create the ambiance of a true city, the retail locations were not limited to the main streets, but were also included along the side streets. There were courtyards and fountains planned throughout the village center. At the end of Harbor Commons' version of "Main Street" was the main lake—a spectacular backdrop for carrying out one's everyday activities. Keep in mind that this community was located just a couple of miles from downtown Orlando.

I spoke with one of the masterminds behind the Harbor Commons development over lunch one day. He had been intimately involved in the development of Celebration, the first full TND neighborhood in the Orlando area. Located near Walt Disney World Resort,

Celebration received both national and international attention for its design and development. I asked him what modifications he thought Harbor Commons would require in order to improve upon the development at Celebration and what specific improvements he had planned to implement based on his experience with the earlier community. Without much hesitation, he explained to me that most of the improvements had already been made. Celebration is quite a distance from any of the key population and business centers within the Orlando metropolitan area. Thus, most of the residents are required to commute, leading to a modified suburban arrangement. There are office parks located within Celebration, but the commute is long enough that those who do not work in one of the adjacent complexes retained long commutes from home to work. Harbor Commons' location near downtown Orlando was critical to its success.

The second key difference was the type of retail businesses targeted for Harbor Commons. Though Celebration featured integrated retail, the quantity, size, and types of businesses were insufficient to support the local community. A local grocery store, for instance, had taken a space in the Celebration retail complex that totaled just a few thousand square feet. While convenient, it was not sufficient to support the everyday needs of the residents, who were subsequently forced to travel by car to the more expansive local grocery store. This defeated one of the intended purposes of the TND concept. The other retail establishments were easily accessible, but they did support the activities of everyday life. Located within this development were a number of specialty shops. There was no full-sized drug store, no bank, and no dry cleaner. Harbor Commons' development team was keenly aware of this deficiency, and thus targeted specific businesses to better support the everyday needs and activities of its local residents. The scale of the town center in Harbor Commons was also much larger and offered greater opportunity for a mix of everyday and specialty businesses.

Harbor Commons' development team also better understood their residents following the lessons learned at Celebration. The developer described the residents as "self-actualized." Though they may be wealthy, they do not typically flaunt their financial capacity. If one of the residents drives a Porsche, he explained, it is because they feel that it is truly superior in its design and engineering and that it meets their needs. They do not drive such an automobile as a status symbol. Remember, he told me, that some of these individuals live in multi-million dollar homes that are not gated and are integrated with homes that are valued at one-tenth of their price. These individuals choose such a lifestyle because they understand that the TND model fills a void, and they seek the advantages of that style of living. In all honesty, I found the conversation to be very insightful as it helped me to understand the client base and the role that we could play in the development of the village center — the heart of this development, this lifestyle.

Harbor Commons' primary development company subcontracted the development of the Harbor Commons Village Center to another developer. We contacted the village center's agent fairly early in their leasing efforts and began to discuss a 3,000-square-foot space on the corner of the most prominent intersection in the development. It was a prime location, at the prime corner. The space was on the first floor with two floors of residences above the restaurant. Concurrently with the conversations taking place at Sumner Springs, we began discussions at Harbor Commons and quickly moved toward an LOI. The negotiation process had begun for Harbor Commons.

❖ ❖ ❖

Shifting back to Sumner Springs, the progress in our negotiations with the developer was much slower than we had originally anticipated. The rapid early pace had cooled. Several versions of the LOI had been traveling back and forth, reflecting changes by our team and changes by the developer's team. Though it appeared that we were close to an agreement in principle during our initial conversations, the detailed negotiations began to reveal that we were further apart than we had originally believed. A number of additional red flags began to surface and raised cause for concern regarding the site. Because the conversations had continued for several months, we were able to observe the developer's attempt at negotiations with other potential restaurant tenants. When we first inquired about the site in Sumner Springs, one of the more appealing aspects of the deal was the restaurants with whom the developer had already spoken. These restaurants were well known, with a strong local following, and would have complemented our concept extremely well. Recall an earlier part of this chapter: complementary restaurants can be a real asset. The conversations with these restaurant companies, however, began to fall through, as occurred with some of the non-restaurant retail tenants as well. Thus, the quality of businesses being targeted by the landlord in the second round of negotiations was quite different than those identified originally. Major national retailers were being replaced quickly with local businesses of different types and scope than were originally targeted. It was evident that the developer was becoming more interested in simply leasing the space. Some of the alternative tenants, we feared, would not draw the natural traffic that we had hoped would support our concept.

As our negotiations dragged on and some of the earlier prospective restaurant tenants backed out, the developer worked to keep us in the mix. He offered us a space directly adjacent to the one we had been discussing. Though this new space had better visibility and was listed at a higher price per square foot, the developer offered it to us for the same price as our original space. It was clearly a concession to entice us to sign the LOI, and it was apparent that we had gained even more leverage. We genuinely appreciated the move, but some of the developer's other activities raised even more red flags. As part of our negotiations, we had asked for some exclusivity regarding the style and type of restaurant. It was our desire to avoid having too many restaurants of the same type within the town center development. We did not mind having complementary restaurants adjacent to ours, but we certainly wanted to avoid being located next to direct competitors. We submitted to the landlord a letter containing a list of businesses that we felt were too close to our concept and thus should be excluded from the development if we were to be included. Our letter was crafted to identify not only specific businesses, but also the types of business that concerned us. We found out that, in fact, the developer was discussing a lease with a business that fit one of the profiles we had submitted, though it was not directly listed. When we confronted the issue, the developer offered a series of explanations for such an action, none of which satisfied our team. We believed that the developer had violated the clear intent of our efforts, and we grew more concerned about the viability of this location.

To exacerbate the issue, there were a series of delays that pushed the development back for months. We were unsure of our potential occupancy date, as the information we received from the developer seemed to change with every discussion. Though we did not have a specific time slotted for opening, we had all the pieces of the puzzle in place and were simply waiting for a site to start our development process. Personally, I was like a horse in the starting gate because the next phase of the project was my prime responsibility. I was at the starting line, ready to run the race, and just waiting for the word "go." While delays are an understandable part of the development process, the manner and general tone of the information provided by the developer proved to be concerning. Even the upgraded space we were offered at no additional charge seemed to prove detrimental in our negotiations, as though the developer had done us some big favor that we simply did not appreciate. We had not asked for the upgrade in the first place. Our negotiations with the developer stalled, and the likelihood of signing a lease for the Sumner Springs location began to fade. Chris had even taken the time to meet directly with some of the prominent members of the local government, as well as some key local residents, to garner support for our position and apply pressure on the developer to aggressively pursue our concept. In the end, however, it simply did not work out. Remember, there is *always* another site. In this particular instance, I believe that Chris was too emotionally attached to the site, given his proximity and involvement in the local community. He had also shared our efforts at PTA meetings and local gatherings, subjecting himself to constant questions regarding our progress at every turn within the local community. It took a while for Chris to admit that the site had actually fallen through, though the rest of us could see what had occurred. We had been negotiating an LOI for over six months, with no real agreement reached in that time. Negotiations stalled, frustration grew on both sides, and it became clear that a deal was not in sight. There was never an official end to the negotiations; rather, they just sort of tapered off—along with the opportunity to build the first 'Za-Bistro! in the Sumner Springs Town Center.

With the Harbor Commons negotiations still in play, we began our search of the city for alternative sites to replace Sumner Springs. Our concept, a European-style street-side café, was really designed for the town center environment. There were several new town center developments popping up in and around the Orlando area; however, most would not be ready for two to three years after the time frame in which we were looking to open our first restaurant. We began considering alternative sites in different parts of the city and no longer limited ourselves to the town center model. This was a big decision, as we were beginning to stray—though just slightly—from our original direction. There were two sides to this argument. The first was that we were abandoning our concept in light of the realities that we were facing, and thus sacrificing a core component of the 'Za-Bistro! brand. On the other hand, we did not want to avoid an opportunity and necessary adjustment of a concept that was too limiting in scope. We did not want to be stubborn and committed exclusively to town center developments simply because we had outlined them earlier in our business plan. We wanted to be flexible, but not so flexible as to bastardize the original concept. It was a fine line to walk, and it required extreme care and balance. At such an early stage in the process, every decision can significantly affect the chance of success or failure. Without the luxury of hindsight, it is difficult to know the potential implications of each decision.

As we began to look at other sites around the city, we could not find anything that met our needs. One of the leading influencers of securing another space was the status of Harbor Commons. Negotiations were progressing well on the Harbor Commons site, and based on the anticipated delivery dates, we had only a brief window within which to secure, develop, and open a site before Harbor Commons, or we would simply have to wait until after Harbor Commons was open. We did not want to be under development at two sites simultaneously, given our lack of experience with the 'Za-Bistro! concept and, to be quite honest, the fact that we had not yet successfully opened a restaurant as a team. We clearly understood that we would need to crawl before we could walk, and we worked consciously to avoid biting off more than we could chew.

We began looking at existing restaurant sites, which, like new sites, have a host of issues that must be considered. Existing restaurant sites often have a history associated with them that can be hard to overcome. Many in the industry speak of sites that have played host to multiple restaurant concepts as being cursed. I am sure that you know of a site or two in your own neighborhood that might have fallen victim to this "restaurant rotation." On the other hand, existing sites are, well, *existing*. They are not prone to development delays. They also do not involve the impact fees and additional costs associated with new construction. These are significant incentives. We looked at some existing sites, but most were not all that attractive. With one site, we began moving forward and requested an LOI, but the terms were extremely poor from our perspective and we soon passed on the opportunity. We continued to pursue the option of new developments as well. New sites are often in more desirable, growing areas, offering significant potential. New sites also have a clean slate and can be more easily designed and constructed to support a particular operation. However, the potential delays and additional costs associated with new restaurant sites can negatively affect the financial position of a new restaurant business. Though we continued to look at new sites in our efforts, we again came up empty handed.

There was one site north of the city, in a developing area, that featured a movie theater and several new restaurants. When we learned that "several" restaurants had grown to more than twenty, combined with the fact that other adjacent developments were being constructed with dedicated restaurant space, we decided that far too many restaurants would be located within a one-mile radius. For a well-developed area, a large number of restaurants may be just fine. But for this area, which was fairly green and undeveloped, we felt that the marketplace was going to be too competitive — oversaturated — with too much supply and too little demand. And so we passed on that site as well. With regard to new developments in emerging markets, it is important to consider both short-term and long-term prospects for the site. Though many developers will focus on the long term and what *eventually* will be included within the development when it is built out, it is important for a potential restaurant tenant to also consider what the business environment will be like in the short term. How long will construction take? What inconveniences may affect the business during the construction phase? Are other tenants actually signed or are they just in discussion? What commitment does the landlord have to building out the entire project versus stopping halfway through — and what impact might that have on the tenants? We continued to look at other sites. With some, the rent was too high. With others, the anticipated delivery date was too far away. And thus, our search continued. Days, weeks, and then months went by. At this stage, we jokingly referred to ourselves as one of the best *virtual* restaurant companies in existence. We had it all — a menu, a logo, a

Web site, plans; you name it. We had everything except the restaurant itself.

❖ ❖ ❖

As our efforts to secure a site continued for months and months, we all grew a bit restless. I had never expected, in my wildest dreams, that securing a site would be so difficult. In all reality, I was a walking time bomb of pent-up energy—ready to begin planning, drawing, and building at a moment's notice. As we approached a year since the initiation of conversations with the developer at Sumner Springs, and no firm location had yet been defined, my restless energy began to overwhelm me. The process of searching for a restaurant site, although necessary, was not very fulfilling. It required a great deal of time and effort, with nothing to show for our investment to that point. But while we were not making the desired progress, we also avoided making some very poor decisions by leasing less-than-desirable restaurant spaces, *and that was just as important.* These were good decisions, though they were not always easy decisions. The question was if we could continue to be patient and wait for the right opportunity. There was a real desire, or perhaps a self-imposed pressure, to secure a location so that we could open the first restaurant.

One Sunday morning my wife and I were on our way to visit a friend who was participating in a triathlon as a fundraiser for Team In Training, the fundraising arm of The Leukemia and Lymphoma Society. I was feeling somewhat depressed that we had put so much time into the development of our 'Za-Bistro! concept, but we simply could not seem to reach the next step of initiating development and construction. Put another way, I was feeling rather empty and unaccomplished. I was also in the middle of some other entrepreneurial projects that were stalled at the time. It was as if much of my professional life was simply stuck in the mud. After watching the triathlon participants of all ages push themselves for two, three, or four hours or more, and then cross the finish line, I noticed that they all had something I had been seeking but was unable to find: a sense of accomplishment. Not only had they accomplished something physically, but each participant had also raised money for a very worthy cause. So with the restaurant on unplanned hold, I decided to sign up with Team in Training for a triathlon myself. I yearned for the exhaustion and satisfaction that each of those race participants exhibited.

As our efforts to secure a restaurant site continued, Jason had identified a site in the city of Maitland about four or five miles north of downtown Orlando. The site was an existing fast-casual concept featuring a menu of pizzas, sandwiches, and salads. Though they were quite a bit different in concept, starting with the fact that they did not offer full service, it was ironic that Chris had earlier identified this particular restaurant as likely being our closest competitor in the Orlando marketplace. The prospect of not only securing a site but also removing a potential competitor from the market certainly had appeal. The local market featured a high average income among the households in the area. Within the immediate trading area were a community center, a couple of schools, a trendy artist's theater, and several businesses. About one mile south of the Maitland site was a development called Winter Park Village, which was extremely successful and drove a lot of traffic. The Winter Park Village featured several national and regional chains, as well as a movie theater. As Jason began conducting some of his initial investigative work, he unearthed several interesting facts that potentially could be used in negotiations to take over the existing Maitland operation and convert it to a 'Za-Bistro! The restaurant itself had an average performance by industry standards. In a facility just less than 3,800 square feet in size, sales did not break $1 million. According to the information we received, the restaurant's owner was a franchisee of the concept, which was started by his friend who lived in Jacksonville, Florida. The franchisee had wanted to open a restaurant, despite never having been involved in a restaurant before, and thus convinced his friend to award him a franchise in the Orlando area. What happened next, as we were told, was truly priceless. Just a few days after opening the restaurant in Maitland, the franchisee called his friend in Jacksonville and asked that he take the restaurant back. He described life in the restaurant business as "ER with food." That's not a bad description! If you have worked in a restaurant at some point in your career, then you certainly can relate to this statement. In his research efforts, Jason also learned of a plan to build a town center in Maitland, just a couple of blocks north of the restaurant site. This certainly increased the appeal of the site, as it better fit the stated goals and objectives of our original model.

As we learned more about this particular scenario, we decided to make a run at acquiring this site even though an active business was in operation there. It was an unorthodox approach, but it appeared as though all participants might have some motivation to transition the site to new owners and a new concept. Besides, our current methods of site selection had pretty much hit a brick wall, so what did we have to lose? Once we began our pursuit, we learned that the restaurant had been listed for sale in a few publications, perhaps just to test the waters. This information confirmed that at least a conversation was worthwhile. As it turned out, the landlord also had some motivation for a change in ownership since the space was being leased at $15 per square foot, which was well below market rates. The landlord had expressed a desire to bump the rent up from $15 per square foot to $23 per square foot. In exchange for this bump in rent, the landlord was proposing to provide additional dollars for tenant improvements in our development efforts should we be successful in securing the store. Though the subject of tenant improvement dollars will be discussed in greater detail in the next chapter, as a general definition, these are dollars offered by the landlord to the tenant to assist with the build-out of the facility. The new lease would include rent at $23 per square foot, with the difference between the current lease rate and the increased lease rate returned to us in the form of tenant improvement dollars. At $8 per square foot, and a facility of approximately 3,800 square feet, the tenant improvement dollars made available to 'Za-Bistro! would amount to approximately $250,000. There were several issues to be considered before making our proposal, as the involvement of the franchisor, the franchisee, the landlord, and our team, each with differing objectives and concerns, presented a unique challenge.

With this complex set of information in hand, we began to draft a proposal that considered the objectives of each party involved. There were a number of non-traditional factors included as part of this deal, making it a bit more complex than the proposals for the previous sites we had pursued. Nevertheless, there was a distinct possibility that we could pull this off, based on the motivations of each member involved in the process. However, I did have some reservations regarding this site — and with any site, to be quite honest. I was capable of building a restaurant anywhere that we selected, but how could we be certain that this was in fact the right site for our first restaurant? Was this the location, location, location that was right for us?

In the end, the deal fell through, but it was certainly a creative approach. Given the final numbers that were presented following the negotiation phase, the deal was not as inviting as it had been previously. Furthermore, the entire complex in which the restaurant was located was being sold from one entity to another. There were simply too many moving pieces to make the deal work, and the economics were not right. So we applied one of our most valuable lessons to date and walked away — again.

7

A Lease on (Restaurant) Life

Most first-time restaurant developers do not have the financial capability to buy or build their own restaurant, including the exterior building, from the ground up. The alternative, of course, is to lease a space from a landlord. Not only is the importance of a lease often misunderstood by first-time restaurateurs, but so, too, are the various components of a lease and their potential long-term effect on the viability of the business. Simple decisions made during the negotiating phase of the lease can cause a significant positive or negative swing in cash flow or available capital. When negotiating the final terms of a lease, it is always wise to remain patient and emotionally unattached. Keep in mind that sometimes the best decision is to walk away. While the terms of a lease may not be able to guarantee success of the restaurant operation, they can ensure failure if they are detrimental to the tenant. I have also learned, through my efforts both as a restaurant developer and as a professional who helps others with the development of their own restaurant concepts, that, unfortunately, many landlords do not go out of their way to assist new restaurant startups. This is evidenced by the many LOIs I have seen over the years. There is a common perception that restaurants have an extremely high failure rate. Regardless of the actual facts, has anyone ever researched *why* restaurant startups have so much trouble? It is commonly accepted that many restaurant failures, like many small businesses, are due to under-capitalization. But, again, I must ask the question: *Why* are these restaurant startups undercapitalized?

I have a theory that one answer to this question has much to do with the lease and the frequent surprises that are sprung upon new restaurateurs. It has more to do with what is *not* in the LOI or the lease than what is actually included. To give you one brief example, let's look at the amount of air-conditioning offered by a landlord as standard for a newly constructed space. A typical retail HVAC allotment is one ton of air-conditioning for every 250 square feet. I have seen LOIs for restaurants, however, that list the standard air-conditioning as high as one ton for every 350 square feet, resulting in less conditioned air provided. Now, consider the fact that although there is no prescribed standard, many of the restaurants that I have worked on require one ton of air-conditioning for every 125 square feet. That is *double* the amount of air-conditioning provided for standard retail spaces. And these are not restaurants that require an abnormal amount of cooling because they have significant heat loads from the equipment. On the contrary, these are, in fact, typical restaurants. When a tenant signs a lease that includes provisions for a standard retail space with regard to the HVAC, it is often well after the lease has been signed that the first-time restaurateur learns of the additional HVAC requirements for restaurants and, subsequently, the obligation to pay for the additional capacity. This is where the situation becomes even more difficult. Oftentimes, the landlord will purchase the air-conditioning units in bulk for all of the spaces within the development. As a result, the capacity of the existing units cannot simply be increased. Nope. In some cases, a landlord will offer the tenant credit for the undersized system, which may or may not equal the full market value. But if the landlord is unwilling to offer a credit for the system to be provided according to the terms of the lease, then a second unit must be purchased and installed. This second unit will require an entirely separate distribution system, additional roof penetrations, and an additional curb and flashing on the roof—all of which amount to additional costs for the tenant. This one example is the reason that I want to spend ample time discussing some of the typical provisions in a lease. Please keep in mind that a lease can be 80 pages or more in length, and we will not be able to address all of the issues that are covered in such a document. More importantly, I am not a lawyer, nor do I really want to be a lawyer. With that said, and with my rear end fully covered as required in today's litigious society, I have acquired insight and experience that can be applied in the negotiation of a lease, much of which was learned the hard way: by making mistakes. I want to share this information in an effort to help other aspiring restaurateurs avoid some of the common pitfalls that can result in unforeseen expenses and, in the end, undercapitalization.

Before we begin reviewing the various components of the lease and their potential impact on a new restaurant business, it is important to revisit an important lesson: everything is negotiable—*everything*. It all comes down to the motivation that each party has on either side of the bargaining table. Throughout our development efforts, we found this to be the case. Whether with city officials, landlords, or even among our own team, we always seemed to be negotiating something. There are numerous books on the subject of negotiating and game theory, and I do not intend to summarize all of that research in a paragraph or two. What I can tell you is that the best strategy in negotiating is to create a win-win scenario, where possible, so that both parties leave the bargaining table feeling good about what has been accomplished or agreed upon. It is important to protect your own concerns. No one will be as concerned for your own needs as you will. You have no stronger advocate for your interests than yourself. It is also important to find out what truly motivates the individual or entity on the other side of the bargaining table. What may be important to one side may not be important to the other, offering an opportunity for compromise across multiple issues. Making a concession on one issue that is not important to you may result in a concession from your negotiating partner on an issue that *is* important to you.

The issues we are about to address are just a few of the key terms that will be included in the full lease. Remember that some of these terms will be addressed in the LOI. The lease, however, will cover each issue in much greater detail, including all legal concerns and ramifications. Because leases vary greatly, the examples discussed in the pages that follow cannot and will not reflect every variation. Rather, the information is provided as a reference and is intended to offer a basis for comparison in other lease negotiations. The issues discussed were chosen because of their direct influence on the daily operations and cash position of a tenant's restaurant business. I have avoided extensive discussion on issues that are predominantly legal in nature. Because the typical lease can be a book in and of itself, I had to draw the line somewhere. After all, there is so much more of this journey left to share.

First, let's discuss the length of the lease. Typically, the lease will consist of a base period for rent and additional optional periods thereafter. For example, a lease may consist of a ten-year lease with two five-year options after the initial period. It may, on the other hand, consist of a five-year lease with three five-year options for the same total length of twenty years. Which, you may be wondering, is a better arrangement? The answer is, as is always the case, it depends. Both the landlord and tenant need to consider the amount to be invested in the site and the potential return during the course of the lease. If the landlord is putting up $100,000 for tenant improvements, he or she may be motivated to sign the tenant to a slightly longer lease in order to help ensure a return on the investment. If, on the other hand, the landlord is not offering any tenant improvement dollars, then he or she may lobby for a shorter lease so that there is a chance that the tenant will move to another space. The landlord's space can then be leased to a different tenant at a higher lease rate, assuming that the lease rate in the market will increase during the first term of the lease. Restaurants, unlike other retail establishments, require a significant amount of infrastructure and construction within a space. There are exhaust hoods, floor sinks, refrigeration lines, and all sorts of custom-fabricated equipment. These factors make the consideration of the lease's structure incredibly important.

Next, let's address the rent. Typically, the total amount of rent is based on a rate per square foot. While it may seem intuitive to negotiate the dollar amount per square foot, there are other ways to negotiate the total rent amount without focusing directly on the rate per square foot. The rent is based on the total square footage, but how often do tenants verify the square footage themselves? Is the square footage correct? What about exterior storage areas? Some landlords include dumpster storage locations in the total square footage number, whereas others do not. This may not seem like much of a difference, but it can add up to thousands of dollars over the course of a year. When challenging the method used to calculate the rent amount, the landlord may object, indicating that the rent is "always figured this way." That may be the case, but how often has the formula used to calculate the square footage been challenged? Even something as simple as the rate per square foot, and the method in which it is calculated, is negotiable.

Perhaps the best strategy used by tenants with respect to the dollars charged per square foot versus the active space of the restaurant is the utilization of outside space. Very often landlords will allow a tenant to utilize space to the rear or side of the restaurant at no additional charge.

Walk-in coolers and freezers can be located outside, with a door that opens into the kitchen space. Though the walk-in is located outside of the physical footprint of the leased space, this configuration will make it appear as though the walk-in is connected integrally to the rest of the restaurant. Other uses for outside space adjacent to the restaurant include bulk dry storage and outside dining. Just think about the additional revenue that can be generated if a restaurant is located on an end cap of a development and the restaurant can add another 30, 40, or even 50 seats outside with no increase in the monthly rent. I had the privilege of working with a seasoned restaurateur in Gainesville, Florida, who was well versed in using the outside areas adjacent to his restaurants. In one situation, he leased approximately 3,000 square feet on an end cap of a strip center development. He then placed the walk-in cooler and freezer in the rear, outside of the restaurant envelope, and an outside dining area to the side. The walk-in opened directly into the kitchen, acting as a pure extension of the restaurant's back-of-house with no indication from the interior that the walk-in was not within the main footprint of the leased space. For the outside dining area, he installed a hard roof, ceiling fans, lighting, wood fencing around the perimeter, plastic drop-down enclosures between the railing and the roof, and even air-conditioning. For all intents and purposes, this outside dining area was a completely functional extension of the dining room that could be utilized almost year-round. Though I do not have the exact figures, I would estimate that his useful restaurant space totaled approximately 4,500 square feet when the project was completed. That is a 50 percent increase in the size of the space, at no additional cost per month in rent. Proper utilization of the exterior space adjacent to a restaurant can significantly affect the cost structure and, ultimately, the financial performance of a restaurant throughout its operational life.

Scheduled rent increases, frequently referred to as "bumps," are usually spelled out in the lease. These bumps can occur at any time within the time frame of the lease — it simply depends upon the agreed terms. The lease rate per square foot can stay stagnant for an entire rent period or it can increase within a given initial term or optional period. There are an infinite number of arrangements to accommodate either the landlord's interests or the tenant's interest. It is important to consider these rent bumps in relation to the business plan. If the rent bump comes at the beginning of year two, and additional expenses for expansion or additional development are slated for the same time frame, it would be wise to put off one or the other so that the expenses do not pile up all at once. Be mindful of when the bumps will occur and what stage the business is expected to be at when they do occur. Consider the future financial burden early in the process, even if only a potential scenario exists. Restaurants are a cash-driven business. As my one-time Cornell professor explained to us, you pay your bills with cash, not with profits. Realize that the landlord wants to ensure the lease rate will reflect the current market value, though that future value is unknown at the time. The tenant will want to minimize any increases in rent. Each market and each location has a unique set of circumstances that must be considered in determining the timing and percentage increase of the rent bumps.

It is also common for landlords to offer an initial grace period for rent following turnover of a space, thereby alleviating the burden of rent during construction or at the beginning of the operation. This grace period may be 30 days, 60 days, 90 days, or longer. Try to negotiate the longest grace period possible. The grace period, if used correctly, should help the tenant by offering financial relief in the early days after opening. Unfortunately, in my daily role as a designer, I regularly watch new restaurateurs use this grace period unwisely. Here is a common scenario I see firsthand time and again: A restaurateur approaches me and tells me that he or she needs to secure my services for design of a new facility. Typically, one of my first questions is "Have you signed your lease?" A common response is "Yes, I did, and the clock already started ticking, so how soon can you finish your drawings? I need to open as soon as possible." This is a prime example of how to waste the benefits of a grace period. It will likely take months for a restaurant to be designed, coordinated, submitted for permit, and then constructed. In the scenario described above, the tenant will be paying rent, possibly for several months, without any revenue from the operation. If approached properly, the planning, design, and permit submission process should be completed prior to the turnover of the space so that the grace period extends into the opening of the operation and provides the tenant with some financial relief. The more that a tenant can accomplish prior to the lease commencement date, the better. Some of the planning can occur during the initial negotiations. With new construction, the grace period will typically start when the landlord turns over the space to the tenant. If the anticipated delivery date of the space is not imminent, this can buy the tenant some valuable time for planning and pre-opening preparations. If the space is already available, or will be available soon, it may be worth negotiating a grace period that starts only after the construction documents have been submitted for permit. If the grace period being offered by the landlord is not sufficient to meet your needs, ask for more. Mistakes in this portion of the lease, as with so many other issues, can significantly impact available cash and the capability of the restaurant owner to meet financial obligations.

Common Area Maintenance fees, or CAM for short, are paid to the landlord by the tenant. These funds cover the repair and maintenance of shared areas within a development or property such as parking lots, walkways, service courtyards, and bus stops. It may also include insurance for the property and property taxes, if these items are not listed separately. CAM fees will usually be based on the square footage of the facility, and will be due at the same time as the rent payments. Together, the CAM fees and rent per square foot usually compose the tenant's monthly payment. It is important to define clearly, however, what is included in the CAM description, as there are potential gray areas and gaps. The roof of the building, for instance, may be covered under CAM in the event of storm damage, while regular maintenance and cleaning may be the responsibility of the tenant. Landscaping maintenance and replacement is another potential gray area. Variances in coverage by the landlord from one lease to another typically center on the property's amenities immediately adjacent to the leased space, such as walkways, parking lots, courtyards, and other comparable features. Variances may also occur in the exterior components of the building, such as outdoor lighting, glass storefront, or similar elements. Read the LOI and the lease carefully to ensure that there are no major gaps in the description of items covered in the CAM fees, as those gaps could result in an unexpected repair bill that must be paid by the tenant.

Some landlords require a clause for percentage rent. In this scenario, once a certain level of gross revenue—referred to as the natural breakpoint— is achieved, the amount of rent due will be based on a percentage of that revenue. This percentage rent would then replace the rent amounts that are calculated on a dollar amount per square footage. Ideally, the rent amount should constitute roughly 7 percent of sales. This will vary, of course, based upon the site, geographic location, volume, and other variables related to the restaurant's operation. Percentage rent is usually based on gross sales and is negotiable. The percentage rent will be greater than rent per square foot, and this is a way for the landlord to reap some of the benefits from the success of the restaurant's performance. Not only are the percentage and the breakpoint negotiable, but so, too, is the entire requirement for percentage rent. The percentage rent clause can be removed from the lease altogether. After all, everything is negotiable.

Unfortunately, landlords are very skeptical of new restaurant startups, based partly on their past experience and partly on industry folklore regarding the failure rate associated with new restaurants. Though the new restaurateur should not take this personally, the landlord will usually do just the opposite, requiring new restaurateurs to *personally guarantee* the rent payments and all other financial obligations under the terms of the lease. That is to say, the guarantors will assume responsibilities for the financial commitments, typically monthly rent and CAM fees at a minimum, for the duration of the initial lease term, active option period, or other time frame established. If the restaurant's developers can guarantee the lease with assets from another business, or with other assets that will satisfy the landlord, then a personal guarantee may not be required. Many restaurateurs request that the corporation that will own the restaurant guarantee the lease, because at the time of startup, the corporation may have significant assets. It is certainly worth a shot, but don't hold your breath. Landlords will want something concrete, something stable that they can go after in the event of default. As with everything else, however, this, too, is negotiable.

There are some tactics that can be used to reduce the personal liability as well, even if it cannot be alleviated completely. First, there is the option of a sunset clause, which will gradually reduce the liability over time. Provided that all required payments are made in a timely fashion and any other requirements set forth by the landlord are met, the liability can be gradually reduced and eventually eliminated altogether. For example, a landlord may choose to allow for a five-year reduction schedule, whereby 20 percent of the outstanding liability will be reduced each year until it is reduced to nothing at the end of the fifth year. A tenant can also negotiate a cap on the liability amount up front. This tactic reduces the total liability for the restaurant owner(s). Yet another strategy to reduce the liability is to guarantee a minimum amount of money to be held in a designated bank account. This minimum balance will assure the landlord that ample funds are available to make the required payments in the event of default. Should the balance fall below the required amount, however, the personal guarantees would likely become active.

There are a host of legal issues that revolve around this concept of a personal guarantee and numerous strategies that are used by both landlord and tenant to protect their own interests. As stated earlier, I do not want to play lawyer. However, there is one aspect of the personal guarantee that I do want to address: multiple guarantees signed by partners in a restaurant corporation. In this scenario, more than one individual will often be responsible for the full liability of the lease in a manner called *joint and several*. Joint and several means that all guarantors will be responsible for the liabilities they are assuming, both collectively and individually. In other words, in the event of a default, the landlord can pursue the entire group or any one member of that group for the full guaranteed amount. To demonstrate this concept, let's assume that a leased space has a collective rent and CAM cost of $80,000 per year. This space has been personally guaranteed by four partners, joint and several, and the initial term of the lease is five years. In an unforeseen turn of events, the financing anticipated to fund the restaurant's development falls through, and the partners are unable to open their new business. Their collective liability is $400,000. When guaranteed joint and several, each member's personal liability, and perhaps their financial obligation, could range from $0 to $400,000. Needless to say, this is quite a variation. In such a scenario, it would be incorrect to merely assume that each partner had a liability of $100,000. Any guarantor should be aware of this fact before agreeing to an arrangement that is joint and several. Not every landlord will require a joint and several guarantee. The inclusion of this condition is common for new restaurant startups, however, as the landlord will seek to minimize risk and outstanding liability resulting from the lease. The key with a personal guarantee, in the event that one is required, is to minimize the liability as much as possible.

Tenant improvement dollars (also referred to as TI dollars) are funds that the landlord provides to assist the tenant with the build-out of the space. This item in the negotiation process varies greatly from one lease to another. In some instances, the landlord may not offer any TI dollars at all; in other instances the amounts can reach well into six or even seven figures. Before discussing the strategies for negotiating for TI dollars, it is important to understand the position and motivation of both the landlord and the tenant regarding this issue. From the landlord's perspective, a tenant will be building the space to suit a particular need, which may or may not be usable by the next tenant. For example, assume that a leased space will be built out to house a Mexican restaurant that has an initial lease term of five years. In this particular scenario, let's say that the landlord provided $60,000 worth of TI dollars to assist the tenant with the build-out. At the end of this initial lease term, the Mexican restaurant does not exercise the option for the second five-year term, and decides to relocate instead.

The landlord now leases the location to a Sushi concept, which simply cannot use the space as it was left by the predecessor's Mexican restaurant and will have to spend significant funds to renovate. The landlord fears investing in TI dollars that will only suit the needs of each particular tenant. The tenant's argument, however, is just as strong. If the tenant were to completely fund the interior build out or renovation of a space, without any TI dollars, then the landlord stands to benefit tremendously. The tenant will have paid for the construction effort, including walls, plumbing, electrical, and HVAC work, which must stay with the space; those "goods" are not transportable. Subsequently, the landlord can then lease the space to a new tenant, leveraging the investment made by the previous tenant. Both sides have a legitimate argument, and it is simply a matter of negotiating the best possible solution to meet the needs of both the landlord and tenant. The length of the lease is one of the dominant factors in determining the amount of TI dollars a landlord may provide. The shorter the initial lease period, the more exposed the landlord's investment will be, thereby encouraging the landlord to minimize the total amount of TI dollars offered. A longer lease, on the other hand, will offer the landlord a better chance for return on the investment, and the TI amount offered is likely to be larger.

Tenant improvement dollars typically will be provided with a stipulation regarding their use. That is, the landlord should require the dollars provided to be spent on the physical improvements to the building, and not for operational or marketing purposes. The landlord may also require that the tenant provide proof in the form of receipts as to how the dollars are used, which is understandable, as the landlord will want to verify that the dollars provided have been used as intended. Because the landlord will be providing funding for use in the development effort, TI dollars can act as an off-the-books loan in some instances. Here is one example illustrating this point: If the market lease rate is $24 per square foot in a given location, the landlord may provide the tenant with two options. The first option might be to lease the space at market rate or just below market rate, say $22 per square foot, with no TI dollars. The second option could be a lease rate of $30 per square foot, and a tenant improvement allowance of $50,000. While the second option would include a lease rate slightly above market value, it would offer a $50,000 "loan" that would not show up on the financial statements of the restaurateur's business. This is not a traditional "loan," but rather a source of funding that would be repaid with higher monthly rent payments in lieu of the more common principal and interest. The provision of funds without the classification of debt can sometimes be helpful. The example above, of course, is just one possible combination of rates and tenant improvement amounts. There are an infinite number of combinations upon which a landlord and tenant can agree.

When reviewing the terms of the TI dollars a landlord will provide, it is also important to tie down the timing and manner of that payment. If those dollars have been allocated by a tenant for use in the construction phase, then those funds should be available in a timely fashion to meet obligations during the build-out. If the landlord will require specific documentation to release the funds, clarify any such requirements ahead of time so that, when the time comes and the dollars are needed, no unforeseen delays will result. If the dollars have been set aside to help pay for the construction but are not available until after the tenant has occupied the space, major problems may result that could delay the opening date or place unnecessary financial strain on the operation in its first several weeks of business.

Most leases for new spaces (that is, not an existing space) will include a separate section or exhibit called Landlord's Work, which describes the construction responsibilities of the landlord for the interior build-out of the tenant's leased space. There are different strategies a tenant can use to approach the negotiations related to this portion of the lease, but I want to stress that the work described in this section of the agreement has significant cost implications for the overall project. As with so many subjects in this book, there are an infinite number of variables, making an in-depth discussion challenging. However, there are some key issues on which I do want to focus. This section of the lease details the required condition of the leased premises at the date of turnover by the landlord to the tenant, including specific components of the building's infrastructure that will be provided. Typically, the conversation will center on a *gray box* or a *vanilla box*, both of which refer to the condition of the interior space. In a gray box, the landlord will not provide the interior slab, interior walls, drywall, plumbing rough-ins, ductwork, or other such features. At turnover, the space will likely consist of the exterior envelope (walls and a roof) and a dirt floor. In this scenario, the tenant must conduct all necessary work to complete the interior build-out. If the landlord is providing a vanilla box, however, the slab, a restroom (or possibly more than one), ductwork, drywall, a drop-in ceiling, and other such elements will be provided by the landlord in accordance with the conditions described in the Landlord's Work section of the lease. Determining which option is better for a particular tenant, or a particular space, will depend on a number of factors, including the lease rate and provision of TI dollars. A gray box, naturally, should have a lower lease rate and/or higher TI dollars than a vanilla box, as more work must be done by the tenant to complete the interior build-out. It is wise for the tenant to run financial calculations both ways to figure out which scenario is best.

Which is usually better? Well, that depends. For example, let's say there is a shortage of concrete, which has happened in the past, leading to higher prices and reduced availability. In this particular scenario, it might be best to negotiate a vanilla box so that the landlord will be responsible for providing the slab. The contractor can trench as required after it is poured and run any utilities that must be installed below the slab (for example, soda chase lines, plumbing, or electrical conduit). On the other hand, the lease may stipulate that the landlord must run ductwork in compliance with the original building architect's drawings. In the event that these locations are in conflict with the final mechanical design of the tenant's space, it may be best to ask the landlord to refrain from completing that scope of work, as the tenant's contractors will only have to remove much of the system later, leading to an increase in construction costs. There are two tactics that can be used to reduce the risk for both landlord and tenant with respect to the build-out. The first is an agreement by the landlord to provide the tenant with a cash allowance in lieu of actual materials or components, provided that the credit(s) reflect fair market value. This prevents unnecessary work by either side. If an allowance is agreed upon, remember to tie down the timing and method of the credit, just as with the provision of TI dollars.

The second strategy is to coordinate the work between the landlord and tenant throughout the construction process, though this can be quite challenging. For instance, the tenant's general contractor can complete the underground slab work prior to the pouring of the slab by the landlord's contractor. Similar coordination can be arranged for the ductwork, bathroom placement, and other such elements of the space. I should warn you that this approach requires an incredible amount of coordination and cooperation between all parties involved, but it is possible.

Now let's look at some additional issues. At the beginning of this chapter, we discussed the impact that the size of the HVAC system can have on the build-out. Prior to signing a lease, it is wise to have a mechanical engineer look at the space and provide a rough estimate for the HVAC requirements. The air-conditioning will be based on one ton per "x" number of square feet. Standard retail is often one ton per 250 square feet, as we discussed earlier. Remember that restaurants can require one ton per 125 square feet or an even smaller area, and it is the tenant's responsibility to make up the difference. The HVAC system is a good place to negotiate an allowance. Additional HVAC might otherwise have to be provided through a totally separate system. In some cases this works out, as one unit might cover one part of the restaurant, while the new units cover other sections. In other instances, however, the existing unit provided by the landlord must be scrapped, resulting in an incredible waste of time, money, and effort.

In a vanilla box, it is common for the landlord to provide a restroom, and in some cases multiple restrooms are provided. The provision of restrooms by the landlord can be a great help, but it can also be a hindrance. Where will the restroom(s) be located? If located in a spot other than the spot called out on the drawings for the interior build-out of the space, they will only have to be moved. How many stalls are included? What are the finishes? Depending on the type and quality of the restaurant, the landlord's standard restroom finishes may be perfectly acceptable—or not. The restrooms are another good candidate for negotiating a credit in lieu of having them provided by the landlord.

Verify that all utilities coming in to the space are sufficient to support the restaurant. Electrical service (total amp load and voltage/phase provided), water service, gas service, cable, telephone, sanitary sewer line tie-ins, and grease trap tie-ins are examples of the types of utilities that should be confirmed. If necessary, contract an engineering firm to conduct a brief review and provide feedback to determine if the sizes of all incoming utilities are adequate. Even if the cost is a few hundred dollars on the front end, the resulting information can potentially save thousands during construction.

Another major cost concern for tenants of newly constructed spaces is impact fees. Remember that impact fees are assessed by the local municipality to cover the cost of additional utility and infrastructure due to the introduction of a new restaurant to the local market. Restaurants do require additional impact fees over and above those fees associated with standard retail. This is a result of additional traffic, water usage, sewer usage, and other similar strains on the local community. As you may recall, these fees can run into the tens of thousands of dollars. Yet, as with everything else, these fees are also negotiable—sometimes. The likelihood of negotiating with a local municipality is far greater in a small town than it is in a larger city. As discussed, our team was able to convince the local city council to waive impact fees altogether for a space that we were considering.

This incentive was offered to us by the local government officials in an effort to lure our restaurant concept into their city. Typically, impact fees are not required for existing locations, a consideration which should not be overlooked or taken lightly by a tenant in search of a restaurant space.

The lease should include a defined date when the landlord will turn over the completed premises to the tenant, with the landlord's work as described in the lease completed, for initiation of the interior build-out. New developments often run into delays, whether at the fault of the developer or due to uncontrollable external factors. These delays affect not only the landlord, but also the tenant and the tenant's ability to properly time planning and design, equipment procurement, hiring, training, marketing, and a whole host of critical business activities. It is imperative to tie down the turnover sequence in the lease. The landlord should provide ample notice as to when the space will be delivered and, more importantly, should be held accountable for the information provided. I have seen LOIs giving the landlord as much as an 18- or 24-month window for delivery. These same LOIs included no requirement for the landlord to provide advanced notice to the tenant regarding the delivery of the space. Furthermore, in the event that the landlord did not meet the defined window for delivery of the space, the tenant's only course of action to recoup any lost time or money was the ability to cancel the lease at that time. When combined, all of this can spell disaster for the tenant. To fully demonstrate the possible implications of this scenario, let's assume that the landlord calls a tenant, who has already signed a lease, to let them know that the space will be ready for delivery in 12 weeks. With this notification, design and construction drawings may be completed and submitted for permit, marketing efforts may be initiated, and a general manager may be hired to assist with the opening process. The landlord may continue to inform this tenant that the space will be delivered according to schedule until week 11. At this point, the landlord indicates that there will be a six-week delay due to problems with the general contractor. Considering all that has already been initiated by the tenant, the restaurateur decides to continue as planned, simply adjusting some of the scheduled dates and activities. Four weeks into this six-week delay, the landlord calls to inform the tenant that the problem has not been resolved, and another eight-week delay is anticipated. The tenant is in an awkward position, as significant dollars may have already been committed to meet the initial deadline(s) offered by the landlord. Management has been hired. Advertisements have been placed. Equipment has been ordered and must now be placed in storage, resulting in additional costs. At the beginning of this chapter, I addressed the common perception that restaurateurs suffer from undercapitalization. I believe that unexpected events with repercussions that are not prevented on the front end, often due to the restaurateur's lack of development experience, are some of the reasons why. This emphasizes the importance of addressing these types of issues up front and in writing. In this particular case, the tenant should have negotiated a shorter, more acceptable turnover window for the leased space. Specific communication should be required in writing by the landlord to inform the tenant of the progress related to the turnover of the space. Most importantly, the tenant should try to negotiate a penalty clause and/or an exit clause in case the landlord does not deliver the space within the time frame defined.

In many instances, a lease will contain exclusives and/or use restrictions. The former refers to the exclusivity of a particular business concept or business practice within a given landlord's development. An exclusive may be granted for an Italian-style restaurant, or it could be granted for local pizza delivery, certain games, music, outside dining, or alcohol. This would imply that the only business allowed to operate the stated concept type or service would be any business that has been granted the exclusive for such activities. Use restrictions are often included at the request of the landlord or local municipality. Such restrictions might include limitations on outdoor music or alcohol service after a specified time. Tenants should study their own lease to determine what parts of their business can be covered by exclusives to avoid direct competition within a particular development. Tenants should also carefully study exclusives granted to other businesses within the development to ensure that they do not conflict with certain elements or services that are key to the tenant's concept or which may hinder possible expansions of the concept or services in the future. Though it is difficult to convince a landlord to grant a tenant an exclusive for something that *might* be offered in the future, everything is negotiable. Likewise, use restrictions should be reviewed to ensure that they will not hinder the operation or revenue potential of the business.

While some tenants may feel that exclusives granted to other businesses are extremely limiting to their own operation, these exclusives also exist for protection of the businesses owned by those same tenants. In certain instances, a landlord may become hard pressed to lease the spaces that remain unoccupied, due to slow sales or a sluggish market. Keep in mind that a landlord's revenue is based on rent from occupied spaces;

an unoccupied space provides no income for the landlord. As a result, landlords may begin to alter their perception of the ideal tenant in an effort simply to lease the space and generate income. This can have a lasting effect on the entire development, as well as the businesses that are located within that development. Should a landlord decide to lease three of twelve available spaces to similar concepts, the impact on those three businesses will be significant — they will cannibalize each other. The use of exclusives helps ensure that the entire development and the businesses it contains will remain healthy and viable. In many instances, however, exclusives may not be available. Often, they can only be granted when a single landlord resides over the entire development. In a downtown area, or an area where multiple landlords exist within a given proximity, exclusivity may not be an option. Where exclusives are granted, they should be backed up with penalties for the landlord and the tenant if either falls out of compliance with the requirements of the exclusive. A stipulation is meaningless without repercussions in the event that one or both sides fail to comply. Get this guarantee in writing.

Despite all that has been discussed regarding the lease, there is far more to cover. Again, we cannot cover everything here, but there are some additional issues that deserve recognition and discussion. In lightning-round style, here are some additional issues to consider. A tenant can include a financing contingency in the lease. That is, should financing not be obtained within 45 or 60 days, for example, the tenant would have the right to opt out of the lease. Are any of the adjacent parking spaces allocated for a specific use? Will this use affect your operation? Can you claim any of these spaces for your business? What rights to do you have for signage, either at the restaurant or on the development's marquee? Are there any special requirements you will need during the construction phase? In our case, we included a clause in the lease to ensure that the landlord would provide ample access for our seven-foot-diameter oven during construction. Failure to do so would result in additional costs for our team, as the storefront would have to be dismantled and re-assembled. Some of the sites we considered featured structural members that would have prevented access for the oven altogether. If a space with such conditions were secured, we would need to have the oven delivered in pieces and assembled on site by the manufacturer's certified installers, doubling the cost of the oven. Where is the trash dumpster located, and who has access to it? Who pays for trash removal? Who pays for each of the utilities? What are the landlord's minimum insurance requirements, and how will they affect your business?

Is there a collective marketing fund to which the tenant must contribute? How will those funds be utilized, and what influence does each tenant have over the use of such funds? Regarding maintenance, what *specifically* is the landlord responsible for, and what maintenance items fall under the responsibility of the tenant? Will the landlord require the use of a specific contractor to perform roof work or comparable specialized work? Are the listed contractors competitive in their pricing and quality of performance? Does the landlord have an ownership interest in or benefit from any of these contractors? Is there a requirement for these contractors to meet other competitive bids? What happens if the restaurant doesn't make it? What capacity will the tenant have to sublease the space to another tenant? Will the landlord require a final approval of such a sublease, and will the landlord be reasonable if such a situation rears its ugly head? Will the landlord have any obligation to assist in finding an alternate tenant? What ongoing commitments would the tenant have during the period that the space is not occupied by an active business?

In the end, there are a few key lessons that should be retained from this discussion on the lease. The first is (yes, I am going to say it again) *everything is negotiable.* That does not mean that a particular request will be granted, but if the question is not asked, there is no possibility that the request will be approved. The next lesson is *get it in writing.* Make sure that the agreement can be enforced and that both parties can be held accountable for their actions and inactions. If accountability does not exist, agreements are useless. Finally, have the lease reviewed by *legal counsel.* Leases are legal documents with a long life. They can have a significant impact for extended periods of time, both professionally and personally. There are numerous clauses in a lease covering what-if scenarios that seem unrealistic and far fetched — until they actually occur. Leases are one of the most important documents that restaurateurs come in contact with, and their importance should be respected.

In our case, the Harbor Commons negotiations had continued to progress despite our roadblocks in other locations, and the 'Za-Bistro! team signed a lease for a space within the village center. The space was not to be delivered for another ten months after the lease was executed, so there was still time to continue our search for another site. Harbor Commons was our first executed lease, but it was generally anticipated that it would be our second restaurant location, as we would continue to pursue another site for the first location, based on the time frame provided by the landlord.

Because our initial planning efforts for Sumner Springs and Maitland revealed that the 3,081 space in Harbor Commons was simply too small for our needs, we soon increased the size of that facility by another 700 square feet to 3,781. It was not just the size of the space, but also the configuration that was a problem. It was a long and narrow space, facing the street. Also, there were large structural columns that were driving some of the design possibilities and limiting the potential efficiency and impact of the space. Preliminary design explorations for the original, smaller Harbor Commons space configuration featured a single row of tables along the window, which was dwarfed by the huge oven and display kitchen in the center. Though we could have made it work, it just did not feel right. In addition, our projections for the concept and our anticipated volume indicated that we could have utilized more than the approximately 100 seats that the original space would have accommodated.

While the structure of a lease can be controlled, there are some aspects of the development process over which the aspiring restaurateur has absolutely no control and which can only be watched from the sideline. The economic and political climates of both domestic and foreign affairs are prime examples. During our planning efforts, we were simultaneously facing the aftermath of September 11, 2001, a recession, war in Afghanistan, preparations for the second war in Iraq, and other results of the global war on terrorism. It was a very difficult time to speak with banks and developers regarding the development of a new restaurant concept. New restaurants involve a great deal of uncertainty in the minds of lenders and landlords, and there was already plenty of uncertainty in the air. During this time, we spoke with several different banks regarding a conventional loan, but we were turned down by each of those potential lenders. Though we had planned to pursue an SBA loan, it was looking more and more like the SBA option would be our only option, as conventional lenders were not keen on investing in a restaurant startup at the time, regardless of our credentials. We had spent a tremendous amount of time chasing potential sites and lenders with little to show for our efforts, and our numerous conversations with all of the landlords and banks provided a great basis for comparison for a young company like ours. It allowed us to glean a bit of knowledge and strategy from each discussion, and to combine it all into a single overall strategy for our negotiations.

❖ ❖ ❖

It had been almost seven months since the signing of our lease in Harbor Commons, and the search for our "first" site was still in high gear, but with no concrete leads. We had received a notification from the Harbor Commons developer that the space would be delayed by about two months, which bought us some extra time. That same week, Chris received a random call from the general manager of a restaurant, who was interested in information regarding the executive education program through UCF's hospitality school. As the dialogue continued, Chris soon learned that the person on the other end of the phone was actually the general manager for the restaurant we had previously pursued in Maitland. The conversation revealed that the sale of the development, which was partially responsible for the breakdown of our earlier discussions, had been completed. Chris recognized that there might be another opportunity to pursue the same restaurant we had considered previously. It wasn't long before Jason contacted the new landlord and once again began conversations regarding the restaurant space in Maitland. The restaurant had been listed for sale for the better part of that year with no final agreement reached.

The proposal made to the new landlord was nearly identical to the proposal sent to the previous landlord. This time, however, there was a focus on our part to emphasize the additional foot traffic that our restaurant would likely generate. The previous restaurant had a strong lunch business, but there was one good rush in the middle of the day and that was about it. The dinner business for the existing restaurant was not as strong as it could have been. Our concept would be driving traffic during both lunch and dinner, and there was the discussion of a regular breakfast if the landlord desired it—not just Sunday brunch. In a nutshell, the new landlord was intrigued by the proposal. He was not anxious, necessarily, for the deal to go through, but he was willing to explore the opportunity, as he liked our concept and our team's credentials. He wanted the deal between our group and the then-owners of the restaurant to be transparent; in other words, he did not want to tie up his company in an agreement between the restaurant owners and us. Any further negotiations for this particular site would hinge upon our ability to reach mutually agreeable terms with the existing tenant.

With the restaurant still on the market and no serious offers on the table, the franchisor and franchisee of the Maitland restaurant were both far more receptive the second time around to our proposal to take over the existing business and convert it into the very first 'Za-Bistro! Some of their demands from our previous conversations were modified, including the actual dollar value desired for compensation in the purchase. In the end, we were able to reach an agreement. It was a long and arduous process—much more complex and difficult than I had originally anticipated—but our first site seemed within grasp.

While I continue to emphasize that *everything is negotiable*, there is one factor that most directly affects one's ability to negotiate: the willingness and ability to walk away. A tenant cannot afford to sign a lease with terms that are not desirable or beneficial to his or her business. If either party does not have the ability to completely walk away from a deal, then that party is in no position to negotiate effectively. Particularly with respect to the pursuit of a restaurant site, or a site for any retail business for that matter, it is easy to get caught up in the emotion of the moment and feel as though a particular location is a must-have. Typically, this is not the case—there is always another site. If, on a rare occasion, a tenant is certain that he or she has found the one and only best site on the planet, it is important to focus closely on the terms of the lease in order to protect the long-term interests of the business. Again, it is easy to get caught up in the emotion of the process and overlook the negative aspects of a particular location, talking oneself into a business situation that may not be as positive as originally anticipated. Once that lease is signed, it is signed. That's it. Done deal. There is no turning back. Despite the excitement that comes with searching for, and hopefully finding, a restaurant site, the time to scrutinize a particular situation is *prior* to signing the lease. A prospective tenant should conduct as much research as possible on his or her own. Don't rely on the data from a broker; get down-and-dirty, firsthand information. Talk with local businesses. Attend local community meetings. Put forth the effort to find out what this site has to offer from a non-emotional, business perspective.

So there we were. We had finally done it. We had reached an agreement and signed a lease to develop the first 'Za-Bistro! in Maitland, just north of downtown Orlando. The Harbor Commons lease was signed as well, but delivery was expected a few months later. This project had finally come to life, and things were about to heat up very quickly. The design and planning would be starting immediately.

I was still training for the triathlon, though the training would soon be over, as the race was approaching. Also, my wife was about six months pregnant at this time. Life was going 100 miles per hour, and I no longer had to concern myself with any extra energy. While the triathlon "start" buzzer was still a few weeks away, the 'Za-Bistro! buzzer had just sounded. We were off!

8

THE DESIGN-BUILD OPTION

I received a call one day from a first-time restaurant developer inquiring about design services offered by my firm. He had just signed a lease for a very attractive site right on the beach, on the coast of the Gulf of Mexico. I asked him some specific questions so that I could figure out where he was in his planning process, what his concept entailed, and how sophisticated his approach had been to that point. He explained that he was interested in a restaurant consisting of approximately 185 seats, a full bar with at least 20 seats, a full kitchen, a dance floor, new restrooms, and a host of other amenities that would make his concept the new "hot spot" in the region. It all sounded great, until I learned that his space was only 2,000 square feet — total. Big problem! At that moment, it became my responsibility to let this gentleman know that he would not be able to accommodate all that he wanted in the space he had leased. Unfortunately, I am quite frequently the bearer of such bad news. These situations occur more regularly than I would like. The problem was that this particular restaurateur had already signed the lease. Only after he was committed was he realizing that the concept he wanted to develop would have to be significantly altered if it was going to reside in his newly acquired space. This is not an isolated case by any means. Seeking the assistance of a design professional, or someone with experience and design capabilities, to review the space *before* signing the lease in an effort to ensure that the concept would work would have been a much better approach.

Many restaurant owners rarely realize the importance of learning how to read a plan. Design is a language, and it should be viewed in a light similar to other methods of communication. The restaurant owner does not have to be fluent, necessarily, in the language of design, but having enough knowledge to get by is essential. As with any language, a little studying will go a long way. The sole purpose of design documents, which consist of both graphic and written information, is for the design team to communicate with the owner and contractors. That's it—nothing more. It is unrealistic and impractical, for obvious reasons, to build a restaurant and *then* ask an owner if he or she likes what has been created. The design team must instead present the owner with a set of drawings that *represent* the restaurant for approval. If the owner cannot read a drawing, the universal language in the world of construction, then there will be a breakdown in communication. And if the owner approves the drawings without the capability of fully understanding all that is depicted on the plans, there is a strong likelihood that he or she will experience several unexpected surprises throughout the process. The "that's-not-what-I-wanted" and "I-didn't-approve-that" panic attacks will be plentiful. Visualization is a critical skill. The ability to look at a two-dimensional drawing and *see* the space in three dimensions is an important skill for any restaurant owner to have.

In our situation, we possessed the necessary design expertise in-house. For each site we looked at, I sketched a possible layout to determine what the eventual design might look like. It allowed us the opportunity to determine the number of seats that the space would be able to accommodate and, as a result, helped us with our financial projections. It also helped us to determine the scope of construction or renovation work that might be required and to estimate the potential budget for building out the leased space. Though, in hindsight, there was a great deal of time spent developing designs for restaurants that never materialized, there was also a key benefit that helped to justify the time spent. With each design, we learned a bit more about our own concept and the design features that we wanted to include, as well as the ones that we wanted to exclude. The design process was a catalyst for countless important discussions that would affect the restaurant and its daily performance, both operationally and financially.

Another beneficial aspect of an early design effort is the potential for coordination with the landlord. If the design is completed early enough in the process, it may be possible (particularly in a newly constructed space) to provide the landlord with detailed planning information and request that the contractors constructing the building shell work around your space requirements. This may result in the relocation of a window, the revising of a door configuration, or the integration between the landlord and tenant's HVAC systems. The potential savings as a result of this early planning effort are significant — but only if the design process begins at the right time. Whether the initial design talent can be tapped internally or must be hired externally, every restaurateur should strongly consider seeking the assistance of a qualified design professional to help with such an exploration before the lease is signed. It is a small investment relative to the dollars that will be on the line in the form of a long-term lease commitment. The design would not have to be fully developed; on the contrary, only a rough sketch is required.

As part of the lease signed in Maitland, we had negotiated a grace period for rent of 110 days. The design effort was a bit behind schedule in my mind, as we were unable to obtain architectural drawings or full access to the site while the negotiations were occurring. The space was still occupied, and the existing restaurant was fully operational. It was not until the lease was signed that I finally received architectural drawings for the Maitland restaurant, which delayed my ability to begin detailed planning, even on a preliminary basis. Not ideal, I know, but this is where reality meets theory, and reality wins every time. It would become my responsibility to work diligently and catch us up. The overall timeline was also a concern. The anticipated delivery of the Harbor Commons space was just around the corner; we did not want to be under construction on two sites at the same time, especially for a new concept just starting out. With the Harbor Commons deadline looming over our heads and the established grace period for rent in Maitland clearly defined, we realized that our entire design *and* construction process had an available timeline of 12 weeks, allowing for two weeks of training before opening the restaurant. We had broken down the schedule into four weeks for design and eight weeks for construction, with an overlap in there for the permitting process, which was a huge unknown as we could not confirm how much time it would take for the city to review our drawings. That was tight, bordering on unrealistic! This timeline would not have been as concerning if we were building out an existing restaurant concept, but that was not the case. This was the first of a new restaurant concept, and there were numerous decisions that would have to be made. Based on past experience, I was extremely concerned about the timeline and not confident we could pull it off.

We had finally obtained the architecture for the Maitland space, but plans from previous tenants are rarely (if ever) 100 percent accurate. Outlets, lighting, HVAC configurations, plumbing, and electrical rough-ins are often adjusted in the field during the construction process to accommodate unforeseen challenges not reflected on the drawings. As a result, we would be forced to wait until the previous occupants had closed the business and vacated the space before we could obtain access to begin our detailed work. Further delaying our efforts was the fact that the previous tenants had decided not to inform their employees that the existing restaurant would soon be closing, thereby limiting our ability to access the restaurant and begin working on our construction documents while the business was still operational. We would simply have to wait.

❖ ❖ ❖

Now let's switch gears and discuss the actual design and construction process for a bit—specifically, design-build. What is design-build? Well, I'm glad you asked. In the early days of construction, as in back when the pyramids were being erected, the architect and contractor were usually one and the same. A master builder was responsible for overseeing the process of creating a structure from start to finish, from the first drawing until the final stone was placed and the Pharaoh was pleased. As the process has evolved over time, however, a separation between the design and the construction disciplines has emerged. This is a bit unhealthy in my opinion, as the work of architects and contractors are clearly dependant upon one another. Recently, there has been a strong shift back toward the design-build format, where these two trades are working in a more integrated way. Hardened industry veterans will have a very strict definition of design-build, but mine is a bit more forgiving. In my view, design-build encompasses the continued involvement and cooperation of both design and construction expertise throughout all phases of the development effort. The more rigid definition of design-build requires that these entities exist under the same corporate structure. To me, that is not quite as important; it does not matter whether the design and construction are officially part of the same company, but rather that they are on the same team and working together—from start to finish.

In order to understand what the design-build option has to offer, you first have to be familiar with the typical design and construction process most commonly used today and in the recent past. In this more common scenario, a design team is hired to develop the design documents required to build the new (or renovated) facility. During the course of this design process, a rough budget is provided by the design team or obtained from contractors interested in working on the project when it is ready for construction. Then, following the design process, the documents will go out to several contractors for bids. These contractors will offer pricing based on the documentation the design team has developed. Once the bids are collected and reviewed, a contractor will be selected to perform the work.

In the design-build format, the design and construction tasks are approached in a much different manner. First, a team is assembled that is capable of handling every task required throughout both design and construction. From drawing and coordination to overseeing the trades in the field, the skills required to see the project from concept to fruition are all possessed on the same team, from Day One. This team may consist of separate firms, such as an independent architect and an independent contractor, agreeing to work together on the project. It may also consist of a single firm that can handle everything in-house, under one roof. This team will include members from all of the different disciplines needed to develop the restaurant such as mechanical, electrical, plumbing, structural, foodservice, landscape, and potentially many more. These professionals will see the project through, from a blank sheet of paper until the final punch list is completed and the facility is operational.

There are numerous advantages to using the design-build method for development, which is evident by its growing popularity. Perhaps the most important advantage is the single point of responsibility that the design-build team inherits. In the more traditional arrangement, a designer and contractor frequently end up at odds at some point during the construction phase. The contractor will insist that the documentation was not clear while the designer will maintain that it was. This is not unusual. These finger-pointing exercises usually occur when a problem arises, with both sides focused on shedding responsibility for the error or misunderstanding. Keep in mind that in the world of construction, assuming responsibility for a problem also means assuming responsibility for the cost to fix that problem—a cost that no member of the team, including the owner, is eager to pay. Trust me, these discussions are not fun.

The design-build format also allows for a streamlined process. Given that the key members of the construction team are selected at the beginning of the process, some drawings and documentation are no longer necessary. They can actually be eliminated. For example, custom-designed millwork counters may not need to be designed initially by the architect, with drawings for fabrication of the counters repeated by the millwork shop. Instead, the millwork contractor, if he or she is on board during the design phase, can develop the shop drawings and have them serve as part of the design package. This will alleviate some of the work required by the architect and allow the architect to focus on other pressing issues. Also, some drawings can be eliminated and replaced with simple detailed notes on the drawings. If the contractor is on board during the design phase and understands the intention of the note, then certain drawings may no longer be required to ensure successful communication. Remember that the only objective of any design document is for the design team to clearly communicate ideas and instructions to the construction team. If this communication can be accomplished successfully in an alternative format, that is perfectly acceptable. The focus should be on clear communication, and not the format that the communication takes. This approach can result in substantial savings of both time and money.

When the design and construction entities are closely integrated, as they are in the design-build model, it is far easier for the owner to fast-track or speed up a project, if that is required. In fact, this key feature of the design-build model was instrumental in our team's attempt to meet the accelerated timeline established for the development of 'Za-Bistro! in Maitland. Design-build also does an excellent job of helping to control construction costs. Consider that the contractors who are likely to be involved in the construction effort are available to the design team during the design phase of the project. This creates a forum by which the contractors can share their field experience and ideas with the design team, ensuring that the most practical and cost-effective construction methods are included in the design. Whether these are lower-cost materials or alternative construction techniques, the contractor's techniques are extremely valuable during the design phase. It also results in buy-in by all team members and helps to ensure clearer direction for the construction phase of the project. Just because a contractor is involved during the design phase of the project, this does not mean that they have to be involved in the construction phase as well. The opportunity to bid the project via traditional means still exists. Even if different contractors are used for the design and construction phases, the benefits of involvement by a contractor during the design phase remains. With a contractor retained to provide *pre-construction services*, an industry term used to describe the input and guidance offered by a contractor during the design phase, the budgets will be accurate and limit the need for significant redesign after the bid phase. In the more traditional design and bid process, it is not uncommon for the bids to come back higher than expected after the design phase has been completed. A project that comes in over budget will result in a series of design changes that must be made to bring the project back within budget—a costly exercise at such a late stage in the process.

As with any construction process, problems are guaranteed to arise in the field. When these problems surface and decisions must be made quickly, it is a tremendous benefit to have a construction team that is familiar not only with the design, but also with the logic that was used during the design process. When the contractor is part of the original decision-making team, quick decisions can be made in the field that accurately consider the original design intent. This arrangement improves the quality of the impromptu decisions that are certain to occur. There are many other advantages of design-build, but these are some of the most significant.

There are also some common misconceptions about the design-build format, perhaps the most common being the protection of the owner. Many critics of this model feel that the collaboration of the design and construction teams is not in the owner's best interest. The primary fear they identify is that the design and construction teams will act in their own best interest, and not the best interest of the owner, particularly with regard to specifying or purchasing materials, equipment, furniture, and fixtures. The truth is that there are easy ways to combat this fear and still maintain the benefits of the design-build model.

First, you can request from your design-build team the right to work on an open-book basis. If you structure a cost-plus or fixed-fee agreement, explained later in this chapter, the profit will be known to all parties and will allow for the review of actual costs submitted by the manufacturers or subcontractors. This improves trust between the owner and the design-build team, allowing everyone to focus on the best solutions without fear that the design-build team is proposing one solution over another because it is more profitable to them. Second, you can request to be part of the bidding process. Typically, the contractors on the job will hire subcontractors to perform specific portions of work. These subcontractors must bid on the work. Insist on being part of the bid process. You can actually participate in the selection of the subcontractors. You can interview the subcontractors and develop a level of comfort before any final decisions are made. As I am sure you can tell by now, I am a strong supporter of the design-build model.

❖ ❖ ❖

Our search for a design-build team began long before our signing of the lease in Maitland. In fact, we initiated the process almost immediately when we thought that the Sumner Springs location was going to materialize. I spoke with several general contractors, including some of whom I had worked with before on other projects. I was interested in a general contractor who had substantial experience specifically with the development of restaurants. Restaurants are tricky. They have numerous unique, special requirements and conditions that simply do not exist in other types of construction projects. I had narrowed my search to three general contractors, but one in particular seemed to catch my interest more than the others. He was a locally based general contractor with significant restaurant construction experience for both independent restaurateurs and national chains. He had completed build-outs all over the country. There were two things about him that impressed me most. First was his enthusiasm, which was clearly evident. He lived in the same neighborhood as Chris, and he had learned of our plans at a local community event. He tracked down Chris, introduced himself, and indicated that he would be more than willing to assist in any way he could. Second was his vast experience with restaurants. In the process of interviewing general contractors, I presented very specific ideas and design techniques that I anticipated using. Whether it was a discussion about a particular mounting method or brand of material that might be used, I wanted to gain as much insight as possible into the experience and capabilities of each general contractor. During the course of such discussions, this particular general contractor stood out from the pack. To give you an example, I discussed my desire to use a particular surface for the dining counter in front of the oven. The other two general contractors nodded their heads in agreement, supporting the conceptual idea I had proposed. This gentleman, however, agreed that my proposed design solution would be aesthetically pleasing, but he suggested that perhaps I had not considered some of the implications related to the installation and maintenance that would result from the use of this material. That is *exactly* what I was looking for. I wanted someone who would challenge me and apply experiences gained from other restaurant projects. I did not want to hire a "yes-person," but instead someone who would act as an extension of our team, someone who would be looking out for our best interests in both the short term and the long term. His name was Roger, and I was pretty confident that he had both the desire and capability to help us reach our goals despite the challenge that was before us.

Because of the compressed timeline, we simply would not have the luxury of securing hard bids from multiple general contractors. I was also clear with Roger up front regarding my desire to utilize a design-build format. Not only did he agree with the approach, but he further indicated that this was likely the only way that our objectives would be accomplished. The question we then had to consider was the structure of our design-build agreement. This was an important issue even before we began the design effort, as I was likely choosing the general contractor that would ultimately be responsible for the build-out. While I had negotiated an agreement that would allow us to use a different general contractor for the design phase and the construction phase if we so chose, in all reality such a course of action would have significantly reduced our capability to meet the established timeline. Rent payment on Maitland and the start of construction on Harbor Commons were both drawing closer.

There are two common formats for an agreement between a general contractor and an owner: 1) a fixed-cost agreement, and 2) a cost-plus agreement. Each arrangement has its pros and cons. In a fixed-cost agreement, also called a guaranteed maximum price contract, or GMP for short, the contractor guarantees to the owner that the building will be built for a certain price. This is beneficial, as the owner knows the costs up front. It is also beneficial to the owner in that the general contractor has committed to a defined price and will have a contractual obligation to stick to the price quoted even as problems and challenges arise throughout the construction effort. The downside to this format, however, is that a contractor may also have an incentive to make decisions that are in his or her own best interest throughout the construction process in order to preserve margin and profitability. For instance, using less expensive, inferior materials than those called for on the drawing or in the specifications might not be readily apparent to the owner and may result in a lower cost — and thus higher profitability — to the contractor. I am not trying to be a cynic, but it is important for a potential owner to be aware that such incentives do exist. When a contractor has offered a price that cannot be exceeded, a GMP, that contractor will want to avoid absorbing any unforeseen expenses. Rest assured that this contractor will not be overly anxious to incur additional charges resulting from unclear documents or owner changes. Rather, the contractor will be more likely to find a way for someone else to absorb the additional charges — that someone is often the owner. While the contract is supposed to be all inclusive, the contract is based on the construction documents, and the construction documents only. This increases the likelihood that *anything* not specifically identified in the design documents, but still needing to be done, will require additional funds from the owner. This is handled through a *change order*, indicating that something has been added which was not in the original scope.

The other common structure for an agreement between a general contractor and an owner is a cost-plus agreement. In this format, the contractor provides all materials and labor for the construction effort at a fixed markup (percentage) over his or her actual cost. Such an arrangement is usually subject to open-book communication, whereby the owner has the right to review all of the pricing and quotations received by the general contractor to ensure that the charges are correct. This format has its own set of pros and cons. On the positive side, the owner can be assured that the contractor's profit margin will be consistent throughout the job, and that there will be no "blind" items with an excessively high markup. It also helps to form trust between the contractor and owner, as all costs are readily available for review. One negative is that the owner will not be assured of the final costs for the project at the outset; there is no guaranteed maximum price. Another downside to this arrangement is that there is no incentive for the general contractor to keep the costs down on the project. In fact, the opposite incentive exists. The more the contractor sells to the owner and the higher the price of the products sold, the more money the general contractor will make. This is a potentially dangerous situation. Once again, not to be a cynic, but motivated by profit, an untrustworthy contractor might offer only the more expensive options on materials or costly resolutions to unexpected challenges in the field. Reputable contractors would not do this, but as an owner, you should be aware that the possibility does exist.

With either type of agreement, there is a potential for the contractor to play games undetectable to a restaurant owner. For instance, a general contractor can show the owner a quotation from a subcontractor, but how does the owner know that the quotation reflects the actual price that the contractor will pay? Has a side deal been reached? There are an infinite number of ways to the cheat the system. Where there is a will, there is a way. In the end, it comes down to the honesty and integrity of the contractor who is performing the work. It comes down to trust and gut feeling on the part of the owner.

To borrow a philosophy from former President Ronald Reagan: *Trust, but verify.*

There are standard design-build agreement forms, developed and supported by the American Institute of Architects (AIA), which can be obtained and used in the agreement between a general contractor and an owner. In our case, I wanted to try to incorporate the advantages of both the fixed fee and cost-plus agreements, so Roger and I agreed to a hybrid format for compensation (the specifics of this agreement will be discussed in a later chapter). This format, however, did allow for an open-book format and my ability to review all of the pricing submitted by the subcontractors. It would also guarantee the contractor a minimum level of compensation based on the budget discussed. In the event that the project ran over our stated budget, we would only have to worry about the additional material and labor costs, and not the contractor's additional markup. It seemed like a good compromise. As with the lease, the design and construction contracts are legal documents with tremendous long-term implications and staying power. It is wise to get a cursory review of the terms of the agreement from both a lawyer specifically versed in construction law and an unaffiliated contractor.

In the spirit of the design-build format, I had requested that Roger hire the architect to ensure the single point of responsibility. I wanted someone local, given the format and expedited schedule, so issues could be resolved quickly as they arose. And although I had worked with numerous architects in the Orlando market, most firms were either too large for a project of this size or too small, with insufficient restaurant design experience. Since I did not personally know of a qualified architect that met our needs, I was open to working with an architect with whom Roger had previous experience, given that he and the architect would be working closely together. If Roger were to be responsible for the architect, it was only fair to allow him to select someone with whom he could work comfortably. And so I was introduced to our new architect, Mark. Roger had worked previously with Mark, whose credentials included design work for several restaurants, according to his résumé. Although his restaurant experience was not the most extensive I had seen, I was confident that my experience could help overcome any gaps, though I did not expect many. Our restaurant concept was simple in that there was very little equipment in comparison to most restaurant concepts of a similar size.

In an effort to meet the timeline for design and construction, our newly formed design team devised a strategy to divide the design effort into three separate components: 1) a demolition package, 2) a bare-bones architectural package, and 3) an interior finishes package. This approach served several purposes. First, the breakdown in this particular method would allow for some overlap in our efforts. The demolition package could be developed and submitted for permit. As soon as the demolition permit was received, the demolition work would be able to commence at the site in Maitland. Meanwhile, the architect would already be working on the second package, a basic set of architectural drawings indicating all walls, furniture, fixtures, and equipment to be erected within the space. The package would include all information required to obtain our building permit, following a review and approval by the local building department. We would then await our permit, likely while the demolition work was being executed, and the contractor would start on the interior build-out once the second permit was received. Finally, an interior finishes package would be developed, detailing the materials to be used by the general contractor. This third documentation package was scheduled to be ready for use by the contractor upon receipt of the second permit.

The separation of this third package served multiple purposes. First, the selection of finishes would not delay the application for our interior build-out permit. Second, by the time the interior finishes package was completed, we would have a hard cost on the base interior build-out, allowing us to select final finishes that would meet our budget. The second architectural package would include specification for some of the interior finishes from the third interior finishes package, though not in detail. For instance, the second package might call for tile in a certain location; however, the actual tile manufacturer, color, and installation pattern would be included in the third package. Although this approach was a bit more complicated than usual, it was necessary in order to meet the established timeline. I was comfortable with this plan of attack. It appeared to be well devised and would seemingly help us meet our various goals. Roger and Mark seemed comfortable with the approach as well. With a battle plan in hand, the design of our first restaurant was soon underway.

9

A Look Behind the Design

Form follows function. This age-old design cliché just might be the most important characteristic of truly successful design. In layman's terms, this means that *first* the design must work, and *then* one can make it look good. Whether the design process is meant for a building or a product, the requirement is the same. Think back through your own personal experience. I am sure you have encountered a product at some point in your life that looked great, but just didn't work all that well. It did not do what it was supposed to do, or perhaps it didn't perform as well as it should have, despite its visual appeal. It didn't meet the intended purpose for which you purchased the product. It failed.

Some aspiring restaurateurs have a tendency to focus exclusively on the aesthetics and interior design features to be included in the public spaces of their new restaurant. Sure, the front-of-house is incredibly important; no argument there. However, its high visibility often tends to overshadow the planning that is required for the back-of-house, which is usually out of sight from the guest. The back-of-house, essential in the production and delivery of food or beverage to the patrons, will consist of storage, preparation, cooking, serving, ware washing, and other such functional areas. Some even affectionately refer to it as the "heart-of-house," emphasizing that this area is at the center of the facility, supplying the facility's extremities with all they require. For this reason, as we begin to explore the rationale behind the design we implemented for the restaurant in Maitland, I feel compelled to start with the back-of-house operation. But before I do, I owe you a more detailed history about the building itself and the condition it was in when we took possession.

The building in Maitland was constructed in the late 1980s as a Friendly's restaurant. This was clearly evident in some of the physical characteristics of the exterior structure, such as the roof design, brick, and exterior freezer access, which were signature design treatments included as part of Friendly's prototypical store. Inside, the restaurant still had the short-order-style pass-through window that was commonly featured between the kitchen and the sever pick-up area. Following its initial life

 as a Friendly's, the building was converted to a Perkins family-style restaurant, and then finally to the previous owner's fast-casual pizza, sandwich, and salad concept. The building was just about 15 years old when we took it over, and I must say that I was a little surprised to see that some of the cooking equipment on the line was actually the original equipment. The building showed clear signs of its evolution, as the needs of each occupant required some physical changes to the facility in order to accommodate their concept. At some point, a second hood had been added next to the original hood. Even the restrooms showed signs of the transformation that had occurred over time. It wasn't until the early 1990s that the Americans with Disabilities Act (ADA) took effect. The original bathroom stalls were not large enough to accommodate the five-foot diameter turning radius stipulated by ADA codes. As a result, during one of the earlier renovations, a separate ADA-compliant restroom was added at the opposite end of the restaurant—far from the existing restroom facilities. Not only did this second restroom impose upon the dining room, but it also required a separate experience for those with disabilities. Though it was an understandable solution in order to comply with the ADA regulations, I did not consider it desirable for a disabled patron, nor did I believe it to be good design practice. This configuration would have to be evaluated in our remodeling efforts in light of our concept and desired level of sophistication.

Existing Maitland Floor Plan, Before 'Za-Bistro! Remodel

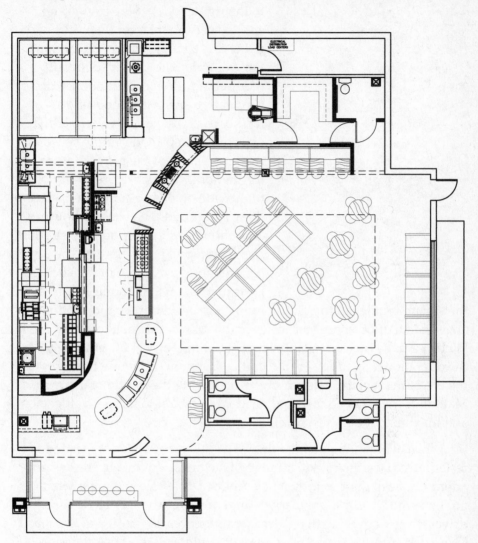

Due in part to the multiple concepts that had occupied the space, and also in part to the changing codes and demands of the general market over the years, the back-of-house space within the restaurant was rather inefficient. The previous tenant's design was capable of accommodating just over 100 seats in the restaurant, which was approximately 3,800 square feet in total size. The space could have supported more seats, but the L-shaped back-of-house configuration limited the seating capacity. Upon entering the restaurant, the kitchen production area was at the left-hand side, and then wrapped toward the

rear of the building and eventually back to the right. Some of the back-of-house spaces were a bit larger than they had to be, due again to the configuration. For example: The L-shaped layout required additional circulation space. Circulation space in a foodservice facility must be carefully planned. The objective is to provide ample space for free movement of people and products throughout the kitchen area, but not to provide any more circulation space than is required. The back-of-house area should be large enough to support the operation—but no larger. The square footage of space in the kitchen costs just as much in monthly rent as the square footage in the dining room, bar, or other revenue-producing areas. Circulation space (the aisles and walkways throughout the kitchen area), when not planned properly, can impact the efficiency of the operation and adversely affect the operation's revenue throughout the life of the facility. After carefully reviewing the existing facility in Maitland, we believed it would need an overhaul to improve efficiency and maximize the public, revenue-producing space.

When evaluating potential design solutions for a new or existing restaurant space, an infinite number of factors can influence the design approach. I call these factors *design drivers.* I don't mean to offer what might sound like an elementary definition of this term, but a design driver is truly anything that drives, or influences, the design of the space. These design drivers come in many different formats. Physical design drivers could include column locations; door locations; existing electrical, gas, or water main locations (especially in existing facilities); stairway locations; egress requirements; and so on. Each design driver will have some effect on the proposed design solution. If the effect is negative, then the costs associated with overcoming the particular obstacle must be studied and evaluated to see if a realistic solution exists. A column, for instance, can be moved in some cases. This is usually an expensive effort, but in certain situations the costs may be justifiable. Operational needs—not just physical elements—can also significantly affect the design of a facility. The desire for an open display kitchen, as an example, will influence the layout of both the front-of-house and back-of-house spaces. Even the style of service can greatly influence the design. Sight lines, containment of noise, and containment of the fluorescent lights that typically illuminate our kitchens all must be addressed while maintaining easy access by the servers to minimize their distance of travel. There is so much to consider, and these are all *design drivers*.

In the case of the Maitland site, we had specific design drivers as well. Our timeline was such that we simply could not wait for access to the building in order to begin our design efforts. Instead, I had to rely on the accuracy of the plans that we had received from the architect of the last renovation. This is not desirable, but it was necessary in our case. In the real world, we start with what is ideal, and then we have to adjust as required. I had also conducted a few site visits as an anonymous patron of the previous restaurant concept in order to verify certain aspects of the building. Keep in mind that the former operators opted not to inform their staff of the restaurant's imminent closing. My objective was to lock in a floor plan—that is, finalize the basic configuration of the restaurant— prior to involving the architect. This approach was intended to further expedite the design process and give the rest of the design team a running head start. Since we had only allocated four weeks for the entire design effort, I was completely focused on streamlining the process as much as possible to ensure that the pending deadlines were met. Having design capabilities in-house was a tremendous advantage in this situation.

Now, let me take you on a little tour of the back-of-house designed for 'Za-Bistro! in Maitland. A great deal of thought and planning went into the design. Was it perfect? No. But there were some valuable design techniques and decisions along the way that are worth reviewing. By sharing not only the features of the design, but also the logic behind the decisions that were made, I hope others can apply some of our solutions to their own operations and applications. For this tour, we are going to follow the flow of food through the facility. In other words, we are going to take the same sequential path that the food takes, from the moment it is received at the back door until the moment that it leaves the back door for the dumpster. I sometimes refer to this round trip as "gate to plate, then back to gate." This is an extremely useful technique that can be employed when reviewing a floor plan, allowing the restaurateur to systematically evaluate each area of the facility. Follow the flow of food. Both product and people will follow this general path. Focusing on the movement through the facility during the design process will help to improve efficiency, which can reduce lost time and product. So let's start our tour where the food enters the facility: at the back door.

When we took over the building, the back door had no protection from the elements. In inclement weather, which is a regular occurrence in central Florida, the interior of the restaurant would be completely exposed whenever the rear door was opened. To fix this problem, we added an awning over the rear door. It was not large, but at least it would allow the door to be opened during a storm without rain pouring directly into the building. It was a relatively inexpensive solution that acted as a bit of a design treatment as well, tackling both form and function simultaneously. The office was located immediately adjacent to the back door. This helped with security in the facility, ensuring that all staff, purveyors, and goods entering or leaving the building through the back-of-house would have to pass by the office. The manager, with windows in the office overlooking both the receiving corridor and the ware-washing area, would be able to keep tabs on critical areas of the back-of-house while working in the office. The office was small, as many restaurant offices are. It was just large enough to house the files, computer, music system, and other essentials, but intentionally small enough to encourage the managers to spend more time on the floor or in the kitchen, rather than burying themselves in the office.

Just off the back-of-house entry corridor were the soda system and the bulk carbon dioxide container required for both the soda and beer systems. These items were placed intentionally at the rear entry, in view of the manager's office, for optimum security. In my designs, I try to limit purveyors' access to the restaurant facility. This design technique increases security and reduces the opportunity for theft. Some of the purveyor-related stories I have heard, though true, are a little hard to believe. In one instance, a restaurant's walk-in cooler and freezer were designed with a dedicated cooler for beer kegs located within the walk-in complex. The only way to access the beer cooler was through the food cooler. Whenever a purveyor had to re-stock the kegs in the beer cooler, they would walk right by all of the food in the everyday walk-in cooler. On one particular day, the manager of this facility caught the beer purveyor walking out the door with two live lobsters under his jacket. The purveyor had stolen live lobsters!

Though the design of a facility cannot completely deter theft, good design can limit the opportunities for such occurrences and reduce the potential for certain actions. If the keg cooler had a separate entrance or a different location, the lobster theft might have been prevented. The location we selected for the soda system, near the back door, would keep the purveyor out of the main production area and in full view of the manager. Even better than that, the carbon dioxide container was located adjacent to the outside wall with a nipple that extended through the exterior, allowing the carbon dioxide purveyor to refill the tank without even entering the facility. Also located in the receiving corridor was a bank of employee lockers. This provided the employees with a convenient location to store their personal belongings during a shift. The psychology of a manager's presence, combined with the absence of locks on the lockers, would help to limit the potential for illegal and improper activities within the restaurant.

At the end of the receiving corridor, I located a receiving station. The receiving station serves two key purposes: 1) It helps to ensure food safety within the restaurant facility, and 2) it protects the restaurant's financial position. First, let's take a look at the food-safety aspect, a topic that has received increased attention in recent years, and will only become more important in the future. The leading cause of food-borne illness outbreaks is cross-contamination within a foodservice facility. Cross-contamination occurs when one contaminated product or surface comes in contact with another product or surface, contaminating the second surface in the process. It can occur when an employee does not wash his or her hands properly after touching a contaminated food product. It can also occur when a utensil is used on a contaminated product first, and then on a second food product without being properly cleaned and sanitized. Improperly sanitized food contact surfaces can lead to cross-contamination as well. In the end, the best way to limit the potential for an outbreak of food-borne illness is never to allow the contaminated product to enter the restaurant in the first place. That is where the receiving station comes into play. I view the receiving door of a restaurant or foodservice facility as a security gate. Product should not be allowed to pass through this gate until it is inspected and approved. A receiving station, when located near the receiving point of the facility, allows the operator to check the food product properly, before accepting any deliveries and allowing the new food products to be stored alongside other food products. A table, a scale, a garbage can, and a sink are all that is required for a receiving station. This relatively inexpensive station gives the staff a place to land and properly inspect the incoming goods. It provides a convenient location to handle the necessary paperwork associated with deliveries. The station also can be used for additional preparation work during non-receiving times. When the staff has a proper receiving facility, they are more likely to inspect the product. When there is no convenient place to check the incoming food products, however, the required inspections are less likely to occur. And if they do not occur, the best, most effective opportunity for preventing outbreaks of food-borne illness — preventing contaminated food from entering the building — will be lost. This is where a minimal investment in a receiving station can help.

I mentioned that the receiving station can affect the financial position of the restaurant as well, and I stand behind that statement one hundred percent. By encouraging the inspection of incoming products, the receiving station will help to ensure that the quantities and weights listed on the purveyor's invoice actually match those that have been received. Imagine for a moment the financial impact over the course of a year if a restaurateur was signing for — and more importantly, *paying* for — ten pounds of product each week, but actually receiving only nine pounds. This unnecessary financial loss can be easily prevented.

There are other tricks that purveyors of questionable character can play. Take a flat of strawberries, for instance. The strawberries on top may look perfect, but they may be strategically placed to hide some of the inferior product on lower tiers. If the inferior product is not discovered during the delivery, and is therefore accepted, it will likely be discarded before being served. The result, once again, is a negative financial impact on the operation. By conducting regular, thorough inspections of incoming products, operators can send a clear message to purveyors: don't try any of your games here! This is not to say that all purveyors are dishonest; however, it would be naïve to ignore the practices that can occur in the real world, especially when they can be prevented so easily.

Once the food products have been received, they must be stored in their respective storage areas — dry storage, refrigerated storage, and frozen storage. Our dry storage was fairly small, but just large enough to support the needs of the operation. The walk-in cooler/freezer combination was located at the far end of the kitchen, with access to the walk-in freezer through the walk-in cooler. Although I typically try to locate the main storage areas as close as possible to the receiving area, a small compromise was necessary in this instance. Food products would have to travel the length of the kitchen, though the space was not all that large, to be stored initially in the walk-in, and then they would continue along the sequential flow of food, with each production area adjacent to the next. There are two reasons that the walk-in freezer was designed to be accessed through the walk-in cooler. First, the walk-in freezer typically maintains a temperature of either 0°F or -10°F. Assuming that the kitchen space will be 80°F or warmer at times, the temperature difference between the two spaces is significant. Opening the walk-in freezer into the walk-in cooler significantly reduces the difference in temperature between the two spaces. This helps the freezer compartment maintain its temperature in the event that the door is left open, and ultimately helps to extend the life of the refrigeration equipment. The second reason has to do with space utilization. This configuration allowed for a larger preparation area just outside of the walk-in box. The inclusion of a freezer door, with direct access from the kitchen, would result in two walk-in doors from the preparation area and would have reduced the amount of available work surface.

Just outside the walk-in cooler and freezer combination was the main preparation area. This portion of the facility, consisting of worktables, sinks, and cooking equipment, was essential to the overall concept and the way that food was prepared in the restaurant. Each worktable featured at least one sink for preparation (multiple sinks allow for the separation of raw and ready-to-eat products during food preparation). The sinks were also strategically located, considering the condensate drain lines so that both the prep sinks and drain lines from the walk-in cooler and freezer coils could share the same floor sink. The cost of an individual floor sink can be $1,000 or more by the time it is purchased, installed, and connected to the plumbing system. As such, it is always wise to think ahead and work to minimize the infrastructure required, where possible, without affecting the function of the facility. Minimizing the number of floor sinks through the layout of the area is just one example.

The real key to this production area, however, was not the sinks, but the rest of the equipment. The entire restaurant would run on only three pieces of cooking equipment. By now you are familiar with one of those pieces—the stone-hearth oven. The other two—a steamer and a six-burner range with a convection oven base—were located in the rear preparation area. A char-broiler was originally planned for the back cooking line, but it was deemed unnecessary and omitted before we opened the restaurant. The fourth piece of production equipment was a blast chiller. The concept behind our food production method was to produce many of the entrée items on premises, but in bulk quantity. The items would be prepared, plated in oven-safe serving dishes, and then blast chilled to bring them down to an appropriate temperature within the time frames stated in the food safety codes. The blast chiller not only ensured that the products would be handled in compliance with all food safety guidelines, but also preserved the food's quality and increased the storage life of the product. The various entrées would be cooked or reheated to order in the oven, out front and in full view of the guest. This cook-chill process had grown in popularity, particularly throughout Europe, but had not yet been widely adopted by individual restaurants in the United States. While some locations throughout the country were using blast chillers, most of the country's leading multi-unit concepts had not yet adopted the cook-chill production method or use of a blast chiller in their restaurant facilities. I would not go so far as to say that the process we were planning to use for food production was on the cutting edge, but we were definitely well ahead of the curve. Many restaurant operators don't realize that refrigerators are merely designed to *maintain* the temperature of a product that is already cold; they are not designed to *reduce* the temperature of a product just out of the oven or a product that has been stored hot and ready to serve. That is where a blast chiller comes in. This piece of equipment is designed specifically to reduce the temperature of the product. In our case, the blast chiller also served as an additional work surface. The location and configuration of the back-of-house production area would allow for additional preparation work to occur during peak periods out of the restaurant patrons' sight.

Even with the limited portfolio of cooking equipment we had selected, we could cook virtually any type of product. We could boil water and make soups or stews on the range top. We could bake desserts or entrées in the convection oven, and we could prepare anything from rice to vegetables in the steamer. We had wet heat, we had dry heat, and we had open burners. Based on the menu, there really was not much more required. Cooking, when you boil it down to the basics (okay, a little pun, I apologize), is the manipulation of only two things: heat and water, or temperature and moisture. The process of cooking either adds heat or removes heat, and the same holds true with water. It is the sequence of such manipulation, the quantity and duration of each of these elements, and, of course, the art with which each item is utilized that enable culinary experts to create the wondrous foodstuff we have come to expect.

This uniquely designed preparation area served some additional purposes with respect to the business model. The main advantage was obvious: there just wasn't much cooking equipment. This would reduce not only the cost of the foodservice equipment package, but also the cost and intricacy of the infrastructure required to support this kitchen. There would be fewer gas, electrical, and water connections, as well as lower overall utility usage. The limited package would also make it easier for future expansion on a larger scale, should the opportunity arise. Maintenance calls, utility costs, and other such operational expenses would be reduced. I do not want the irony of this design to pass you by. Keep in mind that the firm for which I worked, the business started by my grandfather, was one of the largest foodservice equipment dealerships in the United States. And there I was, creating a full-service concept that operated on nothing more than three pieces of cooking equipment and a blast chiller. Though it was a bit ironic, it certainly was not out of character. I am a minimalist. I believe in providing an operation with only what is needed, while still allowing for future expansion or modifications as the operation evolves.

Once the food was prepared, it would either be stored in the walk-in cooler or transported to the front-of-house display kitchen for holding and production. You will notice that both of these areas are next to the back-of-house preparation area — this was by design. You may also notice that access to the display kitchen from the back-of-house preparation area does not conflict with the servers' main access to the ware-washing area. This, too, was by design. In a well-designed foodservice facility, the culinary staff and service staff should meet in areas such as the food pick-up window or the ware-washing area, but never cross paths. Conflicting flow patterns result in accidents, lost money, slower service, and lower employee morale. This access to the display kitchen was essential to the movement of people and product through the facility.

Once the food prepared in the back-of-house preparation kitchen is transported to the display kitchen, it is held in the under-counter refrigerators, ready to be pulled and cooked to order. In other instances, such as the pizza preparation station and the cold food station (also

'Za-Bistro! Maitland Floor Plan

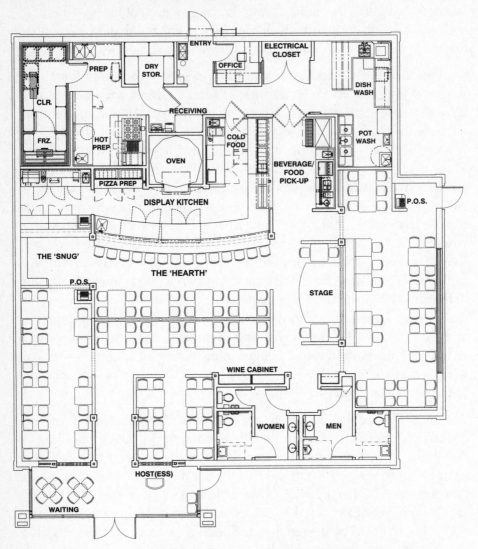

referred to as *garde manger* within the industry), fresh, cold products are moved from the back-of-house and stored, ready for assembly or cooking, as the orders roll in. The long, curved worktable that runs the length of the display kitchen would serve two purposes: First, as a preparation area during off-peak hours in the early morning and in the afternoon. In all honesty, the two small prep tables and the top of the blast chiller in the back-of-house kitchen did not provide a great deal of work space. For this reason, in part, the large worktable was provided with a utility preparation sink within the display kitchen. Second, since the display kitchen had only one piece of cooking equipment, the oven, the large work surface was designed to serve as a buffer during peak production periods. Whether the buffer space was required for products waiting to go into the oven or for products that had just come out of the oven, the oversized worktable would allow for queuing of entrées whenever the need arose. I want to stress that I refer to this work surface as a table, and not as a counter; there is a difference. A table typically consists of a work top, with an open base and legs. A counter, on the other hand, consists of the same style work top but has a fully enclosed understructure consisting of shelves, cabinets, or secure storage areas below. Counters are more expensive than tables. Given the configuration of the dining room and the Hearth display kitchen, patrons seated at the dining bar would only be able to see the top of this particular work surface, and not the base below. So why spend the extra money on a counter if there was no additional benefit? The open-base structure not only cost less, but also allowed extra flexibility for additional equipment below.

I have repeatedly referred to the display kitchen, the foodservice production area in full view of the restaurant patrons. Display kitchens have grown in popularity in recent years. I would like to take a moment to discuss some of the influences a display kitchen can have on a facility's design. If properly conceived and designed, display kitchens can be a tremendous asset to the operation. If not, they can be a nightmare. Today's dining public is far more sophisticated than ever before. The perceived quality, freshness, and presentation of the food are just as important as how the food tastes. Also, the dining atmosphere has a significant effect—positive or negative—on the overall experience. Display kitchens, when properly integrated, can enhance the customers' dining experience.

When food is prepared in full view of the guest, the guest subconsciously believes that the establishment is so proud of its product and preparation methods, it is willing to put them out on display. Additionally, food preparation in front of the guest addresses one of the primary concerns of today's patrons: food safety. Display kitchens offer the guest peace of mind regarding safe food handling. The guest feels that when food is prepared in full view, the culinary staff is more conscious of safe food-handling practices. This approach generally works. Display kitchen staff members are extremely conscious that their every move is being watched, and they tend to take precautions that they might not take in the back-of-house. They are aware of the guest's watchful eye. Another reason for the popularity of display kitchens, and one of the reasons they have experienced tremendous growth, is the element of theater. Display kitchens offer a show for the patrons. It is a form of entertainment that can enhance the overall dining experience.

There are a variety of issues to be considered when determining whether a display kitchen is the right choice for a particular operation. Many of these factors are unique to each individual concept, but there are some global issues that affect every restaurant considering the inclusion of a display kitchen. Display kitchens, by their nature, are in full view. Some of the functions that occur in a foodservice facility are not, shall we say, the most appetizing. I haven't seen too many display ware-washing areas recently, though I have seen one proposed. Can you imagine that? The determination must be made as to which components should be in full view, and which components should be concealed. One of the gray areas is preparation—not the hot or cold production lines, but the main preparation area. Some preparation activities may enhance the guest's experience, while others may have just the opposite effect.

Even though form follows function (yes, there it is again), the aesthetic component is important in display kitchens. When designed properly, every sight line into the kitchen—including into the support areas—is scrutinized. Storage areas must be concealed or kept neat. Built-in equipment may be more desirable than freestanding equipment, presenting a finished look to the patrons. Both operation and construction budgets can be affected by decisions made to accommodate the aesthetic objectives. It is usually more expensive to provide a display kitchen in lieu of a concealed, back-of-house kitchen. Display kitchens should be viewed as an investment. The question is: What is the return on that investment?

Display kitchens often present an opportunity, and frequently a necessity, for the culinary staff to interact with the guest. The requirement for such interaction can impact the operation. The pool of potential employees can be reduced drastically, as not every available applicant is well suited to interact with the guest and convey the desired image of the restaurant. Additionally, the interaction between the culinary team and the service staff can sometimes get heated, as those of you with a restaurant operations background know well. Imagine those heated conversations occurring within close proximity or earshot of the guest. Is that adding to or subtracting from the experience? Please do not misunderstand my position—the potential for guest interaction is a fantastic opportunity. But with that opportunity comes some responsibility as well. The long-term implications a display kitchen can have on an operation should not be overlooked. In the end, we determined that the display kitchen and production in front of the guest was essential for the 'Za-Bistro! concept and, thus, worth the investment. The incorporation of a display kitchen—visible throughout the dining room, with the flame dancing in the back of the oven and our team of cooks working the oven—was a must.

Given our concept's focus on wine, beer, and specialty coffees and teas, we provided a dedicated service bar. This staffed service bar was designed to encourage the servers to sell more specialty drinks. In previous operations where I had worked, I noticed that specialty drinks, such as a cappuccino or espresso, were frequently avoided by servers because it took too long to make them and interrupted the servers' normal workflow. As a result of the perceived inconvenience, servers would tend to avoid selling such items—items that featured a low food cost and highly desirable profit margin. These beverages, when made by a variety of different service staff members, were often inconsistent. To resolve this matter within the 'Za-Bistro! concept, we anticipated that the service bartender would handle these items, improving the consistency of the product and encouraging the servers to sell specialty beverages. In hindsight, though, the design of the bar was one of the biggest flaws of the interior design. This layout did not provide the bartender a secondary way out of the bar space. The only way out was through the hot production line, in front of the oven and through the activity on the line. More importantly, it resulted in a more frequent need to fully staff the service bar. During slower times, it was more difficult to eliminate the bartender because the only access for the wait staff to get their own drinks was also through the cooking line. This was not convenient, to say the least.

There were additional service-related aspects of the overall design worth noting. The pick-up counter was located directly across from the beverage counter and just outside of the ware-washing area, which was in the rear of the restaurant, concealed from the guests' view. These are the only areas that would most frequently be accessed by the servers. Servers could pick up the meals for their tables, retrieve beverages and service items, and drop off their soiled dishes all within a compact area, allowing the service staff to operate more efficiently. Servers would have a shorter distance of travel, and they would not be impeded by bumping into the kitchen staff. This configuration would also require the servers to pass regularly by the pick-up window, which was intentional. The design would provide additional opportunities for the servers to run food to the tables as it was ready, keeping food from just sitting in the pick-up window. Even when the food was not necessarily for the server's own customers, the staff would be more likely to run the food to the appropriate table. It was a team concept. Again, I cannot control the actions of employees, but I can encourage or discourage certain activities by designing a building a certain way. The compact design of the service areas limited the amount of traveling required by the staff, freeing up more time to be spent with the guest. It helped to streamline the steps of service and enable the servers to provide more attention to their patrons. One additional technique demonstrating our early focus on service was the location of the point-of-sale terminals. These terminals are often located in the prime service areas, which would be on or near the beverage counter in our layout. In our design, however, these terminals were located closer to the dining room. This served multiple purposes. First, it would allow the servers to stay closer to the guest and better coordinate when each course needed to be "fired" for service in the kitchen. It would allow a server more time to interact with the guest, as it would require fewer steps during the service sequence. Their locations would also keep the queuing that typically accompanies the point-of-sale system out of the main service corridor, which would be the highest trafficked area of the restaurant. Though it seems like a minor aspect of the design, something as simple as the location of the point-of-sale systems can directly impact the level of service throughout the life of the operation and the satisfaction of the restaurant's patrons.

I should point out that the design that I developed did not utilize any of the existing kitchen facility's infrastructure. The hoods, walk-in cooler and freezer, ware-washing area, office, and other such components from the previous facility would not be reused in the new design. Although it seemed that the layout we developed would efficiently and effectively support our operation, what about the cost associated with *not* reusing the existing layout and equipment? It is a valid question and one that was raised by my father when I was in the middle of finalizing the conceptual layout. In light of this challenge, I went back to the drawing board—literally—and developed an alternate layout that incorporated many of the existing components. This alternative layout reused the walk-in cooler and freezer, the ware-washing area, and other key components, all in their existing locations and condition. I even mapped out the existing floor sinks in an effort to reuse the existing plumbing system. It was certainly a worthwhile exercise, but in the end, the trade-offs were far too great. In attempting to incorporate some of the existing equipment, I also had to consider the status of the equipment that we were trying to retain. The walk-in coolers were beaten up badly. Given that they were the original units, about 15 years old, and clearly not well maintained, I had some serious reservations about their condition and the remaining insulation value of the panels. The electric bills for the previous tenant were extremely high, and the walk-in boxes could have been a contributing factor.

The ware-washing area was not designed to properly support a full-service restaurant operation. Though it would have been nice to reuse the existing tables and dish machine, the trade-offs there were undesirable as well. The dish machine was a low-temperature machine, which is not as effective or desirable as a high-temperature dish machine. Here is a very brief overview on the difference between high- and low-temperature dish machines. Low-temperature dish machines rely on chemicals for cleaning and sanitation. They typically use water that is between 110 and 140 degrees Fahrenheit. If the chemical solution is not correct, there is an increased risk that the china, plastic ware, flatware, and glassware will not be properly sanitized, increasing the risk of cross-contamination within the restaurant. Because these low-temperature machines rely on chemicals for sanitation, they have lower-quality results than their high-temperature counterparts. For example, the low-temperature machines do a poor job of removing lipstick. How would our guests feel, given the focus of our concept on wine, if they received a $40 bottle of wine and four glasses with lipstick stains? The high-temperature machines, on the other hand, rely on heated water with a final rinse temperature of 180 degrees Fahrenheit to properly sanitize the wares in the machine. The water, at this higher temperature, will actually kill any bacteria. It also provides better ware-washing results. Additionally, because the configuration of the dish tables did not allow for enough landing and sorting space for the soiled dishes, it would have contributed to breakage, slow processing, and the need for a higher par level for our smallwares inventory.

'Za-Bistro! Maitland Ware-Washing Layout

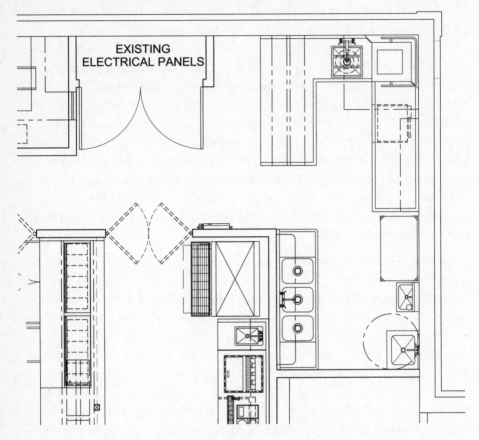

In yet another example of the effort to explore ways to reuse the existing elements of the restaurant, I spoke with our general contractor regarding utilization of the existing plumbing system. We determined, however, that no plumber would be able to warranty the existing system. In other words, if there was a problem, it would be our problem to deal with and not covered by the warranty. There are certain places within the scope of a project to save money, but this was not one of them. If a problem arose with the existing plumbing system, the repair costs and disruption to the operation would be extreme. In the end, it was clear that cutting the slab for an entirely new plumbing system would be the best solution. In all of the above examples, the savings could have been realized during the construction phase, but would have increased operating costs throughout the life of the facility and cost far more than we were saving up front. The building that we were dealing with was

15 years old with minimal additional investment over the years. The decision to remain with our original design was sound, based on the findings of this exploratory effort. Nevertheless, evaluating the existing facility was certainly a worthwhile exercise.

The new design did consider some of the existing conditions. For instance, the electrical panels in the kitchen were to remain untouched. There simply was no justifiable reason to relocate this main breaker panel, as the cost to do so would have been significant. I also considered the existing restrooms in my design. As I discussed earlier, the restaurant was constructed prior to the introduction of the Americans with Disabilities Act and all of its associated compliance requirements. The additional, separate stall, added during an earlier renovation to meet the ADA requirements, was located at the opposite end of the restaurant. Requiring a patron to use a separate facility was inconsistent with the level of

Restroom Layout Comparison, Old vs. New

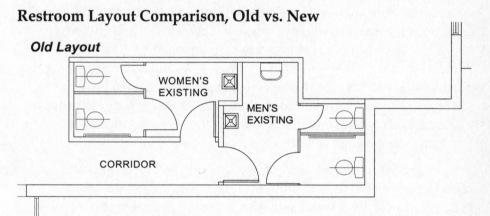

Old Layout

WOMEN'S EXISTING

MEN'S EXISTING

CORRIDOR

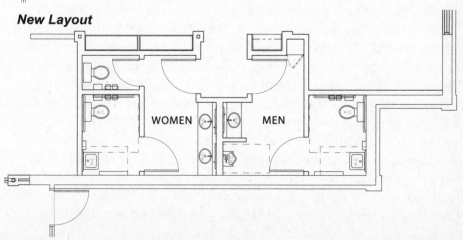

New Layout

WOMEN

MEN

service we wanted to offer our guests. As a result, I was determined to reconfigure the restrooms to include the ADA-compliant stalls within the main restroom and, at the same time, minimize alterations to the existing plumbing stub-up locations. With a bit of work, I was able not only to accomplish this goal, but also to reuse three of the existing toilet stub-ups, limiting the amount of work and cost required to implement this new layout. I share these examples to emphasize that each and every opportunity and challenge has to be evaluated thoroughly and independently. There is no standard, blanket answer for these situations. Each one is unique. We didn't carelessly blow out the existing facility just because we felt like it. No way. But it was important to determine where to save money and where to spend money on a project such as this one. The goal was to spend money where it counts and to achieve the best bang for our buck. That was our objective.

When it comes to the interior design of the front-of-house space, there is never one *right* answer or design solution. In fact, the possibilities are endless. In the end, as I learned, much of it comes down to gut feeling. I began by creating an image board to help organize my thoughts. Remember that at this point, we had already developed the logo, and much of the color scheme was selected. I used these elements as a starting point for my image board. I painted the image board to provide a background consistent with the colors in the logo, and then attached a few images and elements of the logo in various places.

Image boards are very helpful in conveying certain spoken and subconscious elements of the interior image. The images do not have to be completely representative of the final interior design of the space; rather, these images can communicate certain elements or individual ideas that you may want to incorporate into the final design. It might be that a window treatment would be perfect for the new concept, but it is the wrong color in the picture. It could be an architectural element, though the picture may not depict the desired height or proportion. The ability to communicate an idea, rather than the perfect representation of a specific design, is the objective. I poured through restaurant design and image books, industry magazines, architectural and interior design magazines, the Internet, and countless other sources in search of pictures and elements that might help to describe my image for the interior design of 'Za-Bistro! It was an extremely enjoyable, creative, and effective process. I focused quite heavily on the interior architecture, clipping and scanning images of partial, non-right-angled walls, finishes, color schemes, and other such aspects of the interior design package. I gathered sample restroom fixtures, light fixtures, tables, and chairs. I then took all of these images and fastened them to my image board. Some were permanently glued, while others were mounted to foam core board and attached with Velcro so that they could be easily removed or swapped out.

In addition to the image board, I also developed a brief summary and description of the interior design image I had in my mind. The brief overview included below, in conjunction with the image board, helped me to share my vision for the space with the 'Za-Bistro! team, the design team, and even with landlords. The image board and description, in combination, seemed to offer significant insight into our goals and objectives for the space.

This European bistro concept will be anchored by the open-flame oven and display kitchen, fully visible throughout the dining room. The central area will feature a dining counter, called the Hearth, allowing for open interaction between the culinary staff and patrons.

The primary colors of the logo and the restaurant will be maroon and bright blue, with neutral tones for secondary coloring throughout the space. Research on the psychology of colors in restaurants has determined that the maroon will offer a calm environment, while the blue, a cool color, will stir some excitement. The blue will be used as an accent throughout the restaurant: walls, lighting fixtures, tabletop presentation, etc.

To offer the intimacy of a European-style bistro, the dining room will be composed of multiple small dining sections. Half walls with risers and headers divide these sections, resulting in a feeling of separate, private spaces, while maintaining a slightly obstructed view throughout the restaurant's front-of-house.

Some of the walls will be framed with odd angles and multiple depths, to provide interest. The opportunity for different color combinations and patterns will also be explored. We anticipate using faux painting and solid paint colors to achieve the desired effect. The restrooms will receive significant attention and investment. Instead of providing standard fixtures and finishes, the restrooms will further convey the restaurant's concept. Specialty faucets and sink bowls will be combined with fully enclosed stalls (no partitions) and specialty wall finishes.

Now, let's begin our tour of the front-of-house layout. Upon entering the restaurant, the guest is met by the host or hostess and an initial glimpse of the restaurant's dining experience. Entering patrons are able to catch a partial view of the dining and exposition kitchen spaces through the clear glass panels that feature the concept's carefully crafted icon, the flame and wineglass. In order to enter the dining room, the guests pass through a transition space that allows them to leave the outside environment and enter a more controlled environment created by the restaurant's design. The dining room was designed to create a number of smaller, more intimate, semi-private dining spaces without creating a feeling of claustrophobia. This was achieved through the use of a combination of half walls, full walls, cased (wood trimmed) punched openings, and other such architectural features that create interest and variety within the space. There are numerous locations throughout the dining room where patrons can see most of the dining space, but no locations where the entire dining room is revealed all at once. This design technique leads the guest to believe that there is always another space that can be accessed — it is a unique way to increase the *perceived* size of the restaurant.

The feel and comfort of the space was defined in large part by the architectural elements, the color palate, the use of specialty lighting and fixtures, and a number of other key elements. The transitions from one space to another would be seamless yet defining. There were few dead ends in the design of the main walkways, allowing servers and guests of the restaurant at least two ways out from almost any location in the dining room. This would relieve congestion and improve service. Both linear and arched elements were utilized to achieve the desired definition at each level of the cubic space. The architectural design of the space was critical in achieving the desired design objectives, as the wall finishes were quite simple — mostly drywall and paint — in order to stay within our budget. Thus, the architectural elements were responsible for defining the impact of the space. The color palate chosen was coordinated with the colors of the logo. The Bordeaux (or burgundy) color reinforced our focus on the wine element. The beige and gold tones offered a feeling of warmth, while the copper and blue elements were used as accent colors for excitement and intrigue. It took some careful planning and coordination, but the design seemed to accomplish what we had set out to achieve in the space.

The ceiling was raised and acoustic panels were added to address the sound problem that existed in the restaurant's previous configuration. The semi-open design and architectural elements also assisted in reducing the space's ambient volume during peak periods. Several of the half-height walls were designed with a 12-inch frosted glass panel featuring the restaurant's logo in the center in clear glass. The frosted glass caught the flickering glow from the stone-hearth oven and provided an element of movement adjacent to the dining customer. In addition, the frosted glass allowed for patrons to sit on either side of the wall while maintaining their privacy. As an added bonus, even the lighting that penetrated the frosted glass panels would add to the ambiance by reflecting the logo on the tables—another subliminal introduction of the fire and wine that were critical to the concept.

The seating layout was designed with the objective of balancing seating capacity with seating efficiency. A number of restaurants use

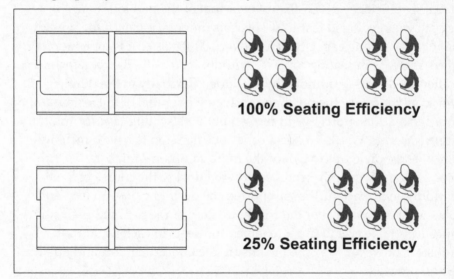

100% Seating Efficiency

25% Seating Efficiency

mostly four-person booths in their dining room and feature a high seating count. However, a closer look at many of these dining rooms in operation reveals that the four-person booths are often occupied by only two patrons. In these instances, the *efficiency* is much lower than the *capacity*. This difference between capacity and efficiency is an interesting one and worth a more detailed exploration. Assume that we have two four-person booths, with a total seating capacity of eight seats. If two parties of four come along, we can seat both parties, four people at each of the two booths. Eight seats accommodating eight people—that is 100 percent seating efficiency. Now, let's look at a slightly different scenario with the same seating configuration and total seating capacity of eight. This time, the two parties are not evenly split. Rather, now we have a party of two and a party of six. The party of two can be seated at one of the two booths, but two of the seats will go unused. The second party—the party of six—however, cannot be seated at the second booth. There is not enough room. With our same eight seats, we were only capable of seating two of the eight patrons. This is a seating efficiency of 25 percent with the exact same seating capacity and configuration. This is a brief look at why seating capacity can sometimes be misleading, and the seating efficiency needs to be scrutinized in light of the anticipated or confirmed average party size. The seating configuration can have a significant impact on the restaurant's revenue.

The use of banquettes and strategic location of a number of tables that could be adjoined to create different seating combinations increased the seating efficiency of 'Za-Bistro! over that of the previous concept. The plan we developed featured 124 seats indoors, whereas the previous tenant had a seating capacity of just over 100 seats. That is more than a 20 percent increase in seating capacity without increasing the rent, insurance, or other fixed costs. Additionally, the added flexibility in the dining room would increase the revenue-producing potential of the restaurant. In our renovation efforts, we improved both the seating *capacity* and the seating *efficiency*. We also made a conscious decision to use 30-inch by 30-inch deuce tabletops in lieu of the more common 24-inch by 30-inch tables, which can quickly become cluttered during the course of a meal. This additional space further supported the desired value, quality, and sophistication statement of the concept. Many of the national chains have reduced the table size to fit more tables and seats in each restaurant. At 'Za-Bistro!, however, we opted to ensure the guests' comfort and quality of the experience.

A wine cabinet, over 9 feet in length, was designed at the center of the restaurant, opposite the oven and display kitchen. From virtually every location within the dining room, a patron would have a view of either the oven, the wine wall, or both. The glass wine cabinet would also do a great job of reflecting the flame from the oven and providing a sense of activity at the opposite side of the restaurant. We made a conscious decision to include a stage area for live jazz performances, as jazz music enhance the ambiance and the concept itself. Two comfortable leather lounge chairs would be placed in this area, each at a 45 degree angle, providing a relaxed seating option for patrons who may choose to visit the restaurant during the off-peak day parts, between lunch and dinner or after dinner. Additionally, this space could be used to support a buffet for parties or Sunday brunch.

The bar, affectionately referred to as the *Snug*, featured a European-style leaning bar. It was not a traditional configuration where the guests could "belly-up to the bar." Rather, it was designed as a social gathering place while waiting for a table or takeout or just enjoying a glass of wine or beer. Though we would have preferred for the Snug to be located toward the front of the restaurant, where it was more accessible, several design drivers required it to be located toward the back and adjacent to the cooking line. The *Hearth*, the dining counter at the display kitchen in the center of the restaurant, was also an important part of the concept. This environment not only provided an attractive option for single diners or small groups, but also provided a truly unique opportunity for the guests to interact with the culinary staff. Due to the design and size of the space, the guests would be close to the action, where the food would be prepared. This is where we believed the primal, romantic effect of cooking in the stone-hearth oven would have its most significant impact on the patrons and their overall experience.

Though the project was on a tight budget, I decided to upgrade the appearance of the facility in two key areas: the display kitchen and the restrooms. There was a reason for this, based deep in psychological theory. The two most popular home renovation projects have long been the kitchen and the bathroom. We wanted to focus our efforts on these same two areas. Not only would this strategy improve the restaurant's design impact, but it would also subconsciously register with the guests of the restaurant, hopefully creating an emotional connection during the course of their dining experience. The display kitchen received a great deal of thought. I had developed several intricate details for the oven façade that included specialty tiles, copper, and other materials intended to draw the interest of the guest. Finish materials and patterns throughout the display kitchen, however, would not be finalized until the third design package, based on our phased approach. The floor plan considered various sight lines from the dining room, especially from the Hearth, to ensure that guests would be able to see only those parts of the operation that were most desirable. The service area that we designed would incorporate front-of-house finishes, including decorative tile and incandescent lighting, to help integrate the space within the dining room's ambiance.

Likewise, a considerable amount of attention was given to the restrooms. The restrooms are often an interesting indicator of the concept's message and the ownership's philosophies. Money spent to upgrade the finishes within the restrooms results from desire, not necessity. Some restaurants view the restrooms as a necessary evil, while others view them as an opportunity to make an impression on the guest — as part of the experience. In fact, many of the old-school quick-service chain restaurants are beginning to upgrade the finishes in their restrooms. These chains are *adding* cost to their restaurants because of the impact that the restroom ambiance has on the overall guest experience.

We not only attempted to upgrade the patron's experience and eliminate the separate ADA-compliant restroom, as was previously discussed, but we also gave a great deal of attention to the fixtures and stalls. The sink bowls we chose were new, trendy, and intended to strike a chord with the local market. They were Kohler fixtures, designed for installation above the counter. That is, the top of the lavatory bowl protruded out from the counter, creating what was a unique look at the time. The faucet was wall mounted, again unique in design. The stalls were designed with full walls and three-quarter height doors for privacy, providing an upgraded feel compared to standard restroom partitions. Keep in mind that this restaurant's anticipated average check was in the $15 range. The restroom was designed in keeping with our desire to provide the $30 experience we had targeted, at a much lower cost to the guest. We anticipated that this particular combination would offer us a unique competitive advantage.

Due to the speed of the design and construction effort, we were advised to seek only an interior renovation permit from the city. We were told that this would speed up the approval process. Consequently, we were unable to include our planned outside dining area in the initial construction effort. Instead, the outside dining area would have to be part of a separate permit after the initial construction effort was completed.

Knowing that this area would be added, however, we planned to include a side door off the entrance lobby during the replacement of the storefront system. We felt that this outside dining area would further support the desired street-side dining environment and European feel for our concept.

The design impact was not limited to the physical building, however. My objective was to carry the unique, European-influenced ambiance throughout all aspects of the environment. One of the best places to do this was through the smallwares (china, glass, and flatware) and the tabletop presentation. Okay, so I was a bit more focused on this aspect than the average restaurant designer, in large part due to my background, but why not? Think about a guest's experience in a restaurant and how few objects the guest actually touches. The flatware is one that subconsciously sends a lasting impression. If, for instance, we were to view ourselves as a $30 experience but offer the guest cheap, lightweight flatware that would easily bend, would we be consistent in our message? I didn't think so. So I paged through numerous catalogs until I found a pattern called Modernaire from Walco, a flatware manufacturer. It was substantial in weight, nice and heavy, and it had European styling. The fork, for instance, had three tines instead of four. These utensils had a sleek, smooth feel. It was just the sort of design treatment I was looking for. Yes, I said design treatment. Such details are most definitely an extension of the design of the space.

There is a strong link between design and psychology. By sheer coincidence, shortly after I selected the flatware pattern, I saw an almost identical pattern advertised by both Pottery Barn and Crate and Barrel. As with the upgraded sink bowls in the restrooms, this particular flatware

pattern would strike a subconscious cord with our restaurant patrons. Whether or not they recognized the pattern from one of the casually sophisticated retailers, the connection and logic were clear. I also wanted to utilize our icon strategically on some of the china and glassware. For the plates, we initially wanted square or rectangular plates. My search, however, revealed that I had champagne taste on a beer budget. The plates that I originally admired were far too expensive for us, and I had to redirect my search. I was still craving a distinctive design treatment, and soon found an alternate option from a Colombian china manufacturer. They offered a plate called a handled food pan. In essence, this dish was a bright, European white plate with sharply raised edges and a handle. That's right, a handle. It was a unique presentation, and if I could add our icon to the handle it would surely set us apart. That's exactly what we did. We also added the icon, frosted, to the wineglass. We even coordinated the desired portion size for a glass of wine with the placement of a portion of the logo, ensuring the accuracy of each and every pour. Other specialty accent pieces such as the sugar caddies, gratin dishes, coffee mugs, and tea pots were selected in cobalt blue, reinforcing the color scheme of the logo. The tabletop is in the guest's full view during most of the dining experience, and our smallwares package was intended to be an extension of our design objectives.

All together, I believe we achieved a unique presentation and helped to support the design objectives in the process. A great deal of time and effort went into our design decisions. More importantly, there was a great deal of logic behind the selections we made. The design of the facility would have a lasting impact on the efficiency of the operation, as well as on the ambiance and impression on the guest.

10

BUDGET-GATE

With a detailed design concept in hand and the imminent turnover of the Maitland restaurant, it was time to formally kick off the design process and bring in the rest of the professionals on the team. Our timeline was aggressive, but my efforts to develop much of the design ahead of time, as well the ownership team's review and comments on the overall design even before involving the architect, would streamline the design effort. The general contractor brought in the architect in the spirit of the design-build model and based on their prior working relationship. He seemed interested in our project and motivated to assist us in our endeavor — at least initially. As the official launch of the design effort drew near, I asked the architect to meet me for lunch at the restaurant in Maitland so that we could discuss various design issues and review my preliminary layout. I refer to our self-developed layout as "preliminary" because, although I had worked out many of the conceptual design issues, I had not yet received any feedback from the engineers to confirm that the layout was free of any conflicts related to their scopes of work. Would there be a structural beam in the way of the hood? Would the existing electrical panels have enough capacity? What other surprises would we find? I had not yet verified the existing field conditions and building structure. In essence, I had the basic concept worked out, but further coordination was necessary in order for the entire design team to move to the next step in the process.

During this lunch meeting, I began to recognize a very different attitude from the architect than the one he presented in our first meeting. As our discussion over lunch progressed, I came to realize that many of the answers I was receiving were either negative or cautionary in nature. I was experiencing a "can't-do" attitude, and I was beginning to get an uncomfortable feeling. I did not, however, want to overreact. After all, the entire design and construction team had committed to the schedule, and the general contractor had indicated that this particular architect was completely competent. Besides, we were days away from starting the formal design process, which was tight to begin with. I did not have time to begin the search for a new architect. Additionally, the odds that I would be able to find an architect with availability to meet our schedule were slim or none. Thus, I convinced myself that I was overreacting, and I let it slide. Everyone is entitled to a bad day. Although there was a strong possibility that we would be working on both Maitland and Harbor Commons at the same time, it was clear that the Maitland project would take precedence.

We had begun discussions with this particular architect very early in our development efforts, anticipating, at that point, that the Sumner Springs location would be the site of the first 'Za-Bistro! At that time, the discussions had progressed far enough for the architect to offer us a proposal. The proposed fee for the Sumner Springs site included the architectural design, interior design, and all of the required mechanical, electrical, and plumbing engineering work. The quote we received was a bit lower than average, given that the architect's scope of work was significantly reduced. The size of the restaurant at less than 4,000 square feet and the amount of work I would be performing on behalf of the ownership team helped keep this fee low. What all designers are really selling, whether they realize it or not, is time. The overall layout and preliminary interior design package I was preparing would significantly reduce the time required by the architect and engineers, which in turn would help limit the design fee. The architect had indicated to me that because the Maitland location was an existing site, whereas the Sumner Springs site was a new building, the fee would have to be adjusted slightly. This made sense, as additional time and coordination are typically required for an existing site. All of the dimensions, wall locations, window locations, column locations, and other such conditions would have to be confirmed. From a building systems perspective, the existing HVAC system, exhaust hood(s), electrical service, and plumbing service would also have to be verified. I've always aspired to be fair in business — tough, but fair. I learned this approach by watching my family's business and their interactions with their suppliers. You want to push enough to make sure that you are receiving the best service you deserve. Push a little too hard, however, and you risk alienating your business partner and actually doing yourself a disservice. Thus, a slight increase in the design fee for the Maitland location seemed reasonable.

It was just two days before the scheduled turnover of the Maitland restaurant from the previous tenant. The turnover date was significant, as it would be the very first time that we would be able to gain full, unrestricted access to the restaurant. It was also the date on which our grace period for rent would begin. The clock would start ticking at the turnover of the space. The previous owners would not allow our design team to begin their exploratory work and confirmation of the site conditions until we had officially received the keys. I was driving back to Tampa from Orlando that afternoon, where I had been on other business, when my phone rang. It was the architect and general contractor on the line together. Having reviewed the earlier agreement and pricing structure of the design contract offered based on the Sumner Springs site, the architect had developed a revised proposal. *No problem*, I thought — until I heard the actual proposal. The architect had determined that his revised fee would be significantly more than his original quote *plus* a separate allowance for interior design. The interior design component, which was included in the original scope of work, was now an additional service. On top of this significant modification, the interior design services were listed as "hourly against a capped fee." I am typically uncomfortable working on a strict hourly basis when it comes to design, whether I am the client or the professional offering design services. Design is a messy, inefficient process by nature. It is subjective. As a result, I find that with a strict hourly arrangement it is rare for either the client or design professional to be fully satisfied. The client will be second guessing the hours spent by the design team, looking over their shoulder, and questioning each and every minute spent on the project, because time equals money in such an arrangement. On the other side of the equation, on an hourly basis, I have rarely seen a design firm charge every hour that they spend on a project to a client. For these reasons, I was uncomfortable with the hourly arrangement. The cap on this scope of work, however, was at least a compromise and would provide a specific, pre-determined cut-off point, which would allow me to budget for our design work. If the work completed for the interior design allowance was not sufficient, I would at least have an opportunity to determine whether or not I should allow the architect to continue the interior design work, or, if the information was sufficient, perhaps either the general contractor or I could handle the remaining design documentation and coordination.

There is no reason to sugar coat this, however. I was livid. In the end, the architect had proposed a 43 percent increase over the design fee for Sumner Springs, and the only justification I received was that this was an existing building whereas the earlier location was new construction. After the architect revealed the fee increase, I expressed my concern and disappointment. Okay, I wasn't anywhere near that polite. There were some heated exchanges in that conversation. From a layman's point of view, I was getting hosed! I had tried to express to him that a 15 percent or 20 percent increase would have been understandable, but 43 percent? Who was he kidding? Again, fully aware of our time pressure with Harbor Commons and the quickly approaching end of a brief grace period for rent in Maitland, the architect stood his ground on the fee increase, indicating that he could hold on the project while I either thought it over or found an alternate design team. We both knew that I did not have the luxury of time. It is impossible to negotiate if you are unwilling to walk away, and in this case, I was not willing to walk away. I agreed to the increase, while expressing my disappointment in the way that the architect had handled the situation. He assured me that nothing of the sort would happen again, and that he and his team were fully committed to our project. I gave the approval for the general contractor to sign the architect's contract.

The architect was officially hired by the general contractor. This was intentional, in the spirit of the design-build format. The idea was that the general contractor would ultimately be responsible for the drawings, and the information contained within those drawings. Furthermore, the general contractor was being paid a fee for his involvement in the design and construction process. Such an approach would help alleviate finger pointing in the event of an error or miscommunication between the design and construction team, as they were actually one and the same. Originally, I had wanted to break the process into two separate stages, design and construction. I wanted to have the general contractor involved in the design process for coordination, budgeting, and sharing design techniques based on field experience. In our initial plan, following the design process, I wanted to put the project out for competitive bids among a selection of general contractors. The bidding process would provide a competitive comparison and, perhaps even more importantly, allow other general contractors the opportunity to scrutinize our plans and offer suggestions regarding materials and techniques. While the bidding phase was part of our earlier plan, our timeline simply did not allow for it. Also, Roger was interested in locking up the business for his firm. As part of our contractual agreement, we developed a structure that would assure Roger that he would be our general contractor and would assure me that the pricing and sourcing that we would receive would be in our best interest.

Traditionally, at the end of the bidding phase a general contractor would be selected based on price, experience, current workload, and a host of other factors. As we discussed in an earlier chapter, there are many types of contracts. It is common for the contractor, following a bid, to be hired based on a guaranteed maximum price. That is to say, the general contractor assures the client that the project, as designed and specified in the design documents, can be built for the predetermined price. When Roger and I began to explore a possible agreement, Roger could not commit to a guaranteed maximum price, as the restaurant design had not yet been completed. There was, of course, the option of a cost-plus agreement.

Aware of both the positive and negative aspects of each contract format, I indicated to Roger that I was interested in developing a hybrid contract that could capitalize on the pros for each format, while limiting the cons. That is exactly what we did. Given our budget for construction, we developed an agreement that was part fixed-cost and part cost-plus. Our final contract stated that the general contractor would provide services on a direct cost-plus basis, but there would be a minimum and maximum fee for the general contractor. In this case, the contract was to be cost plus a fixed percentage with a $17,500 minimum (floor) and a $25,000 maximum (ceiling) for the contractor's fees. In its final format, the contract assured Roger a minimum payment of $17,500. Conversely, if the budget were to exceed our projections for construction, our payment to the general contractor would not exceed $25,000. The base format was still a cost-plus agreement, however, and thus provided an open-book environment that would allow me, as the owner, to review all of the direct invoices and quotes.

You may be wondering about the bid process and the lack of competitive pricing if we were agreeing to a deal on the front end with a general contractor. We actually had a plan to obtain competitive pricing. Roger and I had agreed that each of the major subcontracted disciplines would be bid competitively. In other words, we would get two or three bids for plumbing contractors. We would do the same for electrical, framing, and all key subcontracted scopes of work. I requested the ability to sit in on any discussions or interviews, as the lowest price is not always the best price. A combination of price, experience, commitment to the project, and personality should all be considered in the final selection of either a general or subcontractor. There were still some potential pitfalls in this arrangement. What if the general contractor had rigged all three bids? If our initial construction budget was exceeded, what was the incentive for the general contractor to keep the cost of the project in line? It was not perfect, but I had believed that this arrangement offered a legitimate compromise. With both the design and construction contracts signed and delivered, our development process was officially underway.

Following our acceptance of the facility from the previous tenants, a number of activities had to take place. Some were rather basic, such as the transferring of utilities to our name. However, even these basic activities proved to be extremely enlightening. When I called to arrange the transfer of the electrical service, the electric utility company requested a deposit of $3,700, the equivalent of one month's bill for the previous tenant. *Three thousand seven hundred dollars* for one month in a 3,800-square-foot space? That seemed very high, given the size of the building and their equipment package. I was able to talk the utility company into accepting $3,000 as a deposit (remember, *everything* is negotiable), but the real lesson was that something had to be horribly wrong with the building, as the previous restaurant appeared to be using far too much energy based on its size and type. Further discussions on this topic revealed that the air-conditioning system was incredibly inefficient. The previous tenant left the air-conditioning on the lowest possible temperature setting overnight during the summer months, just to try to keep the dining room comfortable for the lunch rush the following day. My access to the site also revealed the poor state of the facility. It was not clean, and some of the building systems were questionable. The facility did not appear well maintained. These factors, along with many others, influenced some of our decisions during the design process.

As the design process moved forward, the architect indicated a desire to explore other options for the floor plan I had developed. While I was certainly open to this, I was rather concerned about the additional time such a process would take. Having raised this concern with the architect, he assured me that taking a day or two to explore these options would not dramatically affect the schedule. I agreed to the exploratory effort.

I want to emphasize here the importance of communication in the design process. Sometimes the design solutions come quickly, while at other times they do not. In certain instances, the first or second layout may be sufficient to meet the owner's design criteria. In other instances, it may take five, ten, or twenty attempts to reach a suitable design solution. Because design is an artistic process, it includes a vast number of variables, placing an even greater importance on communication between the owner and the design team. Whether the design is for a building or an advertisement, the need for clear direction and communication is equally important. It is the designer's responsibility to ask as many questions as necessary to obtain this clear direction. Conversely, it is the owner's responsibility to offer clear and concise direction, as mixed signals and changes in direction negatively impact the process and, ultimately, the final product. From my perspective on both sides of this process, I can tell you that poor communication is one of the most frequent causes of delays, cost overruns, and lost profitability. Though design is an inefficient process by nature, management of the process to the best of one's ability is essential for a successful, comprehensive solution. Clear communication by both owner and designer is imperative for success in any design effort.

Unfortunately, our architect did not follow the directions we gave, and he did not ask the right questions. As a result, the design options he generated were rejected because they did not address our most basic design objectives. It was not that I was opposed to reviewing another design solution; that was not the case at all. Rather, I was hoping to review a design solution that was consistent with our goals for the project. Our criteria was not considered accurately in the architect's effort to develop an alternate design solution. For instance, the seating capacity in the proposed alternative layout was significantly reduced from the quantity we had achieved. Some of the proposed architectural elements conflicted with the flows and efficiency that were achieved in the earlier design developed and reviewed by our team. In the end, the architect's alternate layouts were a wasted effort, primarily due to a breakdown in communication. This is a perfect illustration of the reason that I do not like to work on an hourly basis as either the designer or the client. In an hourly arrangement, I would have been charged for this evaluation exercise. The architect would have looked at the time spent and expected compensation in return, despite the fact that the consideration of alternative designs was largely a wasted effort. It would have been the first dispute over fees and charges, and it was just the first step in the process. In the terms of our agreement, this portion of the design contract was covered under a fixed fee, and there would be no additional fees for the time spent on the architect's proposal. We did, however, lose several precious days.

As the design effort progressed, the architectural elements within the space took on even greater significance. We intended for the architecture to serve as a key interior design treatment. We planned to create this sophisticated yet casual environment primarily through the use of paint and drywall. Our limited budget also forced discipline. We had to pick and choose the places to splurge, as we did not have the luxury of being able to afford everything we wanted. We spent money on the items that were focal points of the restaurant: the oven façade, the wine cabinet, the restrooms, and the small wares. We spent money on the elements of the restaurant that had the highest and most direct impact on the guest. The oven façade was a clear focal point. However, while it could be seen, it could not be touched by the guest. As a result, we were able to use certain tricks of the trade in order to maintain both our aesthetic and budgetary objectives. We had planned to use copper as part of the façade, but in the end chose a copper laminate instead. It was more expensive than a traditional laminate, but a fraction of the cost of real copper, and, just as important, it required no major maintenance to keep it looking clean and polished. The untrained eye would never be able to tell that the copper was not actually copper at all, but laminate instead.

The store in Maitland was intended to be a first shot at our concept. We knew that we would not be able to incorporate everything we wanted. Instead, our ownership group set the expectation level that the Maitland store would represent 80 to 85 percent of the eventual signature 'Za-Bistro! restaurant. Most restaurant concepts have several distinctive physical features that are considered to be their signature. For us, we had several elements: the stone-hearth oven, at the center of the concept, and the surrounding oven façade; the Hearth and the Snug; the wine cabinet; the open kitchen; the logo and the color scheme; the upgraded sink bowls in the restrooms; and the semi-open yet semi-private design of the dining room. Because of our budget constraints, however, some of the other planned signature design treatments did not make it into the Maitland store. For instance, I had developed a detail that I called the "fire box." It was a recess created in the faux columns that was to feature a blue glass wine bottle, copper clad surroundings (laminate, of course), and a light from below. This was designed to take some of the key elements from our concept and subliminally reinforce them throughout the interior environment. It was a nice detail, but it would just have to wait for the next store.

With the floor plan set, we began turning our design effort toward the elevations of each individual wall. In order to create a bit more separation, I had included an arched header running through the center of the restaurant in my original design. After we finally gained access and began coordinating our design documents with the space, we determined that this arched structure would be far too dominant, so it was deleted. Some ideas stick, while others do not. It is important in the design process, whether as a designer or as an owner, not to become too attached to any one solution. In design, there is no one right answer. We continued to focus on the combined use of half walls and punched openings to achieve the desired architectural affect.

'Za-Bistro! Maitland Interior Elevation

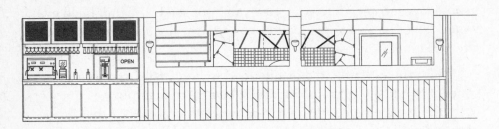

Fortunately, the review of the building by the design team yielded relatively few changes to our layout. The dimensions I received from the previous tenant's renovation drawings had been fairly accurate, and the floor plan was not significantly affected. There were a couple of surprises, however, following a thorough inspection of this site. Two, in particular, affected our efforts. The first was the discovery of two columns buried within the walls of the previous layout. With minor adjustments, they were easily incorporated into our design. The second was a discovery that the existing HVAC roof top units (RTUs) were in terrible shape and needed to be replaced. This would require additional funds that we had not anticipated. Aside from those two factors, we were pretty lucky in that no existing conditions identified up to that point negatively impacted our design direction.

As we progressed through the design process, I continued to emphasize our budget. Our budget of $250,000 for the general construction scope of work was communicated repeatedly to both the architect and the general contractor through a number of different formats, both written and verbal. This amount did not include the furniture, equipment, or other startup costs, but it did include some key fixtures, such as lighting. The ownership team had actually settled on an amount of $75 per square foot as the budget, which equated to $285,000. The shared budget of $250,000 allowed for some contingency and modifications in the event of an overrun. With a contractor on board as a part of the design team, and an architect who was contracted by the general contractor, I expected the design and budget to be in agreement; after all, that was one of the key benefits of this design-build format.

The time during which this design process was taking place was one of the most hectic in my life. I still had a day job, my class at UCF, and several other side projects with which I was involved. My training for the triathlon was still going strong. In fact, the race fell right in the midst of the design effort for the restaurant. My goal was to complete the race in three hours. It was, after all, my first Olympic-distance race. Well, at 3:00:28 into the race, I crossed the finish line — and then collapsed, spending three days in the hospital. Fortunately, it was nothing serious — just heat exhaustion and a chemical imbalance resulting from over-exertion. As I laid in the hospital bed, however, I was still coordinating the design effort for the restaurant. It was a crazy time, and the construction on the restaurant had not even started yet.

When I was released from the hospital, there was really no time to rest or recover. I was back in the full swing of things the following day. Upon my return, I learned that Roger had prepared a budget in conjunction with the architect. It came in at $310,000. I could not believe it. Having communicated the budget of $250,000 clearly many times, I did not understand how we could have missed our target by almost 25 percent. I was quite upset — again. Making matters even worse, we had already begun the demolition effort and were just about to start the actual interior build-out, based on the overlapping, phased design schedule to which the team had agreed. I reviewed my notes and earlier e-mails to ensure that I had communicated our budget constraints clearly and accurately, and I found that I had. In one e-mail to Roger, I had written: *"I want to figure out the best way for us to coordinate the design package with the budget, given that we will likely have the design package completed before we have an itemized budget. How should we handle any budget-driven changes without going back to the architect and incurring additional services?"*

Similar e-mails to both the general contractor and the architect articulated the budget constraints, addressed methods for value engineering, and tried to ensure that we would not be spending design time on items that, due to their expense, could not be used in the eventual construction effort. I saw no need to plan for something that we could not afford. Looking back, I do not believe I could have done anything more to communicate my objectives and goals. Perhaps the most frustrating aspect of this cost overrun was that it negated the most critical reason for employing the design-build concept and paying the general contractor to participate in the design process. It was not the design-build model that had failed, but its execution. With the demolition nearly completed and materials on order, the timeline was more of a factor than ever before. The only comfort I had in this situation was that Roger was aware of the error and he was committed to correcting it. The design and construction process had taken a slight detour, but both Roger and I were focused on getting the effort back on track. We would make the adjustments necessary to bring the budget back in line. The drawings, however, had been completed. One of the objectives of the design-build format is to begin the construction process with an accurate set of drawings that are consistent with the budget. But because the budget for the drawings we had in our possession was far greater than we could afford, we knew that we would have to have the drawings revised by the architect, or we would be building from inaccurate documents. The latter would require a great deal of coordination in the field, but would soon become our reality as my relationship with the architect quickly deteriorated.

As if it were not enough that the architect was 43 percent over his original proposal, upon presentation of the budget, I received a bill for $3,400 over and above the amount that we had agreed upon in our design contract. I was told that this bill was for interior design services rendered over and above the allowance. This brought the total fee even higher. It was now a 67 percent increase over the original fee. Just as important, from a global budgeting and planning perspective, the fees for design services had jumped from 5.2 percent of the construction budget to 8.6 percent of the construction budget. But wait, it gets worse. The interior design package that I received was not even completed. The finishes (specific tile, carpet, and paint selections) still had not been made. According to the architect's time sheets, his firm had spent over 350 hours in about three weeks on our project, and they had not even finished the interior design work. Remember, I had provided the architect with a completed floor plan and numerous preliminary interior elevations. I had done a great deal of his work for him. This whole issue came to a head during a fairly heated discussion between the architect, Roger, and me. The architect was extremely emotional about his position, bordering on unprofessional. He explained that he and his staff had sacrificed so much for us and our restaurant project. He said it was a huge mistake, and he would never do it again. Then he stressed that it was unrealistic to expect all of the interior design work to be completed in three weeks, and *I couldn't have agreed more*. In fact, the intent of the overlapping schedule was to avoid such an unrealistic time pressure. We were to have a completed bare-bones set of documents for permitting that would later be coordinated with our final finish selections and our budget. It became apparent to me that the architect had never fully understood the objectives or the process that I had set for the team. His communication skills were poor at best, and the process, to a large extent, had failed. However, as is often the case when you are an owner, the failures of others do not matter. Ultimately, it is the owner's responsibility to make sure that the process is completed on time and within budget, no matter what obstacles are encountered.

Though I felt we had been wronged in the process, the architect was still demanding full payment. I was prepared to fight this bill. However, given his emotional state and our timeline, he was capable of filing a lien, which could have delayed our loan. As a result, I reluctantly decided to pay the amount he demanded. Following this series of events, the architect was essentially terminated from the project, as we would not be able to rely on his support during the construction phase. Likewise, expecting to receive an updated set of drawings was out of the question. Sometimes the long-term goals must be considered. Though I believed that I was right on this particular issue, had I not decided to pay the architect, my stubbornness and short-term focus could have delayed the opening of our restaurant. My next task, however, was clear. I took home the budget and the most recent drawings and began to study them. I poured over every page, every detail, and every materials finish schedule. I was in search of methods to reduce the construction cost of the project without adversely affecting the design intent and character of the space. I stayed up late at night, several nights in a row, looking at each and every corner of the restaurant for an opportunity to save money. I was on a mission. As was the case with the triathlon, it might require a great deal of personal sacrifice to reach my stated goal, but I rarely miss my target. With tens of thousands of dollars to trim, I had my work cut out for me.

11

DEMOLITION MEN

The overrun in our project's budget, which I affectionately referred to as budget-gate, was incredibly disappointing. After all, we had started working on the costs for our build-out nearly eighteen months prior to the initiation of the design effort. The revised cost estimate of $310,000, based on the architect's final drawings, was far beyond the target of $250,000. As a refresher, this budget included the general construction and some fixtures. It did not, however, include the furniture or the equipment. "What's this restaurant going to cost us?" was one of the first questions the team posed when we decided to pursue the development of what would become 'Za-Bistro! It made sense. The cost was going to dictate much of our initial planning and direction. It would determine how much capital would be required to open the restaurant(s) we had discussed. In our early projections, we determined that we would want a build-out in the range of $62 to $65 per square foot. This was a nice set of numbers, but it was not based on any concrete estimates (another pun — my apologies). In other words, it was wishful thinking. It is also important to keep in mind that looking at a breakdown of restaurant construction costs on a per-square-foot basis can be somewhat misleading, as was the case with the analysis of a restaurant's space allocation percentage covered in an earlier chapter. For example, a 3,200-square-foot restaurant and a 4,000-square-foot restaurant may have comparable infrastructure requirements. Assuming that these two facilities are similar in concept, the higher-priced areas of the restaurant, such as the kitchen and restrooms, would probably have the same actual cost and physical configuration, since the sizes of the restaurants are not dramatically different. But the price per square foot in the 4,000-square-foot location would spread out the cost for the kitchen and restrooms over a much larger area. Thus, while costs per square foot are a reasonable barometer, they are not always accurate.

After conducting extensive research, we determined that a cost of $75 per square foot for our construction budget was much more reasonable, given our concept and stated design objectives. To give you an idea of how early in the process we identified our target construction costs, we established this cost per square foot around the time that we were seriously considering the Sumner Springs location. As we were looking at the Sumner Springs site, we requested preliminary budgets for the build-out of that space, based on some very rough schematic designs that I had prepared. We received proposals from three contractors. The cost estimates ranged from $158,000 to $340,000. This was obviously a wild swing, but each bid included a long list of assumptions by the contractors, as the design was not yet completed. The resulting bids, however, did seem to justify our budget goals. The low bid was low by a wide margin. At this stage, I was not overly concerned with the details included in the numbers, as they were only preliminary estimates. Instead, I was focused on the order of magnitude. Budgets tied to concept drawings are only as accurate as the assumptions that have been made, and those assumptions are subject to interpretation. Some contractors like to lowball the estimate to catch the owner's attention. Other contractors like to budget high, covering the unknowns and the extras that are customary for projects such as these.

Though it may seem like a science, tying down the costs for construction is often more of an art. A number of factors that can influence the bidding may or may not have anything to do with the actual costs of the materials or labor. For instance, let's assume that the local area where a restaurant is scheduled to be built is in the middle of a robust development boom. The local contractors have more work than they can handle, and they almost seem bothered that you are asking them for a quote on your new project. In a situation like this, where the contractors are extremely busy for the foreseeable future, they may throw a high number at the project. The contractor's logic is simple: they do not need the work, but if they get the job they want to receive a premium for fitting it in with the rest of their workload. This is what I refer to as an emotional bid. Conversely, if the local construction business is slow, contractors may bid aggressively in an attempt to keep their crews busy. In some extreme cases, contractors in slower markets may not be concerned about the profit margin of a job. Rather, they will focus on the fact that the revenue from the project will help cover their fixed overhead expenses. National and international conditions can impact the cost of a project as well.

The construction boom in Asia, particularly in China, significantly impacted the cost of raw materials around the world. As a region experiences a massive construction boom, the diversion of materials to a concentrated geographical area affects the pricing of these same materials in other parts of the world. I heard one story about a ship full of raw steel material that was bound for the United States. As the ship approached the United States shoreline, a helicopter with a business executive landed on the ship and cut a deal with the owner of the steel before the ship ever docked in the United States. The ship promptly turned around and set sail for Asia, leaving those in the United States who were expecting the materials, well, high and dry. When materials are in such demand, anything can happen. Ultimately, shortages such as these will be reflected in the pricing and costs of construction. Conditions in one particular forest halfway across the world may affect domestic lumber prices. Natural disasters can have a significant effect on materials pricing due to a depletion of a specific resource, a diversion of labor to assist with the disaster's aftermath, or the inability to transport materials from one location to another. Speaking of transportation, the cost of moving materials from their original source to the point where they will be used as part of a construction effort is significant and directly affected by the cost of gasoline. These shipping charges are typically passed on to the consumer. As you can see, the budgeting effort is very much an art and can be subject to change until a purchase order for the materials is issued. The owner cannot do much to alter these conditions, but nevertheless should be aware of them. These factors may affect decisions such as where to build, when to build, or what construction method to utilize.

My contract with Roger was very clear and designed to hold him accountable for both the timeline and the budget. Though the architect had not performed, ultimately it was Roger's responsibility to work with me and ensure that we would meet our stated budget. He knew this, and he seemed committed to overcoming the earlier challenges resulting from the design process. We worked well together, and we were focused on achieving our objectives. To further encourage Roger to meet our schedule, I drafted an addendum to the original agreement whereby our ownership team would pay him a sum of money, at a set value per day, for each day ahead of schedule he turned over the building. Conversely, Roger would be required to pay us the same dollar amount in the form of liquidated damages for every day past the turnover date that the project remained incomplete. The amount was not significant — only about $350 per day. However, if the project ran one week (seven days) past the turnover date, it would cost the contractor $2,450, or nearly 10 percent of his profit based on his maximum fee. Should the contractor turn over the project a week early, I could justify the additional costs, as they would be offset by an additional week's worth of revenue from the restaurant's operations.

Because of our overlapping schedule and phased approach, we were simultaneously in the middle of the design process and budget-gate, the budget overruns, when the construction process actually began. Roger had hired the demolition crew to come in and begin clearing out the site. Our final design called for the entire interior to be demolished. Not a single wall was to remain inside of the exterior shell. The city of Maitland was extremely cooperative throughout the construction process, as they had become acquainted with our team and our concept. In fact, I would say that they were as supportive of our efforts as they could possibly be. They turned the demolition permit around in just over a week. It was a good thing, too, as the schedule did not allow for much wasted time. In fact, Roger sent me an e-mail one afternoon indicating that he had received a verbal approval for the demolition permit, but did not have the permit in his hands. He was unwilling to lose any more time and was prepared to start the demolition at 8:00 the following morning — with or without the permit in hand. Fortunately, he picked up the permit at 7:30 that morning, and it was hanging in the window when the demolition crew began their work.

With the initiation of the demolition work also came the initiation of my official role as construction coordinator for 'Za-Bistro! It was not long before the first construction crisis reared its head. I was in Chicago on a business trip when I received a frantic call from Chris. He had stopped by the Maitland site to see how the demolition work was progressing and discovered that part of the ceiling, which we had planned to salvage, had been "accidentally" torn down. He had also discovered that the slab in the restrooms had been modified as well, when the objective had been to save and reuse the existing plumbing stub-ups in place. This was of particular concern for a couple of reasons. The first was the history of miscommunication that had already existed on the project between our ownership team and the design and construction team. The second was the fact that we did not yet have a final budget, and I was concerned about the impact that some of these developments would have on our final product. In other words, I did not want to squander money on the front end, where the restaurant patrons would never notice the impact of the dollars spent, and then have to sacrifice the quality or quantity of the finishes at the end in order to meet the budget. We were already at greater risk of such a scenario due to the failure of the design process and termination of the architect's involvement. None of the finishes were finalized. Following Chris's panicked call, I told him that I would stop the job, and everything would have to wait until I returned from my trip.

As it turned out, halting progress on the job site was not necessary as Roger was just doing his job. He had determined that it would actually be more expensive to salvage the existing ceiling than it would be to replace

 it. He also discovered that some of the toilet connections needed some minor work. In both cases, Roger's actions were justified. He requested that I give him the leeway to do his job and act in our best interest, which was a fair request. In return, I requested that he keep me notified of such decisions so that I could keep tabs on the construction status and respond to inquiries from my team. This, too, was a legitimate request. It all came down to two main factors: communication and trust. With both in place, the above concerns could have been alleviated. Without them, however, the process can quickly grind to a halt.

As I stayed awake late each night, combing through the budget and

drawings, looking for opportunities to reduce the budget, I was fully aware that the demolition was nearly completed and the drawings in my possession had already been submitted for permit. The pressure to bring this project in line with our budget was increasing. Roger and I spent numerous hours discussing cost reductions, and soon we were able to find enough opportunities for savings without affecting the original design intent. Believe it or not, in a few instances I would actually say that our cost-reduction efforts yielded design enhancements.

I want to review some of our budget-driven modifications for a couple of reasons. First, I believe that the specific examples may provide some level of insight for aspiring restaurateurs who are forced to participate in a similar process. Second, as you will see, some of these decisions played a role in the remaining stages of the construction process.

One line item that seemed awfully high on the budget breakdown, relatively speaking, was the millwork package. The original intention was to provide molding for all of the arches and punched wall openings throughout the restaurant. The molding would provide a clear definition of the architectural features at first glance and subliminally enhance the sophisticated ambiance that we were attempting to achieve. The punched openings were easy to accommodate, as they were linear. Molding for the arches, however, would have been expensive and time consuming, so they were quickly deleted from the scope of work. The half walls throughout the restaurant were 48 inches high, with the top 12 inches comprised of frosted glass featuring our logo at the center. The detail design for these half walls also called for a chair rail starting at 36 inches above the finished floor (AFF in industry lingo) and stretching down four inches. The rest of the wall, from the base to the bottom of the chair rail, would be covered in wainscot, also sometimes referred to as bead board. The wainscot would protect the walls from abuse, as well as add character to the space. In the course of this budget review, however, everything was on the table. As I studied the elevations, it was apparent that most of the locations where wainscot was identified on the drawings would be blocked by tables or chairs. The direct sight lines to this rather expensive wall finish would be most prominent when patrons were seated — and more focused on the activities at their own table. We were in budget-crunching mode, and while I felt that the wainscot did contribute to the ambiance and improve long-term maintenance, it was promptly removed and replaced with painted drywall in its place. The coloring would be the same, but the wall finish was no longer part of the construction package.

Perhaps one of the most intriguing changes with regard to the millwork package started as a cost-savings idea, but in the end added true character to the space, in every sense of the word. I must share the credit on this one, as the idea was not mine. Again focused on the ambiance required by a sophisticated $30 experience, my original plans had called for a stone dining counter at the Hearth and at the Snug. I was not sure what the ultimate material would be—granite, marble, or one of the many stone alternatives currently available—on the market. However, the budget number for this feature seemed high in relation to the rest of the project.

Chris took, perhaps, the most active role of the team in participating in the design and construction process. Fortunately, he has a natural instinct for design, and he acted as a great sounding board as we moved through the process. When the subject of the stone Hearth and Snug came up, he suggested that we look at the possibility of a wood top (as opposed to stone) for the purpose of cost savings. While it seems like a rather ordinary suggestion, we did not realize until much later just how much this change of material would impact the restaurant space. These two wood tops became defining elements of the restaurant's interior design package, complementing the architectural elements. The wood would wear and patina over time, developing a distinct character not unlike many of the established bars throughout Europe. The bar tops would be mahogany in color with a thick bull-nosed edge. They would become centerpieces of the space, dominant in their positions and configuration. The mahogany would provide a sense of warmth and stability far more consistent with the European theme than the sleek, thin stone tops that were originally included in the drawings. This is a true example of value engineering, which is often a misnomer in the industry today. We had saved a few bucks *and* improved the ambiance of the space. When we talk about some of the distinctive characteristics of the space, the Hearth and Snug are always a part of the conversation. It was a great suggestion by Chris.

The wine cabinet, located along one of the main traffic patterns in the restaurant and directly across from the oven, was originally intended to be a rather elaborate millwork piece. It was meant to balance form and function. At the center of the restaurant, the wine cabinet would be a critical component of the interior design package, while also serving a functional purpose as our wine storage area. The wine bottles would be on display, and servers would be able to pull bottles from the cabinet as orders were placed. The constant presence and activity in and out of the cabinet were merchandising tools, designed to increase wine sales. Originally, I had contemplated the idea of splitting the cabinet in half and providing temperature- and humidity-controlled environments for the red and the white wines. Unfortunately, the piece was far too expensive even without the intricate temperature and humidity controls, and I was forced to search for an alternative solution that would achieve the desired effect at a much lower cost.

I hopped on the Web and started searching for wine display racks. I found all sorts of racks, at all sorts of price points. Some were fairly elaborate stacking systems with an infinite number of possible configurations. Some were designed primarily for residential use and would never stand up to the abuse of a commercial setting. Finally, I found wall-mounted wine racks that stored the bottles of wine properly on their sides, available in sizes that would accommodate one, two, or three bottles deep. They had a chrome finish and looked clean and simple. The space allocated for our wine cabinet was over 9 feet long, so it would take dozens of racks in order to fill the space. I began sketching out our "wine wall" based upon these racks. The two-deep models would provide us with some perceived depth, but still offer significant stability. We would fill the wall space, from about 18 inches AFF to just below the ceiling. After laying out the space based on these racks, I determined not only that we could make it happen, but also that the total cost for all of the racks would be around $1,200, including shipping. Next, I needed to figure out a way to provide the built-in cabinet look that we had originally desired. After considering a number of different options, I decided to use standard French-style doors at the front of the recess for the wine cabinet. In the end, there would be no actual millwork used for the wine "cabinet." We would use only the doors made of wood, painted to match the mahogany throughout the rest of the restaurant, and glass in conjunction with wood and glass panels designed to fill out the space above the doors. Together with the wall-mounted wine racks, the look of a built-in cabinet was achieved at a fraction of the cost of the wine cabinet in our original plans.

More money still needed to be cut from the project. The restrooms had been designed with tile on all of the walls. While desirable, the tile would have to be deleted and replaced with painted drywall. A detailed back-bar shelving structure in the bar was simplified to include a couple of shelves, a glass rack, and mirrors. Vinyl base at the intersection of the floors and walls in the dining room replaced the stained wood originally specified in the drawings. The lighting package was modified, and the number of overall fixtures was reduced in order to lower the material and installation costs of these fixtures; a savings on two fronts. The original design featured a fairly intricate ceiling detail with horizontal members, recessed lighting, and draping cloth. The entire ceiling detail was eliminated, and a simple, black lay-in tile ceiling grid was substituted.

I had targeted a 10 percent reduction in the plumbing and electrical work to help meet the budget as well. This would come as a result of negotiating as well as modifying the specified components. I was relying on the plumbing and electrical subcontractors to help in the process, and they did, to a certain extent. I also took it upon myself to check on some of the prices that had been quoted. The subcontractors who were favored by Roger had provided lump-sum bids. Because I was evaluating each and every line item on the project, I pressed the subs for more detailed quotes that would break out some of the individual costs. In these detailed bids I found some opportunities to save and perhaps some opportunities to right some wrongs. One example that I recall in particular was the pricing for the sink bowls to be used in the restrooms. I wanted to reduce the cost of the project without affecting the design of the space. The sinks in the restrooms were distinctive design features, and I did not want to downgrade them as I thought they were critical to our concept. It would have been easy to save over $1,000 by changing to a more basic sink style, but I was unwilling to compromise the original design impact of these fixtures. That said, my request for a more detailed breakdown of the plumbing package revealed that I was being charged over $800 per sink. I found the exact same model sink at The Home Depot's EXPO Design Center for half that price, and that was consumer pricing. How was it that the plumbing contractor, with a direct relationship with the manufacturer, could not obtain the same pricing (or *better* pricing, for that matter) than an average residential customer walking in off the street? I challenged this number and the plumbing contractor would not back down. Whether the pricing difference was honest or not, I was focused on the end result. I had an opportunity to obtain the exact same model for half the price I was being quoted, and that is precisely what I did. I instructed the plumbing contractor to remove the three sink bowls from his package, and I purchased them myself. That alone was a savings of over $1,200, which may not seem like much, but the savings can add up quickly.

This brings up a subject worth discussing in regard to subcontractors and general contractors. It is important to stay in their back pockets, to a point. Given the cost-plus arrangement we had with the general contractor, it was understood that we had the right to review and understand the quotes from the individual subcontractors. A lump-sum bid did not offer the required level of detail, so I pushed for a breakdown. This more detailed document revealed some discrepancies, which I soon challenged. Now, please do not assume that all contractors are evil, dubious individuals. That is *not* the case at all. Unfortunately, in any industry, there are inevitably those who are a little less than completely honest. Requesting a detailed budget breakdown will help identify errors made by those who are honest and will reveal unwarranted charges by those who are not as honest as we would like them to be. It is an owner's right and obligation to push for this level of detail. Proceed with caution, however, because pushing too far and approaching the situation with a preconceived notion that the contractor is dishonest may upset an honest contractor who is working diligently on the owner's behalf. A contractor can be an owner's greatest ally. To repeat a Ronald Reaganism: *Trust, but verify.*

In the world of construction, there are many individuals and firms who focus solely on the lowest bid. I do not. More important than the price is what that price represents. Some contractors know how to artificially develop their numbers so that certain aspects of the construction are hidden from the owner on the front end and issued as an "unexpected" change order later in the process. The lowest bidder on the day the bids are opened may not be the lowest bidder on the day that the doors are opened; this is a significant distinction. When reviewing the bids, I prefer to meet with the subs and evaluate their character and experience. I prefer to look at the total package when selecting a subcontractor, evaluating everything at once. Selecting your team members by price alone is short-sighted. Contractors will move from one job to another after each is completed, while the owner will have to live with the quality of the work, which may not be apparent during the warranty period. These contractors make decisions throughout the construction process that will affect the facility and operation, and often do so in the absence of the owner. That is why it is important to consider such factors as experience, reputation, availability, communication skills, and especially character when selecting general contractors and subcontractors. It also clearly demonstrates why it is in an owner's best interest to participate in the selection process.

Perhaps the most troubling part of our situation was that we had already begun the construction phase. Some decisions that had been made could not be changed. Other issues required making split-second decisions without time to thoughtfully consider their impact on the rest of the project. Buildings are intricate, with a number of interdependent systems. A modification to one component of the facility can significantly impact another, and the effect might not be readily apparent at the time the decision is made. In our case, the elimination and relocation of some of the lighting affected the HVAC ductwork routing in an already tight ceiling. This is just one example; there were numerous coordination efforts moving simultaneously. It was like solving an equation with thousands of variables, and it was my responsibility to make sure that, in the end, we would have a facility that would meet all of our original design objectives—on time and within budget. With signature features such as the oven façade still undefined, I must admit that I was not comfortable with the position I was in or the way our situation had evolved. I approached the design process with the intent of avoiding the exact scenarios I was now dealing with on a regular basis. Last-minute decisions. Plans that were incomplete or did not match the actual construction. Wasted design time. Nonetheless, I had no other options. I had a job to do, and I needed to get it done one way or another.

When the budget review process was completed, I had reduced the construction budget to approximately $278,000. This amount did not include the costs of the actual permit. With a small contingency (much smaller than I had originally anticipated), it appeared that we were back on track with regard to the budget of $285,000, or $75 per square foot. I am going to jump out of sequence just a bit and fast forward to the end of the project, so that I can tell you just how close we came to this revised budget. In the end, after the cost of our permit and three change orders, resulting from changes we made as well as those required by the local inspectors, the final cost of the general contractor's work was—drum roll please—$287,325. This was eight-tenths of one percent over our projected $75-per-square-foot cost. I love reaching a goal. This was rather remarkable with all of the challenges we faced throughout the construction process. We had surprises around every corner, and numerous decisions were made with little or no notice. With each decision, I knew the budget would be impacted. I had to keep a running mental tab on all of the changes and their impacts on both the aesthetic and financial goals of the project. This last-minute, reactionary approach was, of course, not what I intended. Nevertheless, it was reality. And given the variety of unexpected events that surfaced during the construction process, it is incredible that we actually hit our budget. The construction effort was a wild ride.

12

Hang on to your (Hard) Hats

The world of design and construction is rough. There are all sorts of headaches and pressures associated with *this* side of the industry. I recall far too many times during the build-out in Maitland when I sat back in total frustration, hands covering my eyes, and wondering why I continually subjected myself to a job that could be so taxing on both the mind and the body. I will admit, while I often struggled to remind myself of the reason, there was one thing that kept me coming back for more—one clear benefit to the world of design and construction that is almost unparalleled. It is what keeps most design and construction veterans returning, job after job, despite the regular abuse that they face. It is the realization of an idea. To this day, I find that to be the most rewarding aspect of being involved with development—the ability to initiate an idea on paper, nurture that idea through design and construction, and ultimately experience that idea brought to life. I have always found it incredibly rewarding to be able to touch, feel, and experience, firsthand, a project that I have designed or in whose development I have participated. The first official walk-through of a finished project is a surreal experience. As I wander around the space, I look at every wall, every table, every window, and I recall the stories behind the final product. Sometimes I see ideas I had presented, now in their tangible forms. Sometimes I see ideas that were not implemented, and I try to evaluate the facility in their absence.

Second only to the ability to see a design in its final fruition is the ability to watch a project come together. This includes the series of expected and unexpected events that lead to the final product, the means to the end result. In Maitland, the construction of our restaurant project was in full swing. After nearly two years of planning and effort, 'Za-Bistro! was transforming from a *virtual* restaurant into a *real* restaurant. The restaurant was scheduled to open in December. Later that same month, we were expecting to take over the space at Harbor Commons to initiate construction of the second store. This timeline meant that the bulk of our construction effort would be taking place during the holiday season, a time when many construction projects slow down. We had a challenge before us, but it was not the first nor would it be the last. Like all the others, our team would tackle it head-on. Most importantly, I had received assurance from Roger, our general contractor, and his on-site superintendent, Jim, that we would receive the necessary commitments from the subcontractors to finish on time. The two of them were committed to making our dates and had shared the schedule with all of the subcontractors during the bidding process. I must say that both men did a fantastic job orchestrating the construction effort. Roger worked hard with me to help us bring our project back within budget. Additionally, Jim took a personal liking to the project and, I believe, the team, as he labored from before dawn until after dusk on our behalf. Jim was a gem.

As an ownership team, we knew that we had set some very aggressive goals for the construction team. The scope of work that was to be completed in the allotted time frame, without the accurate documentation, was challenging, to say the least. However, we were also supportive — very supportive. I have seen many owners approach their construction team with lengthy lists of difficult demands, conveyed with an attitude that the construction team has an obligation to comply with the owner's request, no matter what the impact may be on the contractors or subcontractors. I approach the scenario a little differently. No doubt, we were demanding. I readily admit that. But following each request, no matter how difficult, I would turn to Roger or Jim and ask how *we* were going to get it done. I was prepared to roll up my sleeves and help in any way possible. I developed "hot lists" of tasks that had to be completed and issued them to the field and the contractor's office to ensure proper communication and coordination. Was this my job? Not really. But if it helped the construction team meet their objectives, I was more than willing to participate in the process and offer my assistance.

I remember one evening in particular during the construction in Maitland. It was about 8:30 at night. I still had an hour-and-a-half drive back to Tampa ahead of me, and it was clear that Jim had no

plans to leave the site any time soon. In his raspy voice — the result of years of chain smoking and late nights like the one before him — Jim turned to me and told me that in more than 30 years on various job sites, I was one of the most supportive owners he had the pleasure to work with, despite the demanding nature of our project. *He* thanked *us*! Though sometimes inconvenient, he knew that the challenges and suggestions I proposed were usually well-conceived and kept our ultimate objectives in mind. I was focused on the end result. Most importantly, however, I think Jim recognized my personal commitment to the success of the project and the extent of my hands-on involvement. I was an active participant in the process, partly because I wanted to be and partly because I had no other choice.

Because of our experience with the architect, as well as our timeline, we did not have an opportunity to revise the design documents. This meant that we would have to build the restaurant from an outdated set of plans, which did not reflect more than $30,000 of modifications we had made. This made Jim's job a lot more difficult, and he was in constant need of advice and direction. Without exaggeration, I can tell you that I would typically receive 10 to 15 calls a day from Jim during the peak of the construction phase in Maitland regarding design decisions that had to be made on the fly. Some days we spoke more than 20 times. Most of these questions were a result of poor design documentation, our budget reduction, or both. It was my job, however, to make myself available and give Jim and his team the clear direction and support they required. Though there were an incredible number of design details that were not addressed in the outdated design documents, Jim confirmed that my rapid, clear direction reduced or eliminated potential time delays. Some of the discussions were very specific, and because I was located in Tampa, I had to rely on my visualization skills, hoping that I was making the right decision with each and every phone call fielded. I did not have the luxury of dropping by the site on a daily basis.

As an example, I received one call from Jim regarding the location of some of the recessed light fixtures just above the Hearth. As part of the budget reduction, we had modified the number of light fixtures in this area. The revised ceiling design, which was modified slightly due to the elimination of the center ceiling detail, raised a question: Below which level of the multi-level soffit should the lighting fixtures be installed? I closed my eyes and visualized the scenario that Jim was describing, the original design intent, and ultimately the answer to Jim's question. In this particular case, the upper level was the best choice, as the lighting fixtures would then cascade a rhythmic pattern of light on the soffit above the Hearth. Sometimes when materials had not arrived, Jim would call to seek advice for an alternative. In one instance, we modified the flooring material. In another instance, we modified the architecture. The issues ranged from the discovery of an unanticipated roof problem to how the molding should meet in a particular corner of the restaurant. The conflicts were both large in scope and focused on the minutest of details. Keep in mind that, with each and every call, I had to keep a running tab on the impact that decision would have on the budget.

Support was also offered in other ways. I made it a point to be on site as much as possible. I thanked the subcontractors for their continued efforts during the holiday season and made myself available for questions and suggestions. I explained to the subs that I viewed them as an extension of our team and hoped they would offer any advice they felt was in our best interest. In one example, the HVAC contractor indicated that the plans called for him to remove and repaint the existing ceiling registers. He said that he could not support the direction in good conscience. We reviewed the status of the existing registers as well as the cost of replacing them, and we decided to replace them.

I wanted the contractors to know that we appreciated their hard work. In some instances, we also rewarded their efforts. Our head chef, Daniel, took it upon himself to make a meal for the entire crew every Friday throughout the duration of the construction process. Job sites typically slow down on Fridays, but not ours. In fact, because Daniel fed the crew, we typically had a very large turnout on Fridays. Jim and Roger appreciated this as well. Not only did the strong Friday turnout give them a better chance to meet their goals, but the meal allowed them to fill their own stomachs with some creatively crafted sustenance. Again, we were demanding but supportive of the team in every way possible.

The camaraderie on the job site proved to be essential to our success, as there were a host of issues looming, which we would have to face as a team—owners, contractors, and subcontractors. The remainder of this chapter is focused on some of the specific events that transpired on the job site. I have far too much respect for true war veterans like both of my grandfathers to call the following accounts "war stories," so I will refer to them instead as *tales from the field*. I cannot share every event—that would add several hundred pages to this book. I hope, however, that these *tales from the field* will provide at least a glimpse into the world of restaurant construction and actual events that can transpire on a job site.

The stone-hearth oven, as you are now well aware, was the centerpiece of our restaurant concept from both the culinary and design perspectives. When it came to the construction effort, the oven was no less significant. The oven was over seven feet in diameter and weighed more than three tons. These units come pre-assembled, making access a major consideration. We had to carefully coordinate a way to get the oven into the building, as few restaurant spaces typically have an 8-foot-wide opening. We could have purchased the oven and had it assembled on site, but that would have required certified factory installers to travel from Bellingham, Washington, to complete the installation, more than doubling the cost of our $20,000 oven. I addressed the access issue with the landlord during our lease negotiations and with Roger and Jim before construction commenced in Maitland. But before we could bring the oven into the space, we had to ship it from Washington to Florida. This sounds like a simple task, but in the world of construction, expect the unexpected, and hope you have a viable alternative.

Before the demolition started, I began coordinating the delivery of the oven for Maitland. Because of their weight and size, these units must be transported by a specialty carrier. A flatbed trailer is used to carry the oven. Unlike a typical freight company, this carrier's hauls most often are dedicated to one destination, as it is difficult to coordinate multiple deliveries on a single trailer. The trailer typically holds a maximum of only two or three ovens. Thus, the real cost for shipping one oven was pretty close to the cost of shipping two ovens. With Harbor Commons around the corner, I had determined that we could save over $1,000 if we shipped both ovens at the same time. The oven for Maitland could be brought directly into the space under construction, while the Harbor Commons oven could rest in the space for a few weeks until we were ready to commence the construction project there. In fact, in the case of Harbor Commons, it would be an advantage to bring in the oven early, as the space would be closed in shortly after the oven was to arrive, according to their construction schedule. An early delivery of the oven for Harbor Commons would also save money by eliminating unnecessary removal and replacement of the storefront. And by using the same forklift to remove the ovens from the trailer and transport them into both restaurant spaces on the same day, we saved the few hundred dollars it would cost for a second forklift rental. I decided to ship both the Maitland and Harbor Commons ovens at the same time. Perhaps it was the remnants from my recent budget-crunching effort in Maitland, but I was still focused on saving money wherever possible, as long as it would not affect the final product.

When the oven was released to ship, I learned that the carrier's policy would not allow them to guarantee a specific delivery date, but that shipments to Florida usually took five days. This was important, as I would have to hire a crew to receive the oven, first in Maitland and then at Harbor Commons. My crew leader, Ben, was a kind, driven, hard-working gentleman with whom I had worked on past projects. He was hired to be in charge of setting and coordinating all of the foodservice equipment and dining room furniture. This was a separate scope of work, outside of the general contractor's realm, typically handled by the kitchen equipment contractor, or KEC in industry lingo. On this job, I was wearing multiple hats, as both the owner and the KEC through Louis Wohl & Sons. Ben was focused on every detail and expeditious in his work, even though he was based in Miami and the job was in Orlando. He got in, got it done, and got out. With our schedule, that was exactly what I needed. The oven was prepared for shipping on a Friday and would be picked up from the factory first thing on Saturday morning. I contacted Ben and made arrangements for him and his team to arrive and receive the oven on Wednesday, indicating, however, that the delivery date was not guaranteed. I also relayed to Ben that my purchase order to Wood Stone, who contracted with the carrier, indicated that a 72-hour notice prior to delivery must be provided to both Ben and me by the freight company. This would allow us ample time to make the necessary arrangements to receive the ovens and rent the forklift.

Early in the afternoon on the following Monday, two days before the estimated delivery date, I received a call from the shipper, indicating that he was in Orlando at the restaurant site and did not see my crew. I explained that we had been told the shipment would take roughly five days and that we were to have received a call prior to delivery. Arrangements had been made for a Wednesday delivery with temporary arrangements made for either the Tuesday preceding or the Thursday following the scheduled delivery date, just in case. He referred to his company's stated policy that no delivery dates were guaranteed. As it turned out, the driving team of two people had an engagement scheduled later that week and decided to split driving shifts throughout the weekend. Between Saturday morning and Monday morning, the team of drivers covered the entire continental United States, driving from Washington state to Florida. We had no idea that the oven was arriving early until it showed up, and now it was my problem to resolve. After explaining to the driver that we were not prepared to receive the delivery on Monday, he told me he had other obligations and would have to take the ovens with him or store them somewhere in Orlando temporarily. Either way, we would be responsible for the additional freight and storage charges. Since this obviously was not a desirable scenario, I began pleading with the driver to offer us some assistance with the situation. I already had a call into Ben as I was trying to schedule him and his crew to come to Orlando for a 7:00 a.m. start on Tuesday. Meanwhile, I was on the phone with the driver and making no progress—until I decided to play the game a little differently.

Looking at the big picture and the number of dollars involved, I offered him a little monetary incentive to assist me in my efforts. I indicated that if he could stay the night, I would pick up his hotel room and throw him a hundred bucks. Although this would cost me some money, our schedule did not allow for any delays. If we did not have the oven on time, it could have delayed the entire construction schedule. At this point, the demolition in Maitland had already been completed and the framing of the walls had begun. The framing was underway around the perimeter of the restaurant, while the center area remained untouched in anticipation of the oven delivery. If the oven did not arrive on time, the framing at the center of the restaurant and around the oven would be further delayed, impacting progress throughout the rest of the project. At just after 6:00 on Monday evening, the driver reluctantly agreed to stay the night in light of my monetary incentive. I was awaiting a return phone call from Ben to make sure that he could have his crew in Orlando the next morning and that the forklift rental company would be able to accommodate our request on short notice. While the driver had agreed to stay until the morning, he indicated that he would have to start unloading the first oven at 7:00 a.m. in order to meet his other commitments. If the crew was not there, he would have to move on. At 8:30 on Monday evening, less than eleven hours before the ovens were to have been unloaded, I received a call from Ben confirming that he had been able to reserve a forklift and he would be in Orlando first thing in the morning to offload the ovens. Before Ben could finish with his update, I hung up and called the driver on his cell phone to let him know that the crew would be there first thing in the morning. We were set, at least for the time being. I could not help but wonder, though, how many other similar scenarios were in my future.

Ben arrived on time to meet the driver, and the ovens were offloaded. First was Harbor Commons. When Ben arrived with his forklift, he was quite surprised to learn that we had ordered the 7-foot Wood Stone oven. In the past, he had only dealt with the 5-foot and 6-foot models. He was concerned, to say the least, as to whether the forklift he had rented would be able to handle the 3-ton ovens. It was smaller than the size that the manufacturer had recommended, but he decided to press on. The smaller forklift turned out to a blessing in disguise as the larger forklift would not have cleared the existing opening into the building. The oven was offloaded without a hitch at Harbor Commons. That site was wide open, and access was not

a concern. When Ben and the oven flatbed truck driver arrived in Maitland, the storefront had already been removed. Access to the space had been part of my frantic coordination the night before. As it turned out, Roger had removed the storefront in Maitland a few days early, anticipating the oven's arrival. Access would not be as easy as we had anticipated, however, as the clearance for the forklift below the existing awning left only two inches to spare — literally, two inches. Given that forklifts are not the most graceful machines, a sudden jerk could have damaged the oven, the awning, or the building — not

to mention the people working to deliver our precious cargo. In the end, they made it. With Ben at the wheel, they carefully drove the oven right into the center of the dining room. And as soon as they pulled out, the framing began in the center of the restaurant, an area previously off limits. It was a carefully orchestrated process, but the additional aggravation was worth the end result. We had our ovens — a day early, in fact. It was time to move on to the next crisis.

Later that week, I received a call from Roger at the Maitland site, indicating that they had found a surprise. The plumber was in the process of trenching the existing concrete slab in order to run his underground drain lines called for on the drawings. There was to be a floor trough in front of the ice machine, designed to catch any fallen ice and provide a place for excess water to drain from the adjacent wet area. The ice machine was located in the service area, which would be subject to high amounts of traffic. This floor trough was included in the original design for both convenience and safety. The plumber had run into a rather unusual circumstance, however, when trenching for this particular floor trough. Throughout the rest of the building, the slab thickness was pretty consistent, with packed earth material below. At the trough, however, the slab was much thicker than in the rest of the building. Little did we know just how much thicker it was. When Roger called, he told me that the plumber had already dug down more than three feet, and he was still hitting solid concrete. We could not identify a particular reason for this additional slab thickness. Our best guess was that the original construction crew, needing to backfill below the slab, had just decided to use concrete in lieu of earth material, figuring that no one would ever know the difference. Well, *we* knew the difference. The problem was that the plumber would need to dig even deeper in order to accommodate the floor trough (and drain lines), which had already been shipped and was on site ready to be installed. The extra-thick slab was requiring the plumber to spend an incredible amount of time and labor, both of which were beyond the scope of what he had anticipated. Thus, we were once again in search of alternate solutions. The problem was the drain location, which was centered on the floor trough we had purchased. We had determined that if we could use a trough with an offset drain, perhaps on the side at one end, we could route a drain line through the existing 3-foot-deep slab trench. Otherwise, further digging would require specialty equipment. Clearly, the additional equipment and labor would result in additional costs and delays, so we opted for the new trough with an offset drain location. The existing trough would be held and used for Harbor Commons. Fortunately, the solution worked.

Not all of the surprises we encountered were negative. There were also some nice surprises as we continued construction. On the south exterior wall we discovered a window, which had been framed out, but was covered up in one of the earlier building remodels. We saw no reason to leave it covered

up, and we opted to include this new window in the construction effort. The south wall elevation had to be modified slightly in order to incorporate the window, but our new source of natural light was easily accommodated. Such an addition had not been contemplated in the design process, as our remodel was officially classified as an interior renovation. The additional window was, however, a nice bonus. A similar modification occurred on the interior of the restaurant. A wall at the end of the Hearth, closest to the service station, was designed to be a full-height wall. Again, giving credit where credit is due, Chris and I were on site one evening and he asked me if we had a punched opening in that particular wall. The walls were framed, but the drywall had not been completed. I checked the drawings and found that no punched opening was

planned there. So we added one. Standing next to that wall, adjacent to the punched opening and the pick-up counter, a manager would be capable of viewing almost the entire restaurant. It would become the single best place in the entire building for a manager to keep a finger on the pulse of the operation—the guests, the servers, and the display kitchen. It was definitely a positive addition with no real impact on the cost of the project. An improvement that didn't cost any additional money—now you're talking my language!

Typically, the construction process does not start until the building permit is in hand. Our demolition permit allowed for demolition work only; on our time schedule, however, we were forced to push the envelope just a bit. The contractors actually began some of what would be considered construction, under the letter of the law, before the building permit was issued. They did not progress past the point when first inspections would be required by the local building official, but they certainly brushed up against it. No harm done, but the limits were pushed. The inspector raised an eyebrow when Jim asked for his first inspection just one day after the building permit was officially issued. Jim and the building inspector developed quite a relationship. In fact, the local inspector was one of the main reasons we were able to maintain such an aggressive schedule. He was there almost every day, as Maitland is a relatively small town, and, during the holiday season, we were one of the few projects running at full steam. It also helped that the same inspector was responsible for multiple disciplines (mechanical, electrical, and plumbing). Most importantly, he provided us with partial inspections. In other words, he would conduct inspections for selected areas within the restaurant and approve the team to move forward in the one area. He would, for example, conduct a plumbing inspection for one wall, and if all of the inspected work met code, the inspector would authorize the team to close up that wall—but that wall only. Most inspectors would not be as accommodating. Typically, contractors can call for an inspection only when the scope of work has been completed throughout the entire building. Even then, the contractor is usually at the mercy of the inspector's schedule. We were lucky in that we received support from a variety of different sources. Our building inspector in Maitland was a tremendous help.

Starting the construction effort without the building permit in hand, however, was not without its challenges. In Florida, the Department of Business and Professional Regulations (DBPR) has a division for hotels and restaurants. This is the health department, responsible for reviewing the drawings to ensure that the plans comply with all local health codes. In a typical scenario, the DBPR approval is received prior to the issuing of the building permit. Thus, all comments and concerns from DBPR are relayed and resolved before construction commences. That was not the case with our efforts in Maitland. Construction had begun well before we received the DBPR approval. This did present some risk, as the DBPR comments had the potential to affect our progress on site. As with many aspects of this construction effort, it was a calculated risk. Some of the DBPR review comments were addressed easily. For instance, we had more preparation sinks than required by code, and the reviewer wanted to understand why. In her experience with other facilities, she had discovered that some sinks were intended for improper uses, such as preparation of raw foods, ready-to-eat foods, and sanitation in the same sink, and she wanted to make sure that was not the case in our facility. It was not. In fact, we exceeded the number of prep sinks required, ensuring that each sink would have a designated purpose, which would help reduce the risk of cross-contamination. Another aspect of our drawings that confused the reviewer was the provision of space for a second, under-counter dish machine in addition to the main dish machine. I explained that we had planned for the potential future purchase and use of the second dish machine if volume demanded additional ware-washing capacity or if a second machine was required for washing wineglasses. Because food residue from dishes and flatware can build up on the glassware in certain instances, the option of adding a second machine exclusively for glassware was part of our planning ahead and left our options open. The under-counter dish machine would not be purchased as part of our initial equipment package. The utilities required to operate this second dish machine, however, would be. This is a great technique to use for either future flexibility or budget reduction. Provision of the plumbing or electrical rough-ins during the initial construction can allow for the incorporation of additional equipment in the future. Commercial foodservice operations *need* flexibility, and proper planning and design can ensure that the required utilities are provided at the outset to ease and encourage future modifications. Some of the DBPR comments came as a result of misunderstandings, and most were easily explained.

Other comments, and subsequent requirements, were not as easy to deal with, however. The first was the requirement for a food guard at the Hearth. I call this a food guard, though many call it a sneeze guard or breath guard. It has always seemed more appropriate to me to call these food guards, as they are designed to guard the food. Do we really want to guard a sneeze? Guard *from* a sneeze, now that makes sense. Anyway, the DBPR reviewer indicated that due to the proximity of the Hearth, a dining area, to the adjacent preparation area, a food guard would be required. Although it was not included on my original drawings, and although several restaurants around town with similar configurations passed inspection without a food guard, I had anticipated that this food guard would be required. In fact, my budget reduction exercise was the only reason I left it off the drawings originally. If the food guard was either desired or required, it could be added at a later date, with relatively little effort. What I found puzzling was my inability to obtain clarification or approval on the requirements for this food guard ahead of time, specifically regarding the height. Typically, a standard food guard has detailed requirements, consisting of specified heights and angles, to ensure that the food products displayed are adequately protected. In the case of a vertical shield — a simple vertical barrier — the specifications were not as clear. I knew that it would be a standard vertical glass shield, hopefully transparent so as not to obstruct or interfere with the view to the oven from the dining room. I asked the reviewer if an 8-inch-high glass food guard would be acceptable, and the response I received was baffling. I was told that the height requirement could not be confirmed in advance. Instead, we would have to build the food guard and install it, and upon final inspection, the field inspector would be able to determine if the food guard met the DBPR requirements. I beg your pardon! Let me get this straight: I am supposed to build and install this food guard, and then once it is completed the inspector will tell me whether it passes or not? Talk about a high-stakes game of poker! What happens if it doesn't pass? And even then, how could I be sure that the second configuration would pass if they could not give me any guidelines up front? What about the additional costs? What about potential delays? This is why some inspectors and reviewers have a poor reputation in the field. I am in full support of enforcing the codes, which is what the inspectors are hired to do. It is in the best interest of the owner, the staff, and the general public for all codes to be enforced — in a reasonable and consistent manner. This, however, was not reasonable. I drafted a letter with my responses to all of the comments and questions posed by the reviewer. In that letter, I clearly stated that an 8-inch-high vertical food guard would be provided to meet the request of the plan reviewer. I could only hope that my documentation of the actual height of the food guard to be installed would give me some leverage if the inspector did not approve of the unit. It was no guarantee, but I was planning my rebuttal just in case it was required. Ultimately, we passed the inspection. The height and configuration that I had chosen were accepted by the field inspector.

The trouble with many of the health codes enforced by local health departments is that often the requirements are unspecific and open to interpretation. The requirements for hand sinks in a kitchen are a perfect example — specifically the quantity and location requirements. I have spoken directly with Florida state officials on this issue. My sister was an assistant for a renowned Florida state senator, and even she could not get a clear definition. In the end, such codes are open to the interpretation of the individual inspector. And if the restaurateur submitting the plans disagrees with the inspector's

Display Kitchen Hand Sink Locations

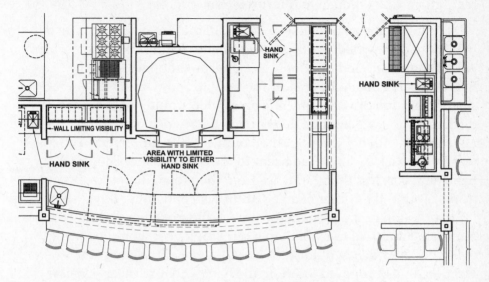

interpretation, there is little or no recourse. The rule of thumb for locating hand sinks in a kitchen, as explained to me by several state officials (who would not give me anything in writing), was that a hand sink should be "readily accessible and within approximately 20 feet of any preparation or ware-washing area." While this sounds reasonable, the interpretation of this statement leads to some gray areas. For instance, I designed a hotel project (coincidentally also in Orlando) where this particular subject surfaced. The hotel's main kitchen contained two work areas that were sharing one hand sink. The trouble was that there was a walkway between these two areas. In the inspector's interpretation (this was a different DBPR inspector than the one who reviewed the Maitland restaurant), the walkway was going to be a heavily trafficked area, and each work area would require its own, dedicated hand sink. Essentially, this particular inspector believed that the constant flow of people and products in the aisle would not make a single hand sink, located near the walkway, readily accessible to both areas of the kitchen. I should point out that this walkway was all of four feet wide, and it was not a major thoroughfare in the kitchen, but rather a secondary walkway. Nevertheless, despite our pleading, the inspector required the addition of a separate hand sink, five feet away from the first. That's right, in the end we had two hand sinks 60 inches apart from one another. Though it sounds ridiculous, this is what can result when regulations are left open to interpretation.

The inspector who reviewed the Maitland drawings confirmed that we had provided a sufficient number of hand sinks. The problem was with the selected locations. Her interpretation was that the hand sinks needed to be "readily accessible and within *full* view of *any* preparation or ware-washing area." She would not commit to a distance. The reviewer had determined that two of our hand sinks did not comply with her interpretation of the code requirement. The first was in the back-of-house, adjacent to the cooking line. Though the hand sink was less than 24 inches from the preparation area, because it was around the corner of an adjacent wall and out of direct sight from a portion of the preparation area, it did not comply with the requirement. I tried to explain that our employees would be there every day, and they would learn very quickly of the hand sink's location. In its proposed location, the hand sink was clearly visible from half of the preparation area, but it was not visible from the other half, where the hood was located. The reviewer remained steadfast in her position—a new hand sink location would be required. The second infraction cited was in the front-of-house. There was a hand sink located within the footprint of the bar, immediately adjacent to the pizza preparation area next to the oven. These two areas, the display kitchen and the bar area, were separated by a full-height wall to create the perception of two completely separate spaces. It was the reviewer's opinion that this configuration did not comply, as the hand sink was not visible from *all* areas of the display kitchen. There was only a 6-foot stretch, give or take a few inches, directly in front of the oven, where neither of the two hand sinks located in the display kitchen were visible, and that was enough to raise the concern of the DBPR plan reviewer. A hand sink could be seen from any point in the display kitchen, except from that one, 6-foot stretch.

As mentioned above, the display kitchen had two dedicated hand sinks, with an additional hand sink provided in the beverage area that was dedicated for use by the servers. A hand sink in ware-washing and a hand sink in the preparation area equaled five hand sinks in total for a restaurant kitchen that was less than 1,600 square feet. While I could understand the perspective of the reviewer, the requirement for a direct sight line seemed a bit excessive. I must admit, the experience changed the way I design kitchens, as I do not want to experience the same problem on any future projects. In the case of Maitland, however, I needed to find solutions to these objections by the reviewer, quickly! The concern about relocating hand sinks was that the required plumbing would also have to be moved and the plumbing work was just about done, even though we had not yet received our DBPR approval. The relocation of either hand sink would have resulted in additional costs and time delays. So, we were under the gun. It was time to get creative, and that is exactly what we did. In the back-of-house, as I stated earlier, we had exceeded the requirement for the number of preparation sinks. One of the sinks was located directly across from the cooking line and was visible throughout the entire preparation area. I decided to convert this utility sink into a hand sink and delete the original hand sink that was just around the corner. We would then weld on a vertical divider to separate the hand sink from the preparation area. This conversion of a prep sink to a hand sink accommodated one of DBPR's objections without changing any of the plumbing. In the front-of-house, the eventual solution was even easier. There was no opportunity to add another hand sink within the display kitchen, and I did not want to convert the utility sink there to a hand sink, as we had anticipated using the front curved, stainless steel work surface for significant preparation. Instead, I proposed the idea of lowering the wall that divided the bar and the display kitchen from a full-height wall to a half-height wall, providing a direct line of sight to the hand sink from that 6-foot stretch of space directly in front of the oven that raised concern from the DBPR inspector. The proposed solution was accepted, and we were able to accommodate both objections without modifying any of the plumbing work that had been completed already. A little creativity can go a long way in the field, not to mention save a few bucks.

The building department also surprised us during the plan review process. The inspector informed us that, although the stone-hearth oven came with an access panel at the front of the supporting structure, a second access panel would be required at the rear of the oven to ensure proper maintenance and safe operation. To meet this requirement, a hole would have to be cut in the wall behind the oven and a dedicated access panel would have to be installed. We soon realized that this secondary access panel would be in conflict with our receiving station, located just off the rear entry. Unfortunately, that did not matter. The receiving station would have to be eliminated to comply with the inspector's direction and ensure proper clearance in front of the new access panel. This particular situation demonstrates how sometimes two well-meaning design objectives or code requirements can be in conflict with one another. In this case, a secondary access would be required at the expense of our receiving station. Hopefully, the elimination of the receiving station would not adversely affect the operation. Only time would tell.

Perhaps one of the most memorable and frequent experiences at that job site was the frantic, last-minute selection of our interior finishes. Though we had paid a significant sum of money for interior design work, much of that work was eventually omitted in an effort to bring the overall cost of the project in line with the budget. Additionally, despite all of the interior design drawings, no actual finishes were ever specified. Given the budget and timeline (yes, I know — a recurring theme), we had developed a little system for the selection of the interior finishes such as carpet, tile, laminate selections, solid surface selections, and other elements. Roger and I would meet on site with the samples and review the products, the availability, and the cost, keeping in mind that each and every decision was still impacting the cost of the project. The $278,000 budget we derived was just that — a budget. In reality, we had a cost-plus contract, and the final costs would be unknown until all of the decisions were made and the costs tallied. Every decision required strict discipline on my part. Chris was there for some of them and acted as my sounding board, but ultimately the decisions were mine to make. This process produced some unusual outcomes resulting from necessity, as opposed to careful planning. The original plan was to wrap the two columns adjacent to the oven in mahogany wood, either actual mahogany or wood painted or stained to look like mahogany. The coordination for this portion of the construction did not happen, as other issues took precedence. Time was winding down, and we needed to select a material for these columns. I did not want them to be finished in painted drywall. While that was acceptable for much of the restaurant, this was the focal point, and it needed to be a defining statement. While walking through the construction site, considering various ideas and options for the finish of these two prominent columns, I literally stumbled over the solution. There were a few extra boxes of beige floor tile that we had used on the floor in front of the Hearth and in the entry. I checked the dimensions to see if we could use the tile on the columns instead of the wood that was planned. It worked. In fact, it worked so well that when we were in search of wall tile for the display kitchen, I ordered extra quantity of the tile we were planning to use on the floor in the restrooms. The tile was installed at a 45-degree angle on the walls in the display kitchen and accented with copper tiles, which were installed vertically on a standard 90-degree angle. It was a quick solution, and even I was surprised how well it worked.

Perhaps the most intriguing tile-related story involved the final selections made for the oven façade. In our selection of materials, I concentrated carefully on the design and finish of the oven façade. It would not be anything close to what I had designed in my original conceptual elevations; the budget and pace of construction ensured that. But I did find a selection of tiles, and I developed an alternate pattern that would provide a desirable and aesthetically pleasing focal point for the restaurant. The pattern included burgundy and blue tiles, as well as copper-colored glass accent tiles that would glimmer and sparkle in the lights just above the oven. The copper tiles came out of a warehouse in Miami, and I had them sent by rush delivery to ensure they would arrive on time. The burgundy and blue tiles had to be ordered from a different source. When the copper tiles finally arrived, I breathed a small sigh of relief. Later that week, on a day I happened to be on site in Maitland, Jim picked up the blue and burgundy tiles from the tile distributor's warehouse, only to find that they had arrived broken. All of them! The tile was supposed to be installed that day, as it was just before the final inspection, and the day before our first all-staff meeting. As soon as I received the call from Jim, I jumped in my car and started scouring the city for replacement blue and burgundy tiles, also considering the possibility of changing the design altogether. Fortunately, I had the copper tiles in my possession—at least I could plan a new design scheme around them.

The restaurant was located just a couple of miles north of a designer's district. I must have stopped in five or six stores, finding nothing in stock that met my design objectives. On a mad dash and with time ticking away, I jumped back into my car and tore off, still on a mission to find replacement tile. At such a critical time in the project, I needed to be on site to assist with coordination, not driving aimlessly around the city in search of alternate material. Nevertheless, it had to be done. Growing more anxious with every minute, I began to broaden my horizons for possible solutions. As I headed back toward the highway on my way to yet another tile store in a different part of town, a storefront sign caught my attention. It was a pool tile store. I pulled in and hopped out, almost before I could undo my seatbelt. With a sense of urgency, I asked the store owner to show me everything he had in stock in either a blue or burgundy tile. As

luck would have it—with extra emphasis on *luck*—this pool store actually had tile that seemed to meet the criteria, and it was in stock. I borrowed a few samples and took them back to the restaurant. The colors matched remarkably well. I laid out a couple of different tile patterns on the bar top and finally decided on one that would work. I then drove back to the pool store and purchased the tile we needed. It was installed the next morning—*during* our all-staff meeting. Every time I look at the oven façade, I recall that story, which is a telling example of the way our construction process evolved.

That one little story exemplifies what occurs during the construction process, whether for a restaurant or for any other building type. It inspires me to summarize and share some of the realities of life in design and construction—some words of wisdom, if you will. *It is important to expect the unexpected. Even the best-made plans must often be set aside to accommodate the events that present themselves. Go with the flow. Sometimes, the solution that has evolved can be even better than the solution that was planned. Don't be too tied to your original solution, as typically there is more than one right answer.* Who would have thought that I would wind up in a pool tile store purchasing the tile for one of the most important design features in the restaurant with only an afternoon to spare? Given the more than 18 months that had elapsed from the time we began initial drawings for Sumner Springs to the time that I was forced to make this quick selection, the irony of the situation was incredible. So much time available, and yet such an important design decision was made at the last minute, utilizing only what was available at the time, without any advanced preparation.

Though the time and financial pressures were ever present, it was important to draw the line between what was acceptable with regard to modifications and what was not. The framing subcontractor and Jim approached me with a proposal that would save them some time. They wanted to eliminate some of the full-height walls, which featured punched openings, and install half walls in those locations instead. While I could understand and support the desire to expedite the workload, I refused to budge on that particular issue. The modification would have compromised the architectural character of the space, and I could not allow that to happen. A similar occurrence

happened while coordinating some of the relocated lighting and HVAC ceiling registers. The space between the dropped ceiling and the roof was extremely tight. This condition caused Jim to pick up the phone and call me more than a few times, as the challenge had far-reaching implications on other scopes of the project. In some of those instances, I again held my ground when it came to quality of the installation, the aesthetics of the space, and the experience of both the guest and the staff within the space. Of course, there were instances when my decisions cost a little more, but it would be up to me to offset any additional costs with cost savings from other opportunities and challenges that surfaced. Sometimes it was hard to keep up with the running tab of all the additions and subtractions, as the changes occurred so frequently and the pace was extremely fast. I tried to keep a physical record of the changes, at least the major ones. Most of the time, however, I kept the running tab in my head, hoping I was guiding the project in the right direction.

More *typical* construction stories surfaced with the arrival and setting of the foodservice equipment. This scope of work, however, was the one with which I was the most comfortable. It was, after all, what I had grown up with. By its defined nature, the setting of the foodservice equipment is always a hectic process. The problem is inherent with the scope of the work and the phase of the construction process when the setting of the kitchen equipment is required. The foodservice equipment is officially classified as part of the FF&E (furniture, fixtures, and equipment) package. Most of the equipment must be set and installed in the kitchen and dining areas after the walls, floors, and ceilings have been completed. By definition, this is toward the end of the job—a time on any job site when tensions are high and deadlines are approaching. The foodservice equipment is not considered to be typical FF&E, however, due to the many utility connections and requirements for the equipment. In other words, it is far more involved to install the foodservice equipment package than tables or chairs. With all of the utility connections comes the required coordination between several subcontractors and, as always in the world of construction, the unforeseen surprises. Realize also that, by the time the site is ready for the foodservice equipment, much of the

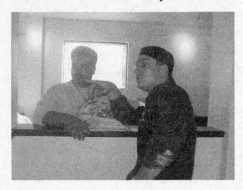

construction team's goodwill has already been spent. Tempers shorten with the mounting pressure. Now, assume for a minute that a piece of equipment arrives with an unexpected connection or an incorrect dimension and requires a modification in the field to make it work. I can assure you that no member of the construction team is going to welcome a drastic change with open arms late in the process. Such changes are usually expensive and time consuming and are not well liked by the trades. Ah, this is the world in which I learned the art of construction and, more importantly, the art of diplomacy and creative thinking on the job site.

Our restaurant in Maitland was no different than any other foodservice project; we had our share of surprises. One of the refrigerated pizza tables was shipped incorrectly, and the wrong model was sent to the warehouse. Dealing with the factory on this issue was difficult, as they could not see their mistake by reviewing their own documentation. I had a surreal conversation with one of the customer service representatives, who tried to explain to me that her paperwork had indicated that I had the correct unit. I had to let her know that I was looking at the unit, and I did not care what her paperwork said—it was the wrong unit. I was forced to speak with multiple supervisors before the problem was finally acknowledged and the correct unit was shipped. This refrigerator, which was supposed to be on site before the installation of the chef's counter, arrived a week later than planned. As a result, it took six men to lift the refrigerator over the counter and set it in its place. I should probably mention that the unit was also slightly larger in length than depicted on the equipment cut sheet, and when it was set in place, there was no more than one-eighth of an inch to spare. Sometimes, it is better to be lucky than good.

The stainless steel custom fabricator had a few errors to deal with himself, particularly with regard to the chef's pick-up counter. Some of the dimensions taken in the field by one of his crew members were

incorrect, and as a result the counter did not fit. In this particular instance, the counter was designed to be installed between two fixed walls with a required cut-out in the center for one of the existing columns. The foodservice equipment arrived on a Friday morning, as did the stainless steel fabrication. In order to maintain the schedule in this late stage of construction, the equipment would all have to be in place by Monday morning at the latest to allow the other trades enough time to make the final electrical, mechanical, and plumbing connections. As soon as I realized the problem with the pick-up counter, I notified the custom fabricator's shop. Mistakes with stainless steel fabrication typically require significant time and money to correct. We, as you know, had neither. I explained the mistake to the shop owner, and he promised to send someone to the site on Saturday morning. And on Saturday, one of the fabricators showed up, but without any tools. He drove all the way from his shop, over two hours away, just to look at the problem I described a day earlier. So I picked up the phone to ask the shop owner what he was thinking. I could not figure out why he would ask one of his employees to drive four hours round trip with no tools or capability to fix the problem. It took every ounce of energy in my body at that moment to resist getting too worked up on the issue, as I was focused on numerous other problems as well. I was persistent as I explained that the counter would have to be fixed on Sunday morning—and it was. The fabricator drove another four hours, with his tools this time, to fix the counter on site. This reminds me of a few more words of wisdom with regard to the development and construction processes: *Work hours are NOT Monday through Friday, 9:00 a.m. to 5:00 p.m. Work hours are whatever it takes to get the job done, and get it done right.*

There were other challenges. We received some standard, buy-out, stainless steel worktables with leg sets wider than the holes with

which they were supposed to align. One instance in particular, the delivery of the tables and chairs, required a great deal of time and coordination. A shipping error had occurred, and it looked as though the dining tables and chairs would not be available for the first all-staff meeting. This was not acceptable, and certainly not the first
impression that I wanted our staff to have of 'Za-Bistro! I was able to convince the manager at the trucking terminal where the furniture had been shipped, in a rare moment of weakness, to allow me to back up a second freight truck to the first truck that held the furniture and transfer the tables and chairs directly from one truck to the other in order to get the furniture to the restaurant on time. This was typically forbidden and clearly against the company's policy. A little persistence and a little convincing go a long way. No, I did not have to resort to monetary incentives this time—though I cannot say that I would have ruled it out. In the end, through all of the trouble and surprises, most of the restaurant equipment was set within a day, with clean-up work happening throughout the rest of the weekend. Not too bad. We were still on schedule.

The entire construction team had been keeping up a pretty good pace, and the restaurant was really starting to come together. There was plenty of work left, however, and as with most construction projects, the stress level and intensity skyrocketed as the end of our construction phase drew near. Toward the end of a job, there are so many different components coming together at once. Within such an intricate effort, just one gap or coordination error can have an enormous ripple effect. Buildings are a series of interdependent systems. There may be nothing wrong with the dish machine, but if there is a problem with the water supply or the electrical wiring for the dish machine, the operator may not be able to wash dishes. Problem! The gas cooking equipment may be functional as well, but a problem with the gas pressure can shut down the entire kitchen. Big problem! At the beginning of every job, I make a promise to each of my clients. I promise them that there *will* be problems on the job site. To this day, that is a promise that I have been able to keep, and it is not for lack of trying to avoid such challenges. In fact, many within my inner circle have accused me of being far too uptight, as I tend to pour over design documents relentlessly in search of any potential conflicts. The truth of the matter is that the design and construction effort, especially in the case of restaurants, is extremely complex, and some conflicts are difficult to avoid. The design team must visualize every square inch of the facility, in three dimensions. We have to visualize the method in which each and every system within the building will ultimately be integrated. Telephone and data lines. Computer systems. Access for each piece of equipment (that is, can you get it in the building?). Phasing and sequencing of each stage in the process. With an incredible amount of information to manage, it is simply a fact of life — there will be problems on the job site. But following this promise, I also remind my clients that it is not necessarily the conflicts that matter most, but rather *how* those conflicts are resolved.

To run a job, decisions must be made rapidly, weighing many factors. These mini-crises, however, offer an opportunity for creativity. There is almost always another solution; it is just a matter of figuring out what the alternatives might be. My father is the person I admire most with regard to creative job site decision making. He is incredible, as he should be after crafting job site conflict resolutions for more than 30 years. I had the privilege of observing him work both before and after I officially started my career, and I learned a tremendous amount from watching him in action. The ability to develop creative alternative solutions at a moment's notice is an invaluable skill to have on the job site, especially as the end of the job draws near. Remember, that is when the foodservice equipment contractor is most intimately involved with a construction project, which explains my father's adeptness in such a situation. Building 'Za-Bistro! was no different from any other job, as we had our share of last-minute crises as well. But this time, *I* was the owner.

The dining bench, part of the banquette seating arrangement, had been fabricated incorrectly by the millwork shop. The dimensions were wrong and the bench was extremely uncomfortable to sit on. It needed to be fixed. The problem was actually the seat cushion—it was too far back, leaving one's legs dangling awkwardly. I proposed the idea of simply sliding the seat cushion forward, which worked like a charm. This was a no-cost solution, and the modification could be made on site. Mission accomplished. Later that same day, the millwork fabricator delivered the bar top. We had been told earlier that the bar top would not be ready in time. Fortunately, it did arrive on time—but it also arrived wet! The stain and finish on the bar top were still tacky when we installed it. Over 20 feet long and made of solid African mahogany, it took six men and some very careful maneuvering to install the top in its final location. The top had to be secured in place so that the food guard could be installed prior to the final on-site health inspection.

We had ordered specialty blue pendant lights to accent the dining room—one of the design treatments I refused to eliminate from the project, given its importance for the ambiance and feel within the space. It was one of the few places where I decided to splurge. These fixtures would provide sparkle and excitement, adding a dose of energy to an otherwise calming environment. Instead, the fixtures arrived in white, not the cobalt blue I ordered. We hung the white fixtures temporarily so that we could pass our building inspection, and later swapped them out after the blue fixtures arrived.

The condition of the existing floor in the dining room was awful. It was uneven, and the demolition had revealed that several different types of flooring had been used throughout the restaurant space. Uncovering the floor was like an archaeological dig, unearthing the restaurant's history at a single glance. Different flooring materials from different renovations could be seen in all areas of the restaurant. We made a decision to float the floor in the dining room, below the carpet, to ensure that the patrons' areas would be level, safe, and comfortable. The actual process of floating the floor involved adding a topping of cement-like material to create an even, flush surface. This process was necessary due to the poor, uneven condition of the existing floor. Our problem was that the floor needed over 24 hours to dry, which meant that the crew would have to stay out of the dining room for that period of time. Unfortunately, not only was there a great deal of work left to do in the dining area, but it was also one of the main access paths into and out of the restaurant. We needed to maintain the access so that the various trades could continue their work, but we also needed to float the floor to stay on schedule. After Roger, Jim, and I put our heads together, we decided to float the floor in two stages. The first float covered only the edges of the areas that needed leveling, leaving a clear walkway down the center so the subcontractors could continue their work. The next day, after the first float had set and hardened, the construction crew was instructed to walk only on the outside areas where the floor had been floated the day before, allowing the original pathway to be floated in a second phase. The floor was leveled in the middle of the restaurant without hindering the efforts of any of the subcontractors. Problem solved.

As discussed earlier, limited work was slated for the outside of the building, as our construction project was officially an interior renovation. We had scheduled, however, to repaint the outside and recover—and in some cases, add or modify—the awnings around the building. As I reviewed options for the new exterior color with the rest of the ownership team, I soon found myself in the middle of a fairly emotional debate. On one side of the issue, part of our contingency wanted to use a modern palate that included a neutral base with highlights and accents of colors from our logo. On the other side was a contingent that wanted anything but the neutral palate and instead wanted to make a bold statement. This portion of our team felt passionately that the exterior of the restaurant needed to match the color scheme of our logo—burgundy and blue. Each contingent was emotionally tied to its point of view, feeling as though they were right and the other side just didn't get it. Where did I stand? Although I sided with those favoring a neutral palate, to be quite honest with you, my plate was full with everything else that was going on. This was just one issue I had to contend with, and once I saw the emotional ties, I removed myself from the process. I asked the team to take a vote, and I would implement whatever decision they agreed upon as a result of the vote. I was responsible for a schedule, and I was not about to let this emotional debate get in the way of my ability to meet my goals and keep my word. A few days later I received the verdict. A bold statement it would be. The base of the building, where the brick was located, would be painted burgundy, with the rest of the building painted blue, similar to the colors we used in the logo.

Crises always arise during construction. It is the nature of the beast. Focusing on the objectives and needs of each member of the construction team typically reveals a viable solution. When you can demonstrate that there is potential benefit for all involved, the team will buy in so the job gets done — correctly. The involvement of design team members is most beneficial under such circumstances, which once again supports the implementation of a design-build format. Just as a contractor's input is valuable during the design phase, the designer can assist the construction team to ensure that alternate solutions do not adversely affect the original design intent. Problems will arise. Quick decisions will have to be made. When the contractor in the field is making decisions with full knowledge of the original design intent, with support in the decision-making process from the design team, the entire development team benefits.

Relationships throughout the construction process are also critical. I have found over the years that design and construction teams will work hard for owners that understand and support their needs. In the end, relationships trump everything else. This is a relationship business; in fact, most businesses are built on relationships. In this day and age, where we e-mail our friends halfway around the world three times a day but may not see our neighbors for weeks, it is important to remember just how critical relationships are. A tile installer will leave the job site at 4:00 p.m. sharp in many instances. But when the owner or the owner's representative clearly demonstrates appreciation, through verbal exchange or action, for the work that is being done, that tile installer may be willing to stay a few extra hours. We all want to feel that the work we do is important. We all search for some level of satisfaction and extrinsic reward for our efforts, though the reward may take on any number of variations. The relationships on the Maitland job site were no different. My relationship with Jim, our job site superintendent, was fantastic. I respected his work ethic and commitment to our project. I believe his respect for me was based on my level of involvement and willingness to help, even get dirty in the process. That was an important relationship, as it permeated the job site. For the most part Jim also had great relationships with the subcontractors on the job site. He was able to share clear direction with them because he had clear direction from me. Those beneficial relationships extended beyond the job site and our construction team. As an example, we could never have met our schedule if it were not for the support and commitments we received from the local building inspector. He did not *have* to issue partial inspections. He did that because he wanted to. He was emotionally involved to some degree with the project and the people working on the project. I will never forget what happened during the final building inspection. I was on site, standing quietly in a corner, observing with hopeful anticipation. The inspection was going very well. Midway through, it was time to check the plumbing system, and Jim promptly turned to the inspector and blurted out "Well, let's go flush the crappers." Excuse me? This is how we talk to our inspector? The answer is yes—when you have the right relationship. Relationships trump all else.

As the construction process was drawing to a close, it seemed that time started to move even faster than it had during the several weeks previous. We had a very detailed list of tasks that needed to be accomplished and a timeline in which they had to be completed. We were making progress, addressing the outstanding issues one by one, but it just wasn't fast enough. Jim had committed to meeting a specific date for us and, based on his word, we had scheduled our friends-and-family evening. This was a special event where our restaurant ownership team would invite friends and family to try out the restaurant—or more accurately, act as our guinea pigs. Also, as the date drew closer, we scheduled our first all-staff meeting and established a training schedule in order to meet the scheduled friends-and-family date. Over 450 invitations had been sent out, and we were expecting some well-respected community members to attend. After learning of the promise made by Jim and reviewing the tasks left to be completed, Roger told me that the date commitment made by Jim could not be met. Most of the equipment had still not been started up. Some of the final utility connections still had not been made. Much of the flooring had not been installed. Some of the specific inspections required for the building permit had still not been scheduled—

inspections such as the fire system dump test to ensure that the fire system worked correctly and would release the fire-suppressing chemicals in the event of a fire. This, again, is where creativity and job site political finesse can significantly affect the final results. Roger, Jim, and I held a spur-of-the-moment conference in the parking lot, just outside of earshot from the rest of the construction crew. I approached the conversation as I had with many other challenges throughout the process, indicating that we *would* in fact meet our dates, but what could I do to help? I explained that we had already received a commitment and scheduled our training, food deliveries, staff, and friends-and-family night based on those commitments. In essence, I approached the situation indicating that we would succeed. I continued to praise the work that had been completed, but I also focused on the work that remained. The challenge was to figure out what needed to be done in order to hit our dates. In this conversation, I eventually compromised, indicating that some of the non-critical construction tasks could be completed during the training

period, which allowed the contractors additional time to complete their most critical work. Some of the painting, finished carpentry, and punch-list work that was not essential for the building inspection was moved to the back burner so that we could focus on the more urgent tasks at hand. In the end, with a little creative scheduling and some commitments from the subcontractors, we did just that—we hit our dates. We passed the building inspection with flying colors and received a temporary certificate of occupancy hours before our first all-staff meeting. Our training and, eventually, the friends-and-family evening were also held on time.

Given my focus on the major construction issues—not to mention that at this point my wife was $8^{1}/_{2}$ months pregnant and wondering where the heck her husband was—I must admit that I allowed some of the finishing touches to slip through the cracks. Fortunately, we were able to use the training period to address many of these minor issues. It only reiterated to me, however, just how important it is to *sweat the details*. We used a copper cataplana (a clamshell-shaped serving vessel) for some of our entrée dishes. One of the servers took it upon herself to install hooks along the bottom of the soffit over the Hearth and hang the cataplanas just above the seating area. It was a fantastic idea and really finished off the central focal point of the restaurant. We added blue beer and wine bottles to the shelves to add a little sparkle. Pictures were hung. We reached out to the Maitland Historical Society, and they provided us with some stunning historical photographs of Maitland (the birthplace of communications

giant Sprint, by the way). We hung those pictures in the dining room along with other works of art. We had always seen ourselves as a community restaurant, and this was one more way to subliminally reiterate our message and our concept. One of my partners ordered wine labels, framed them in small black frames, displaying the label floating in glass, and hung them strategically in the Snug area. We ordered flowers and vases to place throughout the restaurant. The results of our construction offered a terrific palate, but the finishing touches really brought the restaurant to life.

We paid in the end, however, for some of our hastiness and focus on an extremely aggressive timeline. The Hearth top, as I mentioned earlier, arrived wet. We should have waited until the last coat was dry before installing this critical element of the interior space. Not until much later did I learn that the millwork contractor had skipped a couple coats of sealant in order to get the top there on time. The Hearth top never really looked right. We had the millwork shop owner come back three times, but he only made it look worse. The same was true with the floating of the floor. In our rush to meet the schedule, there were areas of the restaurant that did not set right or which did not receive the proper time, care, or attention, and they were far from level. Some of the tables in the restaurant actually rocked. And there were many more such instances. We did meet our goals, but not without a cost.

Our "Opening Soon" sign was up in the window, and buzz was starting to build within the local community. Late one night (a common phrase when referring to the days just before the restaurant opened), I was at a local restaurant picking up dinner to feed the crew that had been helping me set the tables and chairs. I had on a black 'Za-Bistro! hat, with the brim of the hat turned backwards, as I often wear my baseball caps (some habits are hard to break). I was standing in line to order dinner, and the woman behind me asked when we were opening. She knew of the restaurant and had been keeping an eye on our progress. She had read all about the concept on our Web site and was anxious to try the food. To be honest, so was I. It was a great feeling, being stopped on the street by someone who was anxiously anticipating the arrival of 'Za-Bistro! Furthermore, it was the first time I heard our restaurant name being used by someone who was not directly involved in the development or construction effort. But another feeling I had that evening was not the most comforting. As I pulled into the parking lot, grabbed the burritos for the team, and proceeded to have my first official meal within the restaurant, I could not fight off a moment of concern and self-questioning. Was this the right location, location, location? Was this the right concept? Was this the right time? *Was this entire, all-consuming, draining effort a worthwhile cause, or had I done it all for naught?* What did the future hold? Fortunately, the moment passed as I looked at the amount of cleaning left to do before the staff arrived the following morning. But know this: 'Za-Bistro! was real. We had shed the status as a virtual restaurant, and now it was time to perform. We were only days away from opening the doors. It was an exciting time, though there is no rest for the weary. I had a baby on the way. Plenty of work was left to complete, and our doors would soon be officially open for business.

13

The Main Event—
Owner vs. Contractor

As the construction effort was nearing its end, one of the lessons I
learned in college began to take on a whole new meaning: *You pay
your bills with cash, not with profits.* We were well stocked in the bill
department, as all of the construction invoices began to roll in, not to
mention other pre-opening expenses. In addition to materials and goods
included as part of the construction effort, we were quickly accumulating
financial obligations for the computer systems, phone service, alarm
service, utilities, opening inventories, and advertising, as well as salaries
for the managers and staff who were hired to help with the opening.
These expenses were mounting prior to our opening, meaning that we
did not have a steady stream of revenue to cover what our CFO, Jason,
had termed our "cash burn." This made the closing of our loan even more
important. As you may recall, the original plan was to use our capital as
leverage for loans on each store. Under an SBA-approved loan, we would
invest 25 percent of the total construction amount, with the other 75
percent coming from the SBA.

I had always looked at this team and this restaurant development
effort as a learning experience. I approached the entire process with
an open mind, relying upon the expertise of the people around me.

Financially, I am pretty conservative. I am not overly cautious, but my personality profile places a high priority on credibility—keeping my word. When it comes to financial obligations, I am extremely diligent in keeping my word and upholding commitments in my personal life. Because of my personal views, I was a bit uncomfortable when we as a team decided to proceed with the construction effort prior to finalizing the SBA loan. I was raised with the mentality that if you don't have it, don't spend it—it was that simple. No room for negotiations or interpretations. It was black and white. In our development efforts, however, we were taking on significant financial burdens before the loan was closed. I did not understand the decision, but I realized that I had partners who had far more experience in similar financial dealings, so I reluctantly agreed to the approach. I wasn't completely worried. We had a significant amount of our initial capital still in the bank to cover most of our debts, although we had earmarked these funds for future locations as well. We were deviating, however, from our original plan. If we did have to use the funds we had on hand to finance the entire Maitland build-out, it would have reduced our ability to pay for future development. Perhaps even more importantly, a complete depletion of our war chest would have eliminated any contingency cash available to the operation—our "what if" money.

In the process of securing the loan, we ran into some unexpected delays, and toward the end of construction, the tenant improvement dollars promised by the landlord became essential to our ability to meet our financial obligations. As part of our lease agreement in Maitland, we had negotiated a significant amount of TI dollars, which we were planning to apply toward our construction and startup costs. We had not, however, tied down with our landlord the prerequisites and timing for releasing those funds. Due to the delay with the SBA loan, we needed those TI dollars earlier than we originally anticipated. As our bills came due, we soon found ourselves in an unexpected game of jumping through various logistical hoops so that the landlord would release the funds. We hastily filled out several forms, scurrying to secure the documentation required to obtain our money. We also needed our general contractor's assistance, and he became a bit annoyed at dealing with all of the logistical requirements so close to the end of the job. We explained that we had experienced some unforeseen complications and delays, and that we would like to provide our next payment on time. Though he agreed, this was the beginning of a breakdown in our relationship with Roger.

Jim and I had developed a solid working relationship built on mutual respect. Given his role as the on-site construction superintendent, the bulk of my communication over the course of the construction effort had been with Jim rather than with Roger. Whereas Jim had assumed the role of on-site construction coordinator, Roger had assumed a more administrative role on the project. My communication with Roger was focused primarily on budgetary issues, material selection (in the wake of the architect's performance), and administrative functions. While I believe that Jim looked at my involvement as an asset, I sensed that my level of involvement began to frustrate Roger. Consider my "hot lists" as an example. I devised these lists and updated them on a weekly basis to prioritize all of the outstanding tasks remaining in the construction process. It was a communication tool, designed to ensure that the entire team was on the same page and that we all had the same expectations. When I was issuing these lists, Jim found them to be a helpful tool for both communication and organization. It allowed him to better prioritize and delegate the tasks at hand, not to mention understand the issues that were most important to me and most critical to our timeline. I am not sure that Roger felt the same way about these lists. In addition, there were several misunderstandings between Roger and me which led to growing frustrations on both sides. Let me give you some examples. As you may recall, the demolition effort had revealed that the sub-floor was in bad shape. Following this discovery, Roger and I had a discussion covering the various options and approaches that could be used to correct the floor. One was to float the entire floor, but that was not feasible due to time and budget constraints. Instead, we had agreed to float the floor only in the locations where we determined it would be necessary. The focus was primarily in the dining room, as the new quarry tile and mud bed below the tile would hide any imperfections in the back-of-house areas. The objective was to address any trouble areas within the dining room or other guest areas. As you now know, certain areas of the dining room were a problem. In some locations, tables and chairs were rocking due to slopes or unevenness in the floor. Unfortunately, the floor float and installation of the carpet in some of the trouble spots had occurred during the time between two of my site visits, meaning that I did not have an opportunity to see the problem until it was too late. When I asked Roger how such a problem could have arisen given our discussion on the topic, he indicated that his understanding was we wanted to float the floor in only one part of the dining room. Bologna! Why would I be more concerned about the guests' experience on one side of the dining room than on the other?

Display Kitchen Disputed Tile Location

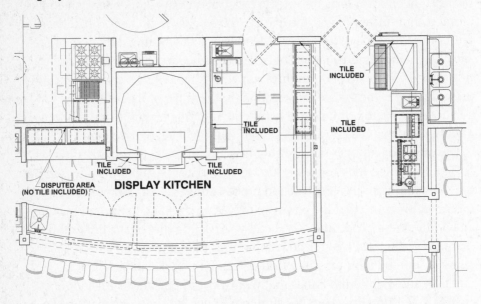

A similar instance occurred with the wall tile in the display kitchen. We had already deleted the wainscot in the dining room and the wall tile in the restrooms, so the wall tile that had been planned in the display kitchen was critical to maintain the casual but sophisticated look and feel that I had been striving to achieve. The display kitchen, as it was labeled and identified on the drawings, included the entire front-of-house cooking and service area. The tile installer started at the service area and began working his way toward the oven. I happened to be on site during this installation process and noticed that the supply of tile seemed quite low in order to cover the full area identified as the display kitchen on the drawings. I pointed this out to the tile installer, only to learn that the area to the left of the oven—between the oven and the bar area—was not going to receive tile. What? Why am I just now learning of this? I picked up the phone and asked Roger how this mistake had happened and what would we do to fix it. There was no mistake, at least in his mind. He claimed that the display kitchen included only the service area and the cold production area, to the right of the oven. It did not include the wall space to the left of the oven. He then went on to tell me that tile for this area to the left of the oven, the disputed area, was not included in the budget that had been provided to date. I was caught off guard. Having reviewed the exact areas that were to be tiled with Roger during our budget reduction exercises, I referred back to my notes and confirmed that I had provided clear direction. The disputed area should most certainly have been included. The tile was not readily available, as there was a lead time of several weeks. Though it was not desirable, we would have to open without tile in the area and then install the tile after we were open for business. The trouble would be finding a time when the tile could be installed without interrupting the foodservice operation and without affecting the guest—that would be difficult. Unexpected problems arise, and I can deal with them fairly well; however, issues like these that were addressed ahead of time but *still* resulted in a problem are the surprises that I find most frustrating. The result is no different than having never identified the potential conflict in the first place.

There were numerous other issues that were similar in nature which arose near the end of the job. In yet another example, for several weeks I had been requesting the millwork shop drawings from Roger in order to review them and provide the millwork shop ample time for production. It was a task that remained on my "hot list" for far too long without being addressed. Week after week, however, the shop drawings were not provided. I am not sure if Roger was focused on other priorities or other jobs, but I knew that this shop drawing review was on the critical path for our timely completion of the build-out in Maitland. I would need to review and approve all of the millwork fabrication drawings before the millwork shop could be released to begin fabrication. Finally, after clearly conveying my frustration on the issue, Roger had the millwork shop drawings delivered to me at the site with a message: "We need these turned around immediately in order to meet our dates." Great! I follow up with no response for weeks, but now I am the one who is going to delay our opening date? I dropped what I was doing, sat down on a stack of tile boxes, laid the plans out on the floor that was full of typical job site debris, and reviewed the plans right then and there. The lack of a timely response by the owner is one factor that often delays the construction team. Well, in this case it was a turnaround of about twenty-five minutes. Roger's inability to provide the millwork shop drawings on time directly impacted the end results of the product. It was this delay that led to the elimination of several coats of sealant on the Hearth top and its delivery while still wet and tacky. The Hearth top was fixed three times, and still was not right. It was a clear result of its premature delivery during the construction process. This delay also resulted in our opening without the wine cabinet doors installed, leaving several thousands of dollars worth of wine exposed and unsecured, not to mention the less-than-sophisticated impression that it left on our early patrons. Some millwork pieces were to have been provided at a later date. They never were. As with the finishing touches from an interior design perspective, here, too, one cannot emphasize this point enough: *Sweat the details!*

Even with all of the construction coordination gaffs that occurred, the most critical issue in the relationship breakdown between Roger and me had to do with the timing of our contract payments. Our contract called for payments to be made by the owner to the general contractor a certain number of days following a specific milestone. For instance, a payment would be due five days after what was termed as "substantial completion." In many instances, where a bank loan is involved, the lending institution will have a strict set of guidelines regarding the releasing of any payments. Only following the provision of an inspection and proper documentation will payments be provided, and they will be representative of the percentage of work that has been completed. In our instance however, due to delays in receiving the loan approval from the bank, we were responsible for policing ourselves. And though one section of our contract stated the timing in which payment was to have been provided, there was another part of the contract that afforded the owner the right to request and confirm proper documentation prior to releasing payment. Due primarily to the compressed construction schedule and extremely aggressive payment schedule, some of the sections of our agreement were in conflict with one another. We had agreed to a cost-plus structure and my right to confirm what our costs actually were before releasing payment. I needed to know what I was buying. Furthermore, my capability to review the invoices was agreed upon with Roger on the front end. The presentation of a consolidated invoice from the general contractor was not enough. Roger's repeated position was that they had met the budget, and, as a result, the money was due according to the contract. Great, but that was not our agreement. In hindsight, it was my mistake to commit to the provision of such payments in a timeline that did not allow for the review of the itemized amounts by category. But the mistake was Roger's as well. Though the payments were due, I decided to hold some money only long enough to conduct the proper evaluation of the supporting documentation for the funds that had been requested. I had a right to know and understand what my costs were, not just to take someone's word for it. Not with this much money at stake. This information was important in the accounting of dollars that had been spent on Maitland, but I also needed the data for the planning of Harbor Commons and future stores. I wanted to be able to analyze how much we had spent and precisely where we had spent our funds in order to make beneficial decisions moving forward. Given all of the last-minute changes resulting from our use of outdated construction documents for the build-out, I needed to know how our money was actually spent. Needless to say, Roger was not at all pleased with my decision. But I had to do what was in our best interest, and I am glad that I did. In my audit of the numbers and documentation submitted to support the costs incurred, I found several discrepancies. As I began to question some of the data, Roger's frustration grew rapidly. He wanted his money, and I wanted my information before I would release the money. This is where it began to get nasty. *Real* nasty.

There were additional factors contributing to the relationship breakdown. Jim had been on site and completely committed to the project from the very beginning all the way through the final inspection. However, based on the compromise that I had made in order to meet the schedule, there was a long list of outstanding items that needed to be completed following the final inspection. Jim had received an offer for a quick job that was scheduled to take about a week. It was a nice paycheck for him, and though I wanted him on site to help finish the loose ends, I had far too much respect for him to request that he pass on such a lucrative opportunity. The job was paying over $10,000 for one week's worth of work. I thanked him profusely for his commitment to our project and our team, and raised no objections to his departure. I was, however, extremely concerned. No one knew the job like Jim did. With no one from the general contractor's firm permanently on site any longer and the building having been turned over to the operations team for training, I was not at all confident that the loose ends would be addressed properly or in a timely fashion. And while Jim had left, my contract was actually with Roger. It would be Roger's responsibility to ensure that the punch list items were addressed. Unfortunately, my fears were confirmed.

With no protagonist on site focused on closing out the job, numerous items began to fall through the cracks. Items on the punch list, originally delayed to expedite our final building inspection and occupancy permit, were not being completed. The wine cabinet doors were *still* not installed. The wood floor at the stage had not yet been installed. The storage closet in the men's room had not been completed. Several problems identified with the plumbing system had not yet been addressed or corrected. Items identified on the change orders (of which there were only three on the entire job) were not being executed. The execution of our punch list items was being regularly ignored. In fact, if you will allow me to jump ahead in the timeline for a brief moment, I can tell you that several of the punch list items were not remedied until more than two months after we opened our doors to the public, which was *three months* after the official date of substantial completion. Jim's absence was readily apparent, as I had feared, and Roger was not making the necessary arrangements to pick up the slack in the wake of his superintendent's departure.

The mutual frustration that Roger and I had with one another continued to grow, because while I was requesting that the outstanding construction items be addressed, I was also awaiting the provision of the required documentation to substantiate the costs that he had listed. I was holding his final payments until such documentation had been provided. We had paid 94 percent of our total contract amount, and I had felt that holding back the final 6 percent was essential to ensure that Roger was motivated to finish the project and address the outstanding issues, especially in light of the lack of follow-through that had resulted after Jim's departure. It should be noted that the contract afforded me the right to retain these funds, based on the incomplete status of the project. And that is when the e-mails began to fly back and forth. The discussions had turned into nothing but arguments, so it seemed that written communication was the only option, not to mention a viable and convenient method for recording the sequence of events. Here is a sample excerpt from one of Roger's e-mails, demonstrating his frustration. Some of the specific data has been modified in order to protect those involved.

E-mail from Roger to Lee:

This is unfortunate. I do not intend to go back and forth again and again on e-mail regarding the closeout of this project any longer. We accomplished your impossible date. We agreed to a contract amount and aggressively protected your budget throughout the project. The construction was a whirlwind effort and the paperwork moved just as fast. We have reviewed the costs together on this project many times. We have provided the backup documentation that you requested. All lien waivers have been accounted for and provided.

I am not going to comment line item by line item on your list below. I will simply remind you that the overall budget was maintained and that it does not matter what category the $150 concrete cost, for example, is in. It is a real cost that has been paid under this budget. When you have met your payment obligations, the subcontractors will be willing to stand behind their warranty obligations, including the floor drain issue. I agreed to help you on your schedule and your budget. I provided the service that was promised. We met our obligations. Your team has not. This is not what I expected given the relationships that exist.

We have received payment on approximately 94% of our contract amount. The HVAC contractor informed us they would be filing a lien on Friday. To avoid this problem, we paid them 100% earlier this week. We have continued to act in good faith to protect our client. The 90 day deadline for the remaining subs to file a lien is approaching. Our lien rights also expire on that date. I request final payment or we will be obligated to protect our lien rights and will advise the subcontractors to do the same.

And, after receiving notification of such a position, here was my response:

E-mail response from Lee to Roger:

It is indeed unfortunate. One issue that continues to be lost in our discussion is the fact that we signed a cost-plus agreement. Thus, we have a right to understand what the costs are. This is why I have been so focused on the costs themselves – it is the nature of the agreement to which we mutually committed. If there was a desire to change the nature of the agreement, we should have discussed that. The end result is a great deal of frustration on both sides due to different expectations. The costs we received, due to understandable changes in "categories," are what we need to verify.

Furthermore, the issue of a delay is concerning as it was over a month ago that we ('Za-Bistro!) requested and held a meeting at your office to try and proactively resolve this matter. We want to get you paid and move on – we just need to understand what it is we are paying for due to the nature of the agreement. We cannot control that it took over a month for you to provide the information requested. You will note that you received a prompt response from me addressing the issues at hand, further demonstrating our desire to resolve this issue.

You are obviously welcome to your opinion on our performance. We proceeded with a great deal of trust during this process. In most cases we were pleased with the performance, in others we were not. Please address the specific issues presented earlier so that we can wrap this up – that is all that is required at this point. In the future, we will not use the same contract structure. Thank you for your assistance.

Despite our ongoing efforts, the situation only escalated from this point. It was time to take a more formal stance. I was forced to draft a letter, in anticipation of potential legal proceedings that might ensue, outlining our position. I want to share with you the content of a letter that I was forced to send to Roger, covering our position as well as several other specific issues that were outstanding at the time. Again, some of the specific data has been modified in order to protect those involved, but otherwise this is the actual letter that was sent.

Formal Letter from 'Za-Bistro! to Roger's Contracting:

It is clear and apparent that your firm is not in compliance with the terms of the agreement between Roger's Contracting and 'Za-Bistro! Restaurant Holdings, Inc. As a result, the information below requires immediate action and resolution.

Additional Information Required

In accordance with section 5.2.1 of the aforementioned agreement, 'Za-Bistro! Restaurant Holdings hereby requires additional information to support the costs submitted by Roger's Contracting. The documentation and expense reports indicating "Home Depot," for example, are insufficient. As per the parameters of the agreement, we are once again requesting the actual receipts to substantiate all costs submitted.

At this time we are formally requesting a comprehensive written breakdown of all items supplied for this project, including both labor and materials. Lump sum amounts by the various contractors are unacceptable. For example, a breakdown of the costs associated with the $4,000 charge for installation of millwork will be required. Due to the cost-plus nature of the agreement, the Owner has the right to review and fully understand the costs associated with the project.

Work Not in Compliance with the Contract Documents

1. *As has been noted previously in writing, numerous components of the plumbing system (i.e., floor drains, trench drain) are not currently functioning as per the design intention and are not in compliance with*

the Contract Documents.

2. *As had been noted previously in writing, certain components of the build-out are not in compliance with the Contract Documents. Specific examples include, but are not limited to, the door swing for the dry storage room and the varying heights in the floor system, which was to be level.*

3. *Certain components of the building system were included on the foodservice drawings, issued as part of the bid set of documents, but were omitted from the designer's documents. Examples include, but are not limited to, condensate drain lines and area floor drain locations. As per section 3.1.3, the Design/Builder shall be responsible to the Owner for acts and omissions by the Design/Builder's hired agents, including the design staff.*

4. *Certain commitments made as part of the value engineering phase were not performed as promised and provided in writing. Examples include, but are not limited to, provision of tile in the entire Display Kitchen, not just the service area.*

5. *Various components of the project, included as part of the base contract, were not provided in a timely manner despite follow-up by the Owner. The delay of these items resulted in an incomplete project, a condition that remained for weeks after the certificate of occupancy was issued. Examples include, but are not limited to, the wood flooring package and wine cabinet doors.*

Summary of Agreement

In accordance with the mutually signed agreement, we are invoking our rights as outlined in the following sections:.

- *The Design/Builder shall be responsible for correcting Work which does not conform to the Contract Documents (3.2.8).*

- *Work not in conformance with the Contract Documents shall be corrected (3.2.9).*

- *Neither progress payment nor partial or full occupancy of the space shall constitute acceptance of the Work by the Owner (5.1.6).*

- *Owner shall have the right to retain reasonable cost to correct or complete incorrect or incomplete Work. Final payment shall be made upon correction of incorrect or incomplete Work (5.1.8).*

- *Payment shall be requested only after Work has been completed and fully performed according to the contract (5.2.2).*

- *The Design/Builder shall promptly correct Work rejected by the Owner or known to be defective or failing to conform to the requirements of the Contract Documents (9.1).*

- *Owner has the right to retain amounts required to correct deficiencies in the Work. If payments due are insufficient to cover the amounts owed to the Owner, the Design/Builder shall pay the difference to the Owner (9.5).*

Action

As per the summary of the agreement, 'Za-Bistro! Restaurant Holdings, Inc. is formally repeating the initial request that the Design/Builder correct all work that is not in compliance with the Contract Documents, including work that was omitted by the Design/Builder's Architect. Furthermore, 'Za-Bistro! Restaurant Holdings, Inc. formally requests that Roger's Contracting provide all necessary detailed documentation to substantiate the costs submitted.

Based on your recent e-mail, it is the understanding of 'Za-Bistro! Restaurant Holdings, Inc. that Roger's Contracting intends to file a lien against the Work performed in Maitland. It is further noted in the same e-mail that Roger's Contracting intends to advise several of its subcontractors to file liens against the aforementioned project as well. It should be noted that the referenced liens are a result of the incomplete Work by the Design/Builder, Roger's Contracting.

Based on the notification received by Roger's Contracting, 'Za-Bistro! Restaurant Holdings, Inc. intends to obtain a bond for the liens that will be filed. We hereby formally request a certified Contractor's Final Affidavit from your firm. Furthermore, it should be noted that in accordance with section 11.4.1 of the agreement, any and all costs associated with this effort and incurred by 'Za-Bistro! Restaurant Holdings, Inc. will be added to a change order and listed as a component of the monies owed, if any, to the Owner by the Design/Builder.

We would hope that the items identified in this letter and previously discussed with Roger's Contracting can be resolved in a mutually satisfactory manner. We remain ready, willing, and able to discuss these matters with you, in hopes of reaching a mutually beneficial conclusion and avoiding legal recourse if at all possible. It should be noted, however, that time is of the essence. 'Za-Bistro! Restaurant Holdings, Inc. is awaiting a response from your firm, which should be provided within 7 days from today's date.

Sincerely,
Lee Simon

Now, there is a subject matter that was referenced in both the e-mails and letter included above that I feel obligated to address, as it was one of the most important lessons that I learned during the course of the construction effort. It is the subject of liens and lien waivers. Before I do so, however, I must caution you that the lien laws are rather complex and vary from state to state. My experience is based on the laws that were in effect in Florida during our construction effort. Unfortunately, the subject matter is one that is rarely presented to restaurant owners and can result in significant potential risk if not handled properly. As you can see by the correspondence between Roger and me, in our instance a "worst-case" scenario came close to presenting itself. Shortly after the commencement of the construction effort, I was bombarded by a series of letters from nearly every subcontractor that had been hired to work on the construction project in Maitland. These documents were all of a similar format, with the same references to state law, and they all bore the title "Notice to Owner." These were notices, required by the state to be filed and issued to the owner on a project, in order for the general contractor and subcontractor(s) to protect their right to file a lien on the project. If a notice to owner is not filed, the contractors waive their rights to file a lien. The next logical question, of course, is what is a lien? And, more importantly, what happens if a lien is filed?

The nature of the construction effort is such that the work is typically completed by a contractor before payment is received. Therefore, contractors are afforded the legal right to file a lien on a job in the event that payment is not received following the rendering of services that were deemed acceptable, compliant with local codes, and in accordance with the contract documents. It is a contractor's form of recourse. Please realize that I am attempting to summarize a complex legal issue in a sentence or two for the purpose of sharing a valuable lesson. Do not rely solely on this information for legal advice.

Lien waivers are a serious issue and should not be taken lightly. A lien, when filed by a contractor on a project, is recorded and shared publicly. An outstanding lien can prevent the owner from conducting certain activities such as selling the property (if it is owned), closing on a loan, and other essential business transactions that are commonly associated with the development of a restaurant, or of any other building type for that matter.

During the construction process, contract arrangements typically require progress payments. In exchange for these progress payments, contractors will issue partial lien waivers — surrendering their right to file a lien for that portion of the job — that match the percentage of payment being provided and work that has been completed. For instance, the contract may call for a 30 percent progress payment. At that time, the owner will provide a payment to the general contractor for 30 percent of the total construction cost, which will then be distributed to the subcontractors. In return, the subcontractors will provide partial lien waivers, waiving their right to lien the 30 percent of the job for which compensation has been provided. When a bank is involved as a provider of a loan to the owner, they will often have a representative review the actual construction progress, on site, to ensure that the percentage being paid represents the percentage of completion. This is important from the lending institution's perspective, as the project is truly their investment as well. In fact, in the case of default on a loan by the borrower, the lender will assume ownership of the project, and thus has a vested interest in the quality and accuracy of the construction effort. Most of the time, the exchange of partial lien waivers for partial payment is rather simple and routine. In other instances, where problems have arisen, the process can become far more complicated, sometimes requiring a physical exchange due to a lack of trust by one or both sides. This physical exchange requires the owner and contractor to simultaneously swap payment for lien waivers.

There is one more critical aspect of lien waivers that directly impacts the way they are managed. Each and every "Notice to Owner" letter clearly states that although payment may be made in full to the general contractor, the *owner* is still responsible for ensuring that the subcontractors are paid as well. In other words, if an owner were to pay the full amount due on the project to the general contractor and then the general contractor takes the money and runs off to a remote Caribbean island, the owner will *still* be responsible for ensuring full payment to all of the subcontractors. This stipulation requires that the *owner* carefully review all documentation to ensure that the general contractor has made proper payments to the subcontractors and that, in return, they have waived their rights to lien the job. The lien waiver should be consistent with the percentage of payment that has been issued, through the provision of lien waiver documents. Rest assured that this condition led me to scrutinize every document that had been provided by Roger to ensure that proper payment had been made. And in my review of the supporting cost data that was eventually provided, I had also discovered discrepancies between some of the waived amounts in certain categories of the reconciliation for our progress payments. More specifically, some of the waived figures were inconsistent as documented in the different progress payments, which raised a red flag. I also found that some of the subcontractors had not received progress payments equal to the percentage of progress payments that we had made to our general contractor. As I began to inquire about the specifics of these instances, what was an already tenuous relationship at best between Roger and me turned belligerent. It was not what I had hoped for, but in accordance with the notices that I had received and the lien laws of the state of Florida, I had an obligation as the owner to protect my interests, as well as the interests of my partners and our company to ensure that payment had been made to the subcontractors. And that is exactly what I did. I held the final payment until I received all of the necessary final full and unconditional lien waivers. It was a shame that such a diligent effort had to end so poorly.

Eventually, I was forced to put the final payment amount in an escrow account, held with our lawyer. This payment was only to be released upon the completion of certain outstanding issues on the punch list and following the provision of the necessary lien waiver documentation. This process became more time consuming, more difficult, and more expensive than it needed to be. However, our relationship had deteriorated to a point where such actions were required. There was a total breakdown of trust on both sides. In the end, most of the outstanding construction issues were resolved, the proper final lien waivers were provided, and the escrow funds were released. It was, to say the least, an unfortunate ending to a long, otherwise-successful construction process. Looking back, I realized that the amount of coordination and teamwork that was required to take us from the start of demolition to a temporary certificate of occupancy in just 48 days made this turn of events personally disappointing. But, as always, I had a new set of pressing issues to focus on as we were preparing for our final health inspection, training, and opening 'Za-Bistro! for business.

14

Welcome to 'Za-Bistro!...
How Many in Your Party?

T he restaurant was abuzz with activity, although the activities were
drastically different from those a just few days earlier. I was absolutely
bewildered at the pace of progress in the days preceding our first all-
staff meeting. Within a 48-hour period, the interior painting was finished,
the carpet and tile installation completed, the tables and chairs set, the
computer systems installed, the kitchen equipment fired up—it was
beginning to look and feel like a real restaurant. But numerous reminders
remained of the construction site that had recently occupied this same
space. Several piles of rolled-up construction plans, each with seemingly
infinite creases, tears, and scribbled details from use throughout the
course of construction, still remained throughout both the front-of-house
and back-of-house areas. Some of the contractors' toolboxes remained on
site. Construction debris was still evident throughout the restaurant, as
the contractors had not yet fully completed their work. Drywall, scrap
electrical wires, razor blades, painting supplies, and other such materials
were scattered randomly on the floors and counters. But this space was
about to undergo a dramatic shift, even if only in its perception, as the
physical changes from this point on would be rather minor in light of the
overall construction effort that had just taken place. I recall one particular

instance that truly captured the transition of the space from a job site into a restaurant. The morning of our first staff meeting, the tile installer showed up to complete the front façade on the oven (remember the tile fiasco?). He arrived about one hour prior to the start of the meeting and set up his tools so as not to disturb the presentation and question-and-answer session. After setting up his tools outside, where noise from the tile saw would not be as disruptive, he ventured back inside to take a few measurements. After reaching for his tape measure, he reached for a cigarette and his lighter. But before he could light the cigarette, I informed him that smoking was no longer allowed in the restaurant, and I would appreciate it if he would relay the message to his fellow contractors. That was it, the line in the sand. From that point on, the space was treated like a restaurant rather than a job site. The once-bustling crew of contractors, sporting torn jeans and foul language, had been replaced by our kitchen, service, and management staff, all of whom were eager and excited to launch this new restaurant concept, 'Za-Bistro! They were the team that would help make our restaurant dream come true.

By construction standards, it seemed as though the restaurant was near completion. By the standards that would be used by our staff and patrons, however, the place was a wreck. The night before the first all-staff meeting, I stayed well into the evening hours to help clean up. I began wiping down the counters, putting away tools, and throwing out trash that remained throughout the job site. One of the managers showed up to help around 9:00 p.m. or so. The following morning, the staff started to trickle in one by one. We had set up theater-style seating in the middle of the restaurant, with all chairs facing a screen where a PowerPoint presentation would be displayed. Nearly 60 people were scheduled to show up for this first meeting; a meeting where we would begin the process of handing over the restaurant to the operations team. Chris started the presentation, welcoming the newly formed operations team to *their* restaurant. He stated that the ownership team had taken the first step to bring 'Za-Bistro! from concept to reality, but it would be the hosts, servers, cooks, dishwashers, and managers who would be responsible for taking the next step. Each member of the ownership team took a moment to speak with the new 'Za-Bistro! employees, explaining the journey we had taken in order to arrive at the point where they were joining the effort—just before we were ready to open the doors. We explained everything from the origin of the name to the philosophy behind the menu and the food preparations. We discussed the design of the restaurant. We discussed elements of the business plan and growth models presented to lenders and potential investors. We wanted the employees to understand where we had come from, where we were, and where we were going. As an ownership team, we felt that a thorough understanding of these factors by the entire staff was essential to our success. It was a rather emotional moment. So much work and effort had gone into this project, and now it was time to pass the torch to the operations team.

With the operations team now controlling the restaurant, the construction effort quickly took a backseat to the training and preparations that were underway in advance of opening for business. Whereas the contractors formerly had free reign over the space, they were suddenly required to complete any outstanding work around the ongoing training that was taking place, almost around the clock. For this reason I had tried to push for completion of as many construction issues as possible prior to the beginning of the training period, but as you are aware, it did not necessarily work out that way. The operations team was now on site every day and, by default, became involved in the completion of the construction punch list items. My wife and I were just days away from the birth of our daughter, so I was much more reluctant to make the nearly two-hour drive as regularly as I had over the past several months. As a result, I had to rely much more on the managers as my eyes and ears on site. Though this was certainly helpful most of the time, it also added another level of complexity, as there were an additional four to six people involved, and maintaining control of both the logistics and finances became a far greater challenge. Jim was still off site. We had lost our protagonist in the field, and the completion of seemingly simple tasks became far more difficult.

Throughout most of the project, I was solely responsible for coordination and costs. Given the way the situation had evolved, with the operations team on site and my constraints just before opening the restaurant, I had lost much of that control by the end. Unfamiliar with the level of effort required to maintain our budget, and focused more on the needs of their employees, the operations team quickly began suggesting a multitude of modifications and additions to the building, each of which cost money to complete. Some of the suggestions were valid and well received. For instance, the tile had been deleted throughout the restrooms, but the suggestion was made to add tile back around the men's urinal for ease of cleaning and sanitation. I felt this was an extremely logical modification, and approved it with a cost of just under $200. Some of the other changes, however, were more extreme. The managers began coordinating directly with the millwork contractor for the cabinets that were to be installed in the manager's office. The configuration they were requesting, in my opinion, was a bit more elaborate than what was actually required. Both managers had backgrounds with large restaurant or hotel corporations, and I am not sure that they fully understood the concept of having to watch every penny. By the time the millwork cabinets were installed, the bill came to just over $1,000, not including the actual desk that had already been installed. Having learned of the total cost only after the cabinets were installed, and in spite of the direction I had given to keep all costs to a minimum and to run them by me prior to approval, there was little I could do. It was extremely frustrating given the hours I spent trying to control every penny on the project. There were other similar suggestions and modifications, but I was able to stop some of them before implementation. For example, before we ever served our first meal, one of the managers was convinced that we needed a fourth point-of-sale station for the servers. With two terminals in the dining room—one at each end—and one in the bar, the addition of a fourth terminal seemed unnecessary to me for a 124-seat restaurant. Our point-of-sale equipment provider agreed. Based on this confirmation, we convinced our manager to use the equipment we had already installed for a while before making such a drastic decision, which would cost us a great deal of money. It was not just the additional equipment that would result in unnecessary expenses, but the installation of that equipment as well. We did not have any cabling run to the newly proposed additional point-of-sale location, and tearing up the freshly painted walls to run the wiring was not at all desirable.

Given the constant barrage of recommendations I received as the coordinator of the design and construction efforts, allow me to share a lesson that I learned the hard way. When the operations team takes over the space, numerous opportunities will be identified for improvements or changes to the facility, especially in the case of a new restaurant concept. I would suggest that anyone responsible for approving such suggestions first record all ideas along with an associated cost. The next step would be to wait at least 30 days after the doors are opened so that actual operational experience can be used to prioritize the items on the list. Critical items, however, should of course be addressed immediately. As a final step, available funds should be allocated to the list of prioritized modifications to determine which ones will be approved and implemented. This will ensure that the money spent in the wake of the restaurant's opening will provide the best value and offer the greatest improvement of the facility in order to better support the restaurant's operation. Implementing such an approach will also prevent the spending of precious funds on unnecessary items or on modifications that will not significantly impact the operation, at least in the short term. It was a mistake not to establish strict ground rules.

With ongoing training and punch list items being addressed in the background, there were still tasks with which I had to contend, such as the final health inspection. Without it, we would not be able to serve any food for the upcoming friends-and-family night, and our opening would have been delayed. When the health department approved our construction drawings, a pre-requisite for the building permit, our drawings were returned along with a thick packet of forms and instructions. This packet detailed everything that must be accomplished before calling for our final health inspection, from having the "employees must wash hands" sign in the restroom to ensuring that soap and towel dispensers were at each hand sink. The instructions stated that we must have all of our equipment up and running at the proper temperatures. All refrigerators had to be holding temperatures below 40 degrees Fahrenheit, with built-in thermostats or thermometers inside the boxes to verify the refrigerators' performance. Some of the requirements presented a bit of a challenge due to the uniqueness of our concept. For instance, one checklist stated an inspector would be checking to ensure that a rendering tank, which is typically used for storing spent oil from deep-fat fryers, was located on site. But we did not have a fryer. Was it still required? We could not get a straight answer, so we took a risk in calling for the inspection without having the rendering tank on site. I say that this was a risk, as the scheduling was still critical. Though the main portion of the construction effort had been completed, and a certificate of occupancy had been issued, the final health inspection was on the critical path if we were to open on time. Furthermore, we were at the mercy of the inspector's schedule and could not obtain a confirmation as to when the inspection could be completed. Only when I actually called for the inspection did I learned why this was the case.

Fully aware that health department officials do not like conducting inspections more than once, the management team and I were meticulous, ensuring that all of the requirements for the inspection had been addressed. We reviewed the entire set of instructions from the health department several times to confirm we were in full compliance. Only after we were ready did I call in for the inspection. That was when I learned of the standard practice associated with opening health inspections within the state of Florida at the time—and it was ridiculous. The procedure required that the inspection request be called in to the main state health department office in Tallahassee. Following the call request, DBPR then used regular mail—*snail* mail—to forward the inspection request to the local inspector. The restaurateur must then wait until the mailed request arrives and the local inspector contacts the restaurant owner to schedule the inspection. This entire process can take more than a week. How crazy is that? Realize that by the time an inspection can be called in to the state's agency, the staff has been hired, training is ongoing, advertising may have commenced, and a host of other commitments may already be in place. There are real costs being incurred by the restaurant owner, and no revenue is coming in to offset the cash burn. An extra five to seven days at that point is a big deal. With modern-day access to instant information, I am not sure why the state would mandate an unnecessary delay at such a critical time. According to the letter of the law, no food is permitted in the restaurant prior to the inspection—even for training. Great! So I have cooks who have left their previous jobs and are now on my payroll, but they can't even train for their new jobs. Where is the sense in that? Requirements such as these lead to animosity between industry and certain government agencies. Though it took longer than anticipated, the inspector eventually arrived and was quite pleasant on the first visit. We passed the inspection with flying colors. We were ready. Bring on the customers—and their revenue. We needed it!

Before we opened our doors to paying customers, we had scheduled our friends-and-family evening. Friends and family of the ownership team, as well as some local officials and key personalities, were invited for a dining experience. We featured an abbreviated menu so that the servers and cooks would be able to focus on proper execution. Two friends-and-family nights were planned, and then we would open our doors for business —to paying customers. The opening of almost any restaurant is rough. Even the national chains encounter bumps in the road, despite their extensive past experience and team of trainers.

I vividly recall the feeling that I had the first time I walked into the restaurant as a customer. It was a bit surreal. My wife, just two weeks from her scheduled delivery date and *extremely* pregnant, made the trip with me, as did our son. Entering the restaurant as a customer was an experience that I wanted to enjoy and savor. I had dreamt of that moment for a long time. Walking in that first night, I scanned the dining room to see who was there. At one of the first tables, near the entrance, was my friend Marc, whom I have known since the age of five. Our next-door neighbors and some other friends had also made the trip from Tampa. My aunt and uncle were there too, driving in from the center of the state. The restaurant was abuzz with activity. Smiles on servers' faces. The clinking of glasses at the service station. The sound of tickets printing on the cooking line. The barking out of orders to the line cooks. The scraping sound that came from moving dishes around in the oven. The hum of conversation throughout the dining room. It was a real restaurant—finally! Service the first night was remarkably prompt. I was quite surprised. The unfortunate server assigned to my table was extremely nervous, as he remembered me as one of the owners from the presentation just a few days earlier at the first all-staff meeting. Had he known me, he would have realized that I am the understanding type, aware that he was serving his very first meal in a brand new restaurant. I was there to enjoy my first dining experience in the restaurant I had helped to create.

That first night, everyone was raving about the food. I only hoped that they were being honest, but experience since that first night tells me they were. The second night, which I had hoped would be even better than the first, was not. In the middle of the shift, the point-of-sale computer system crashed and all of the orders that had been entered were lost. It was an unwelcome complication for a staff that was already confused and trying to figure out what to do, but it was a real-world scenario that could happen again, and the experience was worthwhile. There were plenty of kinks that needed to be worked out, but that was to be expected. The bottom line: We were serving food!

Following the second friends-and-family night, the restaurant opened as planned. It was a soft opening, with little advertising and a mere "Now Open" banner hanging in the front window. Think of it as an extended friends-and-family-style training environment, but with paying customers and a full menu. It was not until nearly three weeks after the official opening that we held our grand-opening party. That day and that evening, 'Za-Bistro! hosted an open house, cocktail-style event. Most of the local business and community leaders were in attendance, all welcoming us to the neighborhood. It was at this event that Chris presented a plaque to each of the owners. He had taken the first ten dollar bill that we received at the restaurant and broken it into singles. Each owner received a plaque that read "The First Dollar." It had the 'Za-Bistro! logo at the top, the city and state, the date of the official opening, our names, and one of the first dollar bills. Apparently, there was some fine print that came with that plaque that I did not see at first glance. Okay, it wasn't actually printed there, but it should have been: "In Case of Emergency—Break Glass!" But more on that a little later. I received my plaque a few weeks later, as I did not attend the grand opening; I was at home with my wife, my son, and newborn daughter.

15

Hang-Ups at Harbor Commons

While construction was in full swing in Maitland, the design effort had already begun for our second site in Harbor Commons; the two projects were overlapping. We were expecting delivery of our second location within a month after the scheduled opening of our first store in Maitland. This was, after all, the main reason that Maitland was subject to such an aggressive schedule. The Harbor Commons oven had already been delivered and was sitting on site while the landlord's contractor finished the building shell around this very expensive piece of equipment—the heart of our operation. By the time Maitland opened for business, the design documents for Harbor Commons were nearly finished.

As you may recall, our space in Harbor Commons was situated at the main intersection of the village center, a prime location in the center of the multi-use complex. Many of the interior design features in Harbor Commons were the same as or similar to those in Maitland. It was the same restaurant concept. It was not, however, the same architect. I was less than pleased with the performance of the first architect, and I was not about to go through another construction process with an inaccurate set of documents. I reached out to a colleague from an Orlando-based design firm with significant experience in hospitality and retail design. It was a fairly large firm — well over 100 employees — with architecture, interior design, and engineering all under one roof. I explained where we were with regard to our efforts in both Harbor Commons and Maitland. At the time I began discussions with our new architecture firm, the restaurant in Maitland was still under construction. I also described the bad taste I had from the design effort in Maitland, and clearly expressed my desire to avoid such a fiasco again. After a brief discussion and a clear definition of the scope and the fee on the front end (lesson learned), we were able to reach an agreement and begin the design effort for Harbor Commons.

As in the case of the Maitland location, I approached the architect with a well-developed floor plan and some preliminary elevations. Regarding the actual design of the new restaurant, many of the features resembled those from Maitland. The oven was located in the center of the restaurant, in full view. The Hearth, the Snug, the location of point-of-sale systems in the dining room, the flow of people and product, the configuration and style of seating, the color palate, and other critical design elements were all similar to the selections that had been made in Maitland. Fortunately, however, our experience in Maitland led to the incorporation of several improvements in Harbor Commons. Maitland, as you may recall, was only supposed to be roughly 80 to 85 percent of what the ultimate concept would include. The design and construction process, combined with some limited operational experience under our belts, allowed for minor improvements in the second store. For instance, the Snug was more centralized and closer to the entrance, encouraging mingling among our guests and offering a convenient space for those waiting for take-out orders. The Snug was also designed with an opening onto the main access. This allowed the bartender direct access to the pick-up counter to better handle take-out orders, and it also allowed for servers to get their own beer and wine during off-peak periods. The latter would eliminate the need for a full-time bartender and improve the level of service while simultaneously having a positive impact on labor costs. Another change was the elimination of our steamer, which would be replaced by a combination oven-steamer. This combi-oven, as they are commonly called, would offer additional menu versatility and allow for some freshly made baked goods to be produced on site. The interior design package was enhanced with the re-introduction of the fire-box detail and several other intriguing design features throughout the restaurant. Given the nearly 21-foot clearance from slab to slab, a storage

Harbor Commons Floor Plan

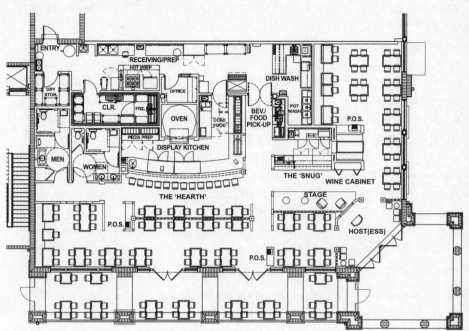

space was located on top of the walk-in cooler/freezer, with access provided via a permanent ship's ladder. Other such minor adjustments were included throughout the restaurant, partly based on our experience and partly due to the fact that the space was configured with different door, window, and column locations—all *design drivers.*

Despite all of the similarities, however, there were two distinctively different factors in the planning and coordination of the Harbor Commons space that significantly influenced our efforts. First, the building shell was not yet completed—it was new construction—whereas the space in Maitland had already existed. Second, the Harbor Commons space was on the first floor of a three-story building in the middle of the village center, with two floors of residences above. These two factors, as you will see, greatly impacted our design and planning decisions for the Harbor Commons restaurant. Also influencing the planning effort was the fact that this restaurant was located in a building that was much larger and more complex than the building in Maitland. The physical configuration—retail on the first floor and residences on the floors above—resulted in the integration of numerous residential and commercial building systems within a tight, confined space. Further complicating the effort were the strict design guidelines developed and enforced by Harbor Commons' primary development company, charged with overseeing all exterior neighborhood design features. This was a separate development company from the one developing the village center, as the village center development rights had been sold to our landlord. Despite the lack of direct ownership, the parent development company was quite interested in ensuring that strict design standards were followed *within* the village center. Regulations included everything from the types of signage to approvals of any and all colors or materials that could be seen by the public, even within the leased space. There was an incredible focus on detail throughout the development, which was beneficial in many respects but also made our planning more complex. In several instances, Harbor Commons' parent development company required separate approvals, even before plans were submitted to the city. This added an additional level of complexity, not to mention additional time required.

I am, however, a rather detail-oriented person, so I kicked it into high gear and began pouring over the plans for the building's shell, keeping in mind our design criteria for the interior build-out of the space. The effort was worthwhile, as I found numerous issues that required attention and coordination with our landlord. In one instance, the original plans called for two sets of double doors (four doors in total) at the main entrance. Not only was this unnecessary, but the proposed design prohibited our ability to efficiently use the space within the restaurant's vestibule. We asked the developer to modify the detail, reducing the doors to one set of double doors. In yet another instance, I attempted to devise a detailed coordination effort between the landlord's work and our tenant's work, as there was significant overlap. The lease required the landlord to provide the sanitary stub-outs for the restrooms. It became imperative for me to coordinate the location of the restroom stub-outs with our drawings to ensure that the work which was to be completed by the landlord would not have to be torn out and reworked by our contractor, a waste of both time and money for all involved. Similarly, the lease required the landlord to provide the concrete slab, which was not yet installed. In light of this requirement, I attempted to coordinate our sequence and schedule of construction with the landlord so that we would be allowed to complete our under-slab rough-in work prior to the pouring of the slab. Again, this was intended to save time and money. I did have the option of asking the landlord for a credit for the concrete slab, but, at the time, concrete was in short supply and increasing in price, so I opted to leave that scope of work with the landlord. The lease called for provision of the main HVAC system by the landlord, with final ductwork distribution by the tenant. It was important to coordinate the location of the HVAC registers with our final floor plan so that the landlord's contractor could install the system in compliance with our design.

Looking at the development effort in Harbor Commons from a global perspective, these were relatively minor issues. Of far greater concern was the coordination for the remote refrigeration lines (required for the walk-in cooler/freezer and ice machine) and for the exhaust hood systems, both for the cooking equipment and for the dish machine. Detailed investigation of the plans revealed that only a 3- by 3-foot chase had been provided by the original architects from our space to the roof. This chase — grossly undersized, given the complexity of the building — was intended for support of not only our foodservice equipment, but also the HVAC equipment needed to provide heating and cooling for our space. The exhaust hood systems alone would require five total duct runs, some as large as 8 by 24 inches. This did not even include the remote refrigeration lines for the walk-in and ice machine, or the connections for the HVAC system. It was a real problem. The chase was not undersized because of our unusually significant infrastructure requirements. On the contrary, our infrastructure was less than a typical restaurant of a comparable size. Rather, it was a significant oversight by the building's original architect.

Decisions were made quickly to change the walk-ins and ice machine to internally located and self-contained compressors, respectively. Though the configuration would introduce more heat into the occupied space and affect the HVAC load, it would reduce the need for remote refrigeration systems. A remote system would require running refrigeration supply and return lines vertically three stories to the roof, and then horizontally another fifty feet or so to a dedicated location. Could this be accomplished? Certainly. The more complex the refrigeration system is, however, the less reliable it will be in the long run and the costlier the maintenance of the system will be over time. Besides, we really did not have much of an option given that the chase would not be enlarged.

The solution for the exhaust hood was not as simple. It required some creative engineering, including the use of special in-line fans (located in the middle of the exhaust duct run, as opposed to the end) and pulling make-up air from the front of the building (as opposed to locating the make-up air fan on the roof), hidden by specialty architectural louvers, For clarification, make-up air is the air returned to the restaurant space to compensate—or make up—for the air that has been removed by the exhaust hood system. If the make-up air was not provided, the exhaust system would create a vacuum and disrupt the balance of air in the space. All of these changes and special configurations were rapidly increasing our construction costs in Harbor Commons, even though the square footage and seating capacity were nearly identical to Maitland.

The potential cost impact required intricate cooperation between our team and the landlord. Unfortunately, this coordination was one of our greatest challenges. Despite the complexity of this planning effort and the need for accurate, detailed information, we were unable to obtain timely or reliable responses from the person who was designated as our key contact from the landlord's team. It was quite frustrating. In one instance, I waited several months—*several months*—for a response. That is simply unreasonable. I was forced to proceed with our design effort, even though several critical pieces of data were still outstanding. I received letters indicating that the turnover of the space to all tenants by the landlord was drawing closer. At the same time, I could not obtain answers to my questions, which were essential to the design and planning effort. As time revealed, the landlord was extremely disorganized with regard to their development efforts. I was concerned that their lack of organization had the potential to directly impact our cost for the development of the Harbor Commons project, and subsequently our company's financial position. I was not about to sit idly by and allow my company to absorb such costs unnecessarily.

As my requests for information grew more frequent and more specific, the landlord developed a dislike for my thoroughness, indicating at one point that he found me more difficult to deal with than some of the national chains in the center. To be honest, I took that as a compliment; it confirmed that I was doing my homework. The landlord frequently questioned why I was the only tenant in the entire village center who was so demanding and causing so many problems. I wasn't causing problems. Rather, I was focused on finding and *solving* the problems before they arose. Had the landlord taken the time to truly understand my motivation, he would have realized that many of the problems I was discovering would impact other tenants, not just 'Za-Bistro! It was an opportunity for them to proactively address similar problems before they were revealed throughout the village center. But the landlord did not seize the opportunity; instead, he viewed me as nothing more than a pain in the backside. It was an opportunity lost, as many of the other tenants eventually had to contend with the same issues I had discovered months earlier. In those instances, however, the tenants incurred additional charges related to the build-out of their spaces, as the problems first surfaced during their construction efforts. This further proves that a landlord's actions can significantly impact the financial well-being of a tenant.

Similar to our development in Maitland, our design efforts in Harbor Commons revealed some unexpected surprises as well. Inexperienced when we signed the lease in Harbor Commons, we committed to an HVAC load per square foot that was far below what we would eventually require. This meant that it was our responsibility to provide the additional HVAC capacity necessary to regulate the temperature within the space. Though this alone would have been enough of an additional burden, the issue became even more complex when we learned that the building's original architects had provided neither the physical footprint nor structural support for the additional rooftop unit that would be required. As a result, I had to independently hire a structural engineer and coordinate supplemental support within the roof's structure for the additional rooftop unit. Time was of the essence; it was important to install the required additional structure *before* the roof construction was completed. Otherwise, we (meaning 'Za-Bistro!) would be forced to penetrate the landlord's newly installed roof membrane, set the new rooftop unit stand, and reseal the roof. This roof work would force us to assume significant additional expense and partial responsibility for the integrity of the new roof, neither of which were desirable. In another example, I was summoned to the site by the architect following the installation of the electrical panel. The main electrical panel had been installed in a location that was in direct conflict with our design, despite the fact that we had submitted our floor plan to the landlord ahead of time—it was in the middle of one of the restrooms. In another attempt to save costs, I reached out to the landlord's contractor and tried to coordinate the relocation before the actual wires were pulled. Unlike our experience with an existing building, in the case of a new building, we had an opportunity to influence the construction effort to better meet our specific needs. And that is exactly what I tried to do, whenever the opportunity presented itself.

Construction progress on the site was well behind schedule, and activity in the field showed no signs of a more aggressive effort to complete the construction project and turn the space over to the tenants. We received notification from the landlord indicating that there would be

an additional delay of four weeks. This was followed by another notice of a two-week delay. And then another, this time a six-week delay. A pattern was developing. Nearly three months after the scheduled delivery date, while I was on site for some coordination, I counted five framers in the entire building complex at one time. Five!

Keep in mind that this was a three-story building stretching nearly a full city block. We averaged 12 to 14 people on the job site at one time in Maitland, and that was a single restaurant. This was a very complex project running months behind schedule. At the pace of progress to date, the completion and formal turnover of the space still appeared to be months away. This is not to say that the project had to be delayed that long. In all reality, the project was not that far from completion. It was a matter of the labor — or lack thereof — that was committed to the project. There were also some issues with the building department that caused delays, but the lack of manpower on the job site really seemed to be the dominant cause. Every time my partners inquired about progress on the site in Harbor Commons, I struggled to provide them with an accurate answer. Could they be finished in two weeks as they have said ? Well, they *could*. Was it likely, given their limited commitment of labor to the project? No, not really. It was also evident that the lack of coordination and attention to detail was taking its toll on the project. On one visit, I discovered that while the chase from our leased space to the roof had been properly framed from the first floor through the second floor, there was a problem on the third floor — no chase. The construction team had neglected to frame out the chase to the roof. That is a significant error. During another visit, I discovered an apartment space on the second floor with no door. I looked at the plans to try to figure out what the architect's intentions were, only to find that the contractor had completely missed a door that was supposed to have been included. These mistakes were eventually corrected, but the resulting costs and delays were the clear result of the lack of coordination by the village center's development team.

I would also like to point out the costs we incurred during this delay. The oven was on site. Given the value and importance of this piece of equipment, we were forced to take out a separate insurance policy covering the oven during the delay. The money I had saved by shipping both ovens together — and then some — soon evaporated in the form of a monthly premium. Also, we had hired an additional manager in Maitland, with the idea that the extra assistance would be beneficial during the opening of that store, and then the second manager would move to the Harbor Commons location when it was ready. However, the ongoing delays kept the manager in Maitland longer than anticipated, resulting in additional, unforeseen labor expenses that we could not recover. And with no accurate estimate of when the space would be turned over for our build-out, the cost of our additional manager was a concern. The design and planning of the Harbor Commons store had been completed — those costs had been incurred. The plans were in with the city for permit — more costs. Altogether, the delays were resulting in significant additional expenses.

I had been meeting with the landlord and his contractor throughout the construction process, but couldn't get accurate answers on issues ranging from construction coordination to delivery dates. Though this was very frustrating, we did manage to use our position to negotiate with the landlord. After all — everything is negotiable, right? In one meeting in particular, we were able to make up some lost ground with the landlord. Among other concessions, we convinced one of the principals within the landlord's organization to issue a credit for the air handlers and ductwork, allowing us to purchase a single HVAC system rather than install a secondary system that would have to work in tandem with the one defined in the lease and provided by the landlord. We convinced him to absorb the cost for the additional structural support that would be required for our new rooftop unit so that the roof membrane would remain intact following the unit's installation. The landlord agreed to move the main electrical panel, at his own expense, to comply with our design and to provide us with a credit for the sanitary stub-outs and fire system sprinkler heads. The landlord made this series of gestures to compensate for some of the costs we had incurred as a result of the delays. These concessions, however, were not significant enough to completely offset the dollars we had lost to that point. And once again, at the end of this meeting, we attempted to get the landlord to commit to a firm turnover date. The date, four months after the scheduled turnover of the space to 'Za-Bistro!, was set — and missed yet again. One of our biggest mistakes with regard to the lease was the lack of a defined delivery date. Without any specific time frame in which the landlord was obligated to turn over the space, the delay could have gone on indefinitely without any adverse affect on the landlord.

With the continued delays at Harbor Commons and one blown date after another, we finally found it necessary to involve our legal counsel. By this time, our sunk costs had reached close to six figures and were significantly hampering our financial well-being. It was not only the delays in completing our space that were of concern, but also the delays in the entire village center. Our original expectation was that we would move into a finished multi-use development. Had we opened as originally scheduled, we would have been opening in the middle of a construction site. Personally, I was also concerned that the landlord's repeated lack of organization or concern for the tenants would result in a focus on the short term as opposed to the long term. In essence, I had a fear that the landlord would try to turnover tenant spaces just as soon as they were ready in order to generate rent — his revenue stream — regardless of whether or not the adjacent spaces were ready to open or all of the landlord's work was complete, as required by the terms of the lease. I had visions of stores opening for business amid cranes, dump trucks, and an entire crew of construction workers, all scaring off potential customers. Opening a new retail business, whether a restaurant or not, is difficult enough without the added pressure of contending with a development that is not ready to welcome paying customers.

I had watched a similar event unfold within a retail development in Tampa. This prominent development on the west coast of Florida had opened up at roughly 50 percent occupancy. As crowds of people ventured to check out the new development, the general consensus was that it was not yet finished and they would come back in a few months when the development was completed. A few months turned to six months for many and the first wave of stores struggled due to lower-than-expected volume and revenue. Some of them were unable to survive the cash crunch and slow business, eventually closing their doors within the first year. By that time, the second wave of tenants had opened, but by then there were several vacancies left by the closed stores or spaces that still had not been leased. Those returning to the development after a long hiatus left again with the same conclusion—the development was still not complete. I was afraid I might be watching the same scenario unfold with the Harbor Commons site—only this time, I was personally involved. We were so concerned about this issue that we arranged for a meeting with representatives from Harbor Commons's parent development company to address our misgivings directly. We figured it was in their best interest to assist us, as the village center was one of the major factors driving home sales within the development, and home sales were the primary concern of the parent development company. Though they were sympathetic, there was really nothing they could do. They had sold the rights to the development of the village center and had to rely on our landlord to keep their word and deliver the final product.

Six months past the scheduled delivery date, and with no indication that a turnover of the space by the landlord was imminent, we sought further legal advice in an effort to determine what our options were, as the costs continued to mount. By the letter of the lease, without a defined delivery date by which the landlord must abide, the landlord was not in violation of the terms of our agreement. Still, our counsel felt that there was consideration for "reasonableness" in that a delay that is adversely affecting another business cannot be allowed to continue indefinitely. I had been documenting all of my discussions with the landlord and the landlord's general contractor, which clearly demonstrated the misleading information we received with regard to turnover dates, as well as the difficulty we experienced during our coordination efforts. This was important—the paper trail for a project like this is critical. At this point, the 'Za-Bistro! team felt that we had been forced to take a stand. In coordination with our attorneys, we issued a letter stating that if we did not receive turnover of the space by a defined date, we would unilaterally terminate the lease. Though we had no right within the terms of the lease to do so, our documented difficulties seemed to provide us with the legal clout we needed. With no response or change of direction from the landlord, we followed that threat with a letter in which we indicated that we had unilaterally terminated our lease. A portion of the letter is listed below, with some modifications to protect the identities of those involved. Once again, the intention of this book is to educate, not disparage.

It is with great regret that we must notify you that our lease is hereby terminated as outlined in our earlier letter to you due to your failure to perform in a reasonable time, and you are now free to re-lease the Leased Premises that 'Za-Bistro! was to have occupied. We will notify your mortgage lender of this termination, as we are contractually bound to do so under the estoppel we executed.

We cannot risk further financial losses and lost business opportunities at this time, as a result of being asked to endure more delays to accommodate your needs. Please understand our frustration with the fact that our "Delivery Date" has been documented and changed at least five times since the first letter to us indicating a delivery date and a Grand Opening date for the center. Our faith in your ability to deliver in the future, at any date certain, on this space or any other, no longer exists as a result.

Further, we have calculated consequential damages related to this non-performance and breach on your part at over $90,000, before considering lost profits, damage to our reputation, etc. Should you decide to pursue a lawsuit against 'Za-Bistro! and the guarantors of the lease, we will be forced to seek recovery of our damages and legal fees in a counter suit. We would advise that you review all e-mails and correspondence between the parties related to past Delivery Dates before making your decision to file suit against the Company and the guarantors. Our attorneys have done extensive research in this regard and feel strongly that under the definition of "reasonableness" as defined under the law, we will prevail, and we are fully prepared to dedicate the necessary resources to do so.

We are available to further discuss this before any legal action progresses.

As with many aspects of our restaurant venture, this was new territory for me. Other members of our team, however, were no strangers to these types of legal maneuvers. In fact, Jason had choreographed the entire strategy in conjunction with our legal counsel—both of whom had far more experience in this area than I did. After all, that was the original concept behind this restaurant team: bring in and lean on the experience you do not have so that the entire team benefits. Though nothing was certain, Jason had explained that such documents were frequently used more as a negotiating tactic than anything else. It was his anticipation that this maneuver would provide us with a better opportunity to negotiate with our landlord and perhaps even recoup some of the financial losses we had incurred as a result of their actions. While it sounded like a great strategy, not everything goes as planned.

I awoke on the Monday morning of a three-day holiday weekend and ventured into my home office to check my e-mail first thing—a weekday ritual that I find hard to break. I noticed a message from Chris. This was not unusual, but the timing was certainly odd. He isn't an early riser, and I found it strange that the message had been sent early that morning, before I woke up. I opened the message, and my eyes got wider with every word I read. There had been a knock on Chris's door at 6:30 that morning. Unsure of who was there and what was going on, he ran downstairs, opened the door, and was promptly served with a lawsuit. The Harbor Commons landlord had retaliated with a formal lawsuit based on our unilateral termination of the lease. They were not interested in negotiating, but rather in enforcing the lease that was already signed. Jason was served later that day, It was certainly not the response we had anticipated. Aaron, the other guarantor on the lease, and I were also served with the same lawsuit.

Once served, there is a specified time limit within which one must respond, and we were soon in discussions with our legal counsel and the legal representatives for the landlord. While everyone was busy determining the next step in this emerging fiasco, I grew extremely concerned that our second oven was still sitting on site. Talk about leverage—they were in possession of our most critical piece of equipment and were threatening to install the storefront at any moment, which would have trapped our oven within the space. I acted swiftly and began making arrangements for what I termed *Operation Stolen Hearth*. I was planning to discretely (well, as discretely as possible, given the size and weight of this piece of equipment) remove our 3-ton oven from the site and store it in a local warehouse, unsure of what the final outcome would be in Harbor Commons. Early on the very next Monday morning, one week after our team was served with the lawsuit, at about 7:00, I arranged for a specialty moving service to *steal* our oven back from the space in which it was being held hostage. Monday morning is traditionally a slow time on a job site, with all of the contractors returning from the weekend. Surprisingly, the effort went off without a hitch. I received a call before 8:00 that morning, informing me that the oven had already been loaded and was on its way to the warehouse.

Given my personal involvement in the coordination efforts related to our legal maneuvering, and the landlord's subsequent dislike for me and my thoroughness, our team agreed that it would be best if I allowed Chris and Jason to handle the dialogue with the landlord in the wake of the lawsuit. I did not want to be an obstacle to progress, so with a focus on the issue itself and not the emotion, I stepped aside. In the end, we reached an agreement with the landlord that was mutually beneficial, though legal restrictions prohibit me from sharing the details with you. I stand by my statement that everything is negotiable, but sometimes the negotiations involve considerable risk. I could not help but think of all the decisions we made in Maitland with the looming turnover date at Harbor Commons as the driving force behind those decisions, which did not materialize as we had expected. Such is life in the *Business of Restaurants*.

16

Life as a Restaurant Owner

This book's focus is not on restaurant operations; however, the initial startup of a restaurant is a critical component of the restaurant development process. For this reason, I feel compelled to share some of our startup stories from Maitland with you now. When the doors opened for business, the operations team took center stage. The revenue for the first week or two was relatively slow, as we did not advertise, and it took some time for the local community to realize we were open for business. This was part of the soft opening we had planned. Within just four weeks, however, we reached our anticipated break-even volume, and the entire team was feeling extremely positive about the prospects for this new restaurant concept, which was literally years in the making.

But perhaps my most satisfying moment in the early days of the operation was on Valentine's Day. It was one of the busiest days in our first year of business. Our volume that day alleviated one of my biggest fears: Given the breadth of the menu and increased focus on full entrées, as opposed to just pizzas and appetizers, *could the oven keep up?* It was a question that had weighed heavily on my mind throughout the entire design and development process. On paper, we had proved that it should work, but it had never actually been tried in a real-world application.

After serving well over 300 patrons in our 124-seat restaurant, mostly for dinner, I finally had my answer: Yes, it could! Without a hitch, the oven and our staff kept up with the demand. Breaking two full turns within the first several weeks of operation was not bad, either. Although this might not be a big deal for some of the high-profile, celebrity-driven restaurants or for the multi-unit national chain restaurant concepts, it was a big deal for a brand-new restaurant concept in the middle of a small town just north of Orlando. We were quite pleased with the performance of the operation in the early days.

As a comical side note, I also found that life as a restaurant owner was quickly changing my perspective on the world. Because we were not a sports bar, Super Bowl Sunday was a rather slow night. Just a few months after we opened our doors, I found myself anxiously awaiting the next Valentine's Day — even hoping that it would fall in the middle of a week to boost revenues — while at the same time dreading the next Super Bowl. That was shocking, even to me.

And if the moment when I realized that the oven was actually working the way we had hoped it would was my most satisfying moment, this next one was a *very* close second. I attended the ribbon cutting for the new UCF hospitality school, which I had been part of in a design-build capacity, from concept to fruition. I had great personal pride in the project. Many extremely distinguished members of the hospitality industry were in attendance, partly due to its location in Orlando — one of the top tourist destinations in the world. The school is located just a few miles from Walt Disney World Resort, Universal Studios, and Darden's headquarters, all donors to the school. You can just imagine the expertise assembled on campus that day. Shortly after the ceremony, I found myself in a conversation with Chris, Jason, and two of the top executives from Darden. In the middle of this conversation, we were interrupted by a phone call from one of our managers letting us know that Joseph Hayes of the *Orlando Weekly*, a local paper walking the line between trendy and mainstream, had written a review of 'Za-Bistro! It was our first official review, and extremely important in both emotional and financial terms, as many throughout Orlando held the newspaper's opinion in high regard. I took a deep breath, paused, and then told our manager to read the review over the phone. Here is an excerpt from the *Orlando Weekly* review:

> *...if every take-your-tray-to-your-table outlet in town was replaced by something the caliber of 'Za-Bistro tomorrow, the world would be a better*

place. Just the sight of the reportedly $20,000 open-hearth, wood-burning oven is enough to draw you in.

The review then continued with a description of the restaurant's interior and our menu:

The interior (Tuscan colors, accents of dark wood) is an astounding change from the counter-service décor of its predecessor, and the focal point, that massive oven, fronted by a high-stooled bar, is quite welcoming.

Some things, particularly the seafood, are superb, including the "ztarter" (lots of "z" puns on tap) of oven-fired shrimp ($7.95) firm, tender, large prawns with a bit of spice, tarted up with lemon aioli on the side and the "Za-Gratin" entrée ($11.95), large sea scallops and shrimp served in a oven-baked casserole with Parmesan and garlic cream sauce. It's better than some dishes I've tried at twice the price. And such beautiful bread, from rough peasant loaves to freshly baked pita.

There still might be a learning curve where other items are involved, mostly in the small things. The chicken tarragon ($9.95) had a mouth-watering aroma of herbs and wine and beautiful fresh mushrooms, but the chicken itself seemed overprocessed. Roasted garlic cloves arrived from the oven pasty and stuck together. The side of roasted potatoes and squash was limp and dry.

The "piz-Zas," while not real Italian pizzas, are satisfying, topped with combinations like portobella mushrooms and smoked mozzarella or andouille, tomato and peppers on top of crusty flatbread-type crust. The "Marcos Pollo" ($8.95), with lime chicken, scallions and Jack cheese was particularly appealing.

Even with its faults, if 'Za-Bistro is the future of chain dining, then bring it on. With reasonable prices, a good, inexpensive wine list and friendly service, I'd rather eat here than at almost any big-box restaurant in town.

Though there were a few opportunities for improvement, the review was extremely strong and exactly what we had hoped for. To demonstrate the power of this review, we saw a 10 percent jump in business the following week, which was directly attributable to the review in the *Orlando Weekly*. And if that was not enough press to introduce our new restaurant concept to the marketplace, a national hospitality publication, focused exclusively on multi-unit restaurant concepts, discussed the 'Za-Bistro! restaurant concept in an article that featured a tour of Orlando, with Chris as the host. The author of the article affectionately referred to Chris as the *Wizard of 'Za*. It was great national exposure to a well-respected readership. And our patrons were also offering up positive comments, primarily through the feedback form on our Web site.

"We came the first night you were open, the 29th, as we have been waiting and watching with great anticipation. We were not disappointed. I have already called several friends, directed them to the website, and insisted they visit you soon. We are thrilled with the food, the menu, the atmosphere and the prices. We will be there often, guaranteed. Keep up the good work! Maitland has needed you and we welcome you."

"'Za-Bistro! was the choice for my son's rehearsal dinner on Friday, April 2, and I am very glad we dined there with 35 of our relatives and friends! Everything was ready when we arrived, our food great, wine flowing well, and [the staff] had only our well-being in mind throughout the evening. I have received so many compliments on the quality of the ambiance, food, and service, and I'm sure that any who can will return to 'Za-Bistro! Thank You!"

"I came by early one day, before you opened, and a guy actually came to the door and asked if I would like to come in and look around and look at the menu!! How awesome is that? Well, a friend of mine and I got there and loved the music and the atmosphere immediately. (Doesn't portray it on the outside.) The service was fantastic. You could feel a good aura among the employees. I am coming back. I am VERY happy it is close to my house!! I am recommending the place to everyone!!"

"We are sooooooo glad you are here! We had an exceptional dining experience. Your menu's diversity and quality is perfect. Very good wine selection. Ambiance is awesome. You are even kid friendly when the need arises. Our service was excellent, from the door to server to helpers to manager. Very attentive and friendly. Pricing is a plus also. We totally intend to let all of our friends, neighbors, and business acquaintances know about our terrific experience. We would love for you to be able to stay here in Maitland. Please keep up your end of the bargain."

"We found you quite by accident while on our way to [another restaurant]. Noticed the 'ZA' in your name and were interested. Were very pleasantly surprised by the setup and the cozy, homey feeling. Loved the open fire. We sat at the bar and watched the food being prepared and listened to the employees having fun. Food was excellent. Wait staff very attentive. We returned Sunday night and have now labeled it our 'newfound place.' We

again sat at the bar area and had a great time watching the fire while the food was being prepared."

What can I tell you? As an owner, those are exactly the kinds of comments that you want to hear. Surprisingly, there were very few negative comments given the newness of our restaurant concept. After all,

the steps of service, menu items, and entire set of operational procedures were untested. The guests clearly appreciated the service they received, as the service staff was averaging 20 percent in tips. This is slightly above by industry standards for a restaurant concept like ours. Also surprising, in a positive way, was the menu mix — or percentage of each category on the menu that was being sold. Having originally envisioned ourselves as a gourmet pizza concept, which eventually evolved into a much broader menu, we were almost shocked to learn in the early days of the restaurant that just 10 percent of our food sales were pizzas. The entrées were a hit with the customers, accounting for the lion's share of our revenue. This phenomenon speaks to that fact that it is up to the restaurant's creators to take the first step, and then sit back and let the customers express what they want the restaurant to become. Too often, I see owners force a certain style of menu or service upon their customers because it is what the *owners* want. This is the difference between the golden rule and the platinum rule. I am a fan of the latter. The golden rule tells us to *treat other people as we want to be treated*. The platinum rule, on the other hand, suggests that we treat other people the way *they* want to be treated, or *do unto others as they want done unto them*. It is a valuable lesson that I took to heart when I first learned of this difference — not only in business, but in life itself.

In the early stages of our operation, we had several discussions with some of the leading national hotel chains. Given our footprint, limited equipment package, menu versatility to serve all major day parts (breakfast, lunch, and dinner, with afternoon and late night easily accommodated as well), some of the hotel companies saw the potential return on investment as a tremendous opportunity. They felt that the inclusion of a 'Za-Bistro! in the right location could not only support the hotel guests, but also draw outside customer traffic in the right locations.

And if all of these positive developments were not enough, Chris had arranged for our entire team to spend a day with Jeffrey Steingarten, the renowned food critic for *Vogue* magazine and frequent judge on the Food Network's Iron Chef America, who was in Orlando researching an article on chain restaurants — a subject that previously had negative connotations in Mr. Steingarten's mind. Subsequently, our little restaurant in Maitland was featured in *Vogue* magazine the following month, in an article written by one of the nation's leading food critics and a *New York Times* best-selling author. Amazing! There was plenty of reason for optimism, given the positive developments we continued to experience. But we soon learned that all was not quite as well as we had perceived it to be. In fact, in the long run, some of our early success proved to be more of a detriment. Slowly but surely, we were pulled back into the reality of opening up a new, unproven restaurant concept.

As our CFO, Jason took the lead on pursuing loans for our development and growth efforts. In the early days, he spoke with several banks and received some rejections, as you are aware. Though I was uncomfortable, having initiated the construction effort in Maitland before the loan was finalized, I did feel better when, in the middle of the construction process, Jason reported that three different banks had tendered offers under the SBA loan program. Jason strongly preferred one of the banks based on its reputation and prestige within the local community. We viewed the bank as a component of our marketing effort, figuring that some of its board members, who were also prominent in the community, would assist with our word-of-mouth advertising if they had a vested interest in the concept. We chose to sign on with this bank, which we felt was our best option. Though we had originally discussed securing two separate loans — one for Maitland and one for Harbor Commons — the bank insisted that the two loans be combined. Then, in the middle of our efforts to close the bank loan, we received an unexpected surprise, which also encouraged the combination of the two loans into one. The SBA reported that it had experienced a 40 percent increase in loan requests over the previous year and, due to insufficient funding, they would soon be forced to shut down. Now we had a critical time element impacting our decision, and we had to act fast. We hastily filled out the necessary paperwork, and our loan was approved the day before the SBA actually shut down. Meanwhile, the sequence and timing of events had forced us to use nearly all of the cash that we had on hand as well as the tenant improvement dollars to cover the construction and opening costs. Our once-plentiful cash reserves had been depleted, at least temporarily. On the positive side, we opened the restaurant with no debt. That is amazing, and quite rare. On the negative side, however, we had little cash on hand for operating capital. That familiar college lesson kept haunting me: *You pay your bills with cash, not with profits.* As soon as the loan was approved, we would replenish the company war chest and use the funds as we originally intended. The paperwork had been filed on time, just before the SBA shutdown was enforced, and the loan was in process — or so we thought.

After the SBA approval of the loan, the bank on several occasions actually changed the terms of the loan. Yes, I said *after* the loan approval. They changed some of the fees. They raised the amount of cash that they wanted us to maintain as reserves for at least the first year. In fact, there were numerous changes, many of which impacted the amount of money we would have access to when the loan was finally closed. Most of these changes, though undesirable, could be accommodated. After all, we were desperate for the cash and had little bargaining power — the SBA was closed, and our loan had already been approved with this particular lender. One change, however, was a deal breaker. Because the loans for Maitland and Harbor Commons had been combined into a single loan, the bank insisted on reviewing the documents and progress for Harbor Commons before they would release *any* funds. They wanted to see final drawings, final budgets, and a whole host of information we were unable to provide. This data was not withheld intentionally, but rather because we could not obtain the information ourselves (need I remind you of the wonderful cooperation and honorable commitments we received from the Harbor Commons landlord?). The bank was adamant, and unwilling to alter its position. In the end, our loan fell through. Jason, a veteran of the banking world, informed us that we had been "re-traded." In my world, there was a much simpler term — we had been *screwed*!

With the loan falling through, and our once-overflowing financial coffers depleted to cover the startup costs in Maitland, we found ourselves in the *exact* position we had worked years in advance to avoid. Most restaurants, and new businesses of any kind for that matter, fail due to undercapitalization—they don't have enough cash on hand. We knew that. But there we were, falling victim to the very same scenario, despite our knowledge and planning on the front end. Just five weeks after opening in Maitland, we were forced to issue a capital call among the partners. This is a great time to stress that owners share not only in the potential profits of an operation, but also in the potential liability. All partners were required to contribute capital, proportional to their percentage of ownership in the holding corporation, or risk reducing their ownership shares. This capital call, as our CFO explained, was intended to bridge the gap until we were able to secure a loan from an alternate source.

At this time we all began focusing more closely on the original financial projections, which anticipated we would be cash-flow positive within 90 days. Ninety days? That is a risky, aggressive projection, with little cushion or room for error. Was it possible? Of course. Was it likely? Well, that is not the type of projection I would advocate. I am a bit more conservative. This aggressive projection, however, became a major issue when, within the first couple of months of operation, we found ourselves floating the restaurant in Maitland on little or no available cash. The ironic part was that we had no debt on the restaurant itself. When describing this unusual situation, I often said it was similar to owning your home outright, with no mortgage, but not having enough cash on hand to buy groceries, and worrying how you might feed your family. It is a mind-boggling paradox. Nonetheless, it was our reality. From almost the first month of business, we were in cash crisis. Fortunately, the business was holding its own in the early days and, as you read earlier, the comments and press that we received were all very positive. But there is no sugar coating the situation—we were tight on cash and watching our daily sales to ensure that we would have enough cash on hand to pay our bills from one week to the next. We were watching every penny. And perhaps most importantly, all we had invested was now riding on the performance of the store in Maitland, where our cash had been devoted. With no lending institution identified as a viable alternative, we were on our own for the foreseeable future. And from this point on, the hits just kept on coming!

While the review in the *Orlando Weekly* gave a glowing account of the reviewer's dining experience, the reviewer from the *Orlando Sentinel* was less than kind. It was not a horrible review, but it was certainly not something that left readers anxious to try the new 'Za-Bistro! restaurant in Maitland. Entitled *Price Is Great, But Overall Quality Is Lacking*, it was not the ringing endorsement we had hoped to receive. More troubling than the impact this mediocre assessment of our performance had on our customers was the impact that it eventually had on our staff. It took a serious emotional toll on our managers, servers, cooks, and other support staff. They had poured their hearts and souls into the startup of 'Za-Bistro!, and the less-than-stellar review absolutely took the wind out of their sails. The melancholy atmosphere was evident in performance at the store level, and eventually in our sales. By that time we were also seeing a slight taper in customer traffic due to the fact that we were no longer the new place on the block. While not entirely unexpected, the impact of this development was magnified by our tight cash position. And with the slight downturn in traffic, we lost some of our serving staff who felt they could make more money elsewhere. The employees who were paid at a set hourly rate were not affected by the drop in volume, but the servers, who relied on tips, were directly affected. Unfortunately, the better employees have a tendency to leave first, as they have the greatest opportunity and potential elsewhere. This was one more disruptive element we had to contend with during an already turbulent period.

Throughout the first several months, we had been asking the management team to report on the labor and food costs, which together are known within the hospitality industry as *prime costs*. Prime costs typically comprise the majority of all expenses in restaurant businesses. The reports we received from our management team indicated that our prime costs were on target with our original projections, which were just over 60 percent. We soon learned, however, that this was not the case. Our accounting review of the first quarter revealed a third-period loss of $16,000, on seemingly steady volume. Worse yet, we were on pace to lose *another* $18,000 in the following period. I was absolutely shocked. How was that even possible? With little cash in reserve, this news was a bombshell. I could not understand how the restaurant could be losing so much money — were we literally handing out twenty dollar bills to each customer at the door as they were leaving? A little bit of research unearthed some of the management team's decisions that led to the restaurant's poor financial performance. For instance, one of the managers had made a habit of tossing out food that did not look fresh or of the highest quality. Now, don't misunderstand me; we were *very* concerned with the quality of food used to prepare our dishes, and we would never serve products of inferior or unacceptable quality. But why were such products received and accepted by this manager in the first place? Why weren't they rejected upon delivery? When we tossed out food that had been accepted and paid for, we were throwing away money. Our investigation also revealed that the managers were not implementing proper receiving procedures, which, as was discussed in an earlier chapter, can impact both food safety and finances. In this instance, they had focused *solely* on food quality and completely overlooked the economic impact of their decisions. In another example of mismanagement at the store level, there were numerous errors with regard to ordering and quantities. It became a regular habit for kitchen staff to run next door to the grocery store to purchase products they had run out of. These purchases cost much more than we would pay our purveyors for the same products. The whole process negatively impacted both food and labor costs. Speaking of labor costs—they were *completely* out of whack. The accountant's report from the first six months revealed that our actual prime costs (food and labor) were approximately 98 percent! It was soon clear that all of the non-prime-cost business expenses were dropping straight to the bottom line and leading to our five-figure monthly loss.

The losses resulted in a need for a second infusion of capital from the partners—still with no potential lender on the horizon. Any potential lender would request to review the actual financials from the operation in Maitland, which were, at this point, a detriment rather than a benefit. When we needed the loan the most, it was appearing less and less likely that a lender would be interested in loaning money to us based on our operational performance. And then came the summer we never expected. As late spring and early summer arrived, we saw another dip in traffic. This time it was a significant dip. But what was the cause? I must admit, it was an unforeseen consequence of our choice of neighborhood. The demographic for Maitland was extremely attractive, based on average age and average income. The average income per household was just shy of six figures. Our original premise was that those who are financially secure do not always want to spend a significant amount of money on a dining experience. We believed that they would truly appreciate our $30 experience at a $15 price tag. And in the winter months, our theory proved to be correct. What we did not realize was that many of the locals took extended vacations in the summer to escape the Florida heat. Some of them had second homes and would spend the hottest months of the year in their alternate residences — a reverse snowbird effect. Others merely took lengthy three- and four-week vacations. Now, if we had thoroughly done our homework, we would have reviewed the traffic patterns from the previous restaurant tenant and identified the potential traffic slow down. However, we had not considered or reviewed the available information. In fact, I later learned the previous franchisee had indicated to one of my partners that there was a significant slow down during that time of year. This information was ignored, however, with my partner assuming that the drop in customer traffic likely had more to do with the previous tenant's concept and its execution than with the location. To be honest, it was a significant error on our part. The information was there for us to use, and we did not make proper use of the data — perhaps due to pride, ego, ignorance, or some combination thereof. We had the opportunity to proactively plan for a summer slowdown, but we did not seize that opportunity. Now our lack of reserves and poor operational controls in the early months really began to take their toll.

By now you are probably wondering what else could possibly go wrong. Well, hang on to your hat, because there are plenty of surprises left to share. The delays and evolution of the situation at Harbor Commons led to a management team consisting of four members, rather than three as originally planned. The gentleman slated to become the managing partner at the Harbor Commons store was hired early to assist with the opening of the Maitland store. However, because the Harbor Commons store was delayed time and time again, we were left with an undesirable scenario in Maitland. We had two managing partners on the payroll, as opposed to one. This was our most expensive staff position, and we honestly did not have the revenue to support two managers at their scheduled pay rate. Further exacerbating the situation, the two managing partners did not see eye to eye on many issues, and a number of conflicts arose as a result. A power struggle ensued, along with a division among the staff. And if that weren't enough, the two managing partners realized that the downturn in traffic meant that achieving the aggressive bonus plan and compensation structure we had presented before they were hired was growing less and less likely by the day. We began to sense a deterioration of their commitment to the concept and the effort we had all undertaken. To state it more bluntly, we were afraid they were losing interest. There we were, grappling with yet another situation that had somehow evolved into the exact scenario we worked to prevent. Part of our original plan was to have a managing partner on site who would buy in to the concept, both literally and figuratively, and have a vested interest in the well-being of the restaurant operation, from both operational and financial perspectives. Instead, our reality included two managing partners in the same store (double the anticipated salary), both of whom were now less committed to the concept than when they started, and neither of whom had a vested interest in the health of the business. Neither had yet invested the money outlined in the Bistro Managing Partner plan. Either manager—or both for that matter—could walk out at any time, leaving 'Za-Bistro! and our team behind, without much recourse. The original program was designed to provide the managing partner with ownership in the store, so that their employment was more than just a job. In the Maitland situation, however, that was likely what these two individuals were thinking at the time—it was just a job. They could leave at any time, and that is exactly what they did. Both managing partners quit. Making an even greater mistake, some ownership team members talked these two into staying after they had submitted their resignations. My father taught me long ago that once someone has quit, they have quit—do not talk them into staying, as their heart is no longer in the effort.

Our personnel troubles were not limited to the store level. A couple of problems arose among the partners, particularly as it related to performance. At one time or another, several of the partners were unable to uphold some of their responsibilities to the company. This was not intentional, but rather a result of competing obligations and responsibilities. This entire effort was a side venture for all involved, and not the primary source of income for any of us. As a result, we each had responsibilities outside of 'Za-Bistro! that were sometimes more limiting than we had hoped or planned. The ever-present financial stress also had some negative effects on the partnership. This situation made our daily lives far more difficult and stressful at best, and endangered the existence of the company and the collective investments of the partners at worst. As the reality of the operational efforts from the early days in Maitland began to sink in, we all grew extremely concerned. We placed greater and greater pressure on the staff to pick up their performance in the short term just to cover the costs of daily operations. And while that reaction is valid to some extent, this pressure led to several short-sighted decisions, which were not in the best interests of the restaurant or the company.

So that must be it, right? I mean, what else could possibly go wrong? It seemed that we had been dealing with problems from every angle — except one. That is when Mother Nature decided to throw her hat into the ring. I guess that I should start with the fact that the restaurant's power source was hit by lightning during the Fourth of July weekend. Lightning literally struck the main electrical box on the street, resulting in a loss of power, and eventually food and business. Unfortunately, the loss-of-power drill would become a familiar routine. We had made it through an unexpectedly slow summer. We were anxious for the return of the school year and the return of our regular customer traffic. Fortunately, school was slated to start earlier than ever that year — students were due back August 1, with teachers reporting during the last week of July. To us, this meant that by the end of July, the summer vacations would be ending and our regular customers would be returning. Almost like clockwork, as the school year started, our customer counts began to rise again. This cause-and-effect manifested just as Chris had predicted it would.

Hurricane season begins on June 1 of every year and does not end until November 30. We were right in the heart of hurricane season. And less than two weeks after classes began, Hurricane Charley was brewing in the Atlantic. Charley was a nasty storm, projected to head straight up the mouth of Tampa Bay. In fact, the forecasted track took the eye of the storm within just a few miles of my house. My parents had lived through Hurricane Andrew in South Florida and, although more than a decade earlier, the aftermath of that storm was still fresh in their minds — and mine.

We braced for the arrival of Charley, watching an endless stream of news and weather reports. The weather-tracking technology had improved greatly since the days of Andrew, and once the storm was in range, the local meteorologists seemed to have a better handle on the storm than the National Hurricane Center. Glued to our television sets, we watched the storm inch closer to Tampa Bay. Coming closer and closer, the storm was headed north-northeast along the west coast of Florida. Then the storm took a quick and unexpected jog to the east, and I realized that the new path would lead to a direct hit on the restaurant. Hurricane Charley blew through, and although the restaurant suffered some physical damage, it was not as bad as I had feared. It was significant enough, but in light of the damage suffered by others in the neighborhood, we could not complain. An architectural firm with which

I worked extensively at the time was less than a mile away, and they lost most of their studio. The windows facing north were blown in, and the resulting damage was significant. We were relatively lucky. While there was major damage all around us, we made it through without any major problems, and without closing the restaurant for an extended length of time. We did sustain some damage to the exterior, as well as loss of power and food. The storm hit on a Friday evening (of course, prime business time), and we were open again the following Monday. With partial power restored and our food purveyors able to deliver food, we opened our doors as a gesture to support the local community more than anything else. We offered only cold foods on the menu, and we sold them at our cost. We made food and gave it away to some of the city officials, rescue workers, and utility crews who had been working day and night in the local area. It was one way we could help the local community. The local community, after all, was our lifeblood, and it was important for us to support our neighbors in their time of need.

One hurricane would have been enough to contend with on top of the other challenges we were facing. Little did we know that we were in the middle of one of the most active hurricane seasons in recorded history. Just two weeks later, Hurricane Frances battered the east coast of Florida, taking a toll on Orlando for the second time. Then, just two weeks after Frances, Hurricane Ivan developed in the waters off the Caribbean and was moving on a path almost identical to Charley's. With two hurricanes fresh in their minds, residents of the entire central portion of the state braced for another hit. The tracks of Charley and Ivan could not have been much closer, until Ivan approached Jamaica. Seemingly aware of the island's presence, Ivan took a jog due west, eventually tearing through the Gulf of Mexico and hitting the Gulf coast in the westernmost portion of the Florida panhandle. We had finally dodged a bullet. There couldn't be *another* storm out there, could there? Right on schedule, just about two weeks after the threat of Ivan, Jeanne formed in the Atlantic Ocean. This particular storm was confused, wandering aimlessly for several days, actually completing a full loop northeast of the Bahamas. But Hurricane Jeanne finally picked her chosen path and began chugging through the ocean toward the east coast of Florida, *again!* Just as Ivan had threatened to follow the same path as Charley, Jeanne threatened to follow almost the same path as Frances, but this storm made good on its threat. The paths were frighteningly similar, as Jeanne came punching her way through central Florida, striking first on the east coast, just a few miles north of where Frances made landfall.

I am a person who tries to look for the humor in almost everything I do. I was amused when, by the end of the six-week stretch, many of the local reporters were struggling to keep the names of the storms straight. They would be covering Hurricane Jeanne, but refer to the storm as Charley, Frances, or Ivan. And talk about Murphy's Law: Nearly every storm hit on a weekend, which was our strongest time of the week for sales. The restaurant made it through the subsequent storms without much physical damage. For the first storm, we had prepared a disaster plan just in case the storm took a slightly different path than had been projected. By the time the third hurricane threatened to hit the restaurant, the staff had the drill down to a science. Some of the tasks on our list were obvious: take down the umbrellas, bring in any outside objects, set up lines of communication after the storm, and other common components of a disaster plan. But we were a restaurant, with a great deal of perishables on hand. Lost inventory meant lost revenue. We devised a plan to empty the restaurant's ice bin, which could store over 1,000 pounds of ice, into bags. The staff then used the bags of ice to pack the walk-in cooler and freezer. We made sure that manual credit card slips would be on hand in the event of a power or telephone outage, as the authorization of credit cards through typical means would not be possible without electricity or data lines. Scratch pads were also on hand so that servers could use them to take orders. We verified that the propane tank, which was the main fuel source for our oven and six-burner range, was full before the storm. By the end of the hurricane season, the hurricane preparation plan could be enacted in record time and with near precision.

While our physical losses were limited, the economic impact, however, was significant. We had chosen early in our restaurant development efforts to locate our concept "among the rooftops." We were a neighborhood restaurant — a model that results in a direct tie between the restaurant and the community. If the community is prospering, the restaurant is likely to benefit. Conversely, when the local community is faced with hard times, the restaurant will feel the impact of the community's hardship in one form or another. In our case, the local community had been struck by three hurricanes in less than six weeks, suffering tremendous economic damage. Some had lost their businesses, some had lost their homes, and others had suffered significant damage. Many were spending large amounts of money on deductibles and repairs that were not covered by their insurance policies. With each storm came the loss of power for many of our local residents, and the subsequent loss of food in their refrigerators. The Orlando market had spent a fortune on hurricane supplies and the replacement of food that was lost during the power outages. Disposable income was shifted to deal with the aftermath from three major hurricanes. Our customers were preoccupied with striving to return to a sense of normalcy following the storms. Dining out at 'Za-Bistro! was not the most important thing on their minds, which only exacerbated our poor financial position. Finally the hurricane season came to an end, and we were able to return to more typical restaurant crises. More than once, for instance, the fire system tripped prematurely, each time forcing the operations team to shut down the restaurant and clean up the mess that was left all over the food and cooking equipment.

What amazed me most, however, was the resiliency of the restaurant itself. Like a cat, it seemed to have nine lives. Despite all of the challenges, some self-created and others completely out of our control, the staff was still serving incredible food in a fabulous environment to a loyal base of customers, and all at a great value. We were, in fact, offering a $30 experience for half the price, just as we had planned to do at the outset. Our average check was right in the range we had aimed for when we first started to develop the 'Za-Bistro! concept. Chris, an eternal optimist, repeatedly told us that we were finally turning the corner. On one of our Sunday calls, I just had to ask Chris, "So, how many corners does this thing have?" We all had a chuckle over that. Fortunately, in the wake of a trying first year, the pendulum began to swing back towards the positive side.

Shortly after the storms blew through, Chris contacted the local Federal Emergency Management Agency (FEMA) representatives to inquire about the possibility of receiving economic assistance in the wake of the hurricanes that had impacted our local area. While the physical damage to the restaurant was minimal, the economic damage was not. After submitting a package that summarized the negative financial toll resulting from the three hurricanes on the restaurant's revenues, FEMA eventually estimated the economic impact at well into six figures. As a result, FEMA then approved a low-interest SBA loan for the restaurant. We would finally receive our SBA loan, though the method for acquiring this loan was *far* from the process we had anticipated originally. And while the loan amount from the storm was less than we had originally planned on receiving for the construction of the Maitland store, the low-interest terms were quite favorable.

After both of our original managers had departed, Aaron reached out to a colleague from a previous employer and brought him on board in Maitland. This new manager brought with him stability and a strong commitment to the concept. Following his arrival, the *Orlando Sentinel* reviewed us again, this time speaking highly of the food quality. Business increased steadily, with year-over-year revenue yielding positive results. Our prime costs were addressed and brought within the scope of our original projections. Conversations were still occurring with prospective investors who recognized the true potential of our concept. Challenges and delays continued with the Harbor Commons site, and as a result, the team continued the difficult, always-exhausting effort to secure a second location. Based on the experiences we had already encountered, none of us really knew what the future would hold. We had survived a number of very challenging and mostly unanticipated events. It took commitment, determination, perseverance, and luck to meet and overcome those challenges.

And though it had been a wild ride, it was — in every sense of the word — an *invaluable* experience. I had learned so much about the *Business of Restaurants*, about other people, and about myself. The entire restaurant development process had made me a better person in many different ways. I was better at dealing with my clients because I *had* walked a mile in their shoes. I was better at business in general, because I learned from both good and bad decisions we made along the way. The lessons learned were not just based in business; there were numerous lessons that impacted my personal life as well. In fact, I felt that what I had learned was equivalent, if not better, than obtaining an actual graduate degree. I had not gone to graduate school for my MBA; rather, this entire venture *was* my MBA, at least for now. And the lessons learned would stay with me throughout the rest of my life, regardless of the eventual success or failure of 'Za-Bistro!

17

LESSONS LEARNED

When I was enrolled in Chris's TCAB class at Cornell, we ended each week with a lecture on Friday morning. Actually, it was more of a discussion than a lecture. The purpose of these Friday sessions was to review the lessons we had learned from the previous week's restaurant concepts. Chris consistently initiated the discussions with the same three questions: What went right, what went wrong, and what would you do differently if you had it to do all over again? These were simple, straightforward questions, but they led to some very intriguing and enlightening conversations. In the spirit of my TCAB class, I wanted to wrap up this book by taking time to reflect upon some of the lessons learned during our restaurant development process. I should stress that these are just a selection of the lessons I learned, which I thought would be beneficial to share. Included in this chapter you will find reminders of lessons already presented. You will also find lessons that have been discussed previously, but have not yet been brought to their logical conclusion. Some lessons involve new information. Others are vivid reminders of earlier advice that had not been fully absorbed or applied. There are lessons that will forever influence my professional and personal life. Finally, there are some important lessons I am legally restricted from sharing (remember, our story included a lawsuit).

This final chapter embodies the primary reason that I wrote this book: for other aspiring restaurateurs to benefit from our experiences. It did not seem sensible for me to learn these valuable lessons and then keep them to myself. Instead, I wanted to capture these lessons and disclose them, hoping that they would prove beneficial to others preparing to embark on their own restaurant development process. The following lessons are not ranked in order of importance, as such a ranking would be completely subjective. They are, instead, organized categorically so that they are at least consistent in theme.

And now, some of the lessons learned:

GENERAL

The *Business of Restaurants* **is upon us.** The shift from the *Restaurant Business* to the *Business of Restaurants*, though this may be an overly academic focus on phrasing, is an important concept to grasp. The bottom line is that the major, multi-unit restaurant companies have changed the way restaurants operate. They are much more sophisticated than they used to be. Just as important, these large chains have also changed the customers' expectations. Customers expect every independent restaurant to meet or exceed the standards of service, quality, consistency, and the overall experience found at any one of today's popular chain restaurants. I stress this point because, if you are opening a new restaurant and want to compete with the chains, you need to know that you will have to play on *their* field, and play by *their* rules. Proficiency in restaurant *systems* is no longer an option, it is a requirement.

You pay your bills with cash, not with profits. Though I first learned this lesson in my college entrepreneurship class, I did not fully understand all that it implied until I began my 'Za-Bistro! journey. Projections are great. Bottom-line numbers for the end of the year are important as well. But the bills show up every month, whether it is a profitable time of year or not. Typically, if you have a strong season in the winter but are slow in the summer, the rent does not change (although, that might be a great point to negotiate). You need to have ample cash on hand at all times. The landlord will not accept a look at your projected bottom line for the year in lieu of the August rent check. If you cannot meet your financial obligations year-round, then you may be at risk of losing your business, perhaps in its infancy. Make sure you have the capital to cover any shortfalls or slower periods, anticipated or not.

Choose your partners more carefully than you choose your spouse. A business partnership is similar in many ways to a marriage. However, many partnerships involve more people and more money than a marriage, which can easily add to the stress level and potential for major conflicts. Partnerships are tricky. Chris used to joke with us about a headline he once read that stated "Man Shoots Partner for No Apparent Reason," to which Chris replied, "Sure there was a reason — it said they were partners!" I am not an expert on partnerships, but having been a part of several, I want to share with you some of the keys that I see to establishing a successful partnership. Perhaps the most important issue in my mind is values. I believe that it is important for partners to share the same value system, just as in a marriage. Would you consider marrying someone who has drastically different values or beliefs than you do? I don't think you would. Now, let me clarify — I am not talking about different *perspectives*, but rather different *values*. Risk tolerance would be a good example of a value component. If one partner is more averse to risk than another, the specific issues become almost irrelevant as the partners will struggle to see eye to eye. It is not that one is right and one is wrong — they are just different, very different. Differing perspectives on a team are incredibly beneficial, and healthy debates on matters of substance should be encouraged. Differing *values* on a team, however, are a recipe for disaster.

In partnerships, it is also important to set clear ground rules before the major activities start. I once heard the following formula for success: *success = expectations + one*. In other words, you have succeeded only if you have met *and* exceeded someone else's expectations. The other party received everything they were expecting, and even a little more. I like this definition. The most important part of the equation, however, is the word "expectations." If expectations are not clearly defined on the front end, how can they possibly be exceeded? If two people have different expectations, one's expectations might be exceeded, while the other's basic expectations could remain unmet. This disparity can be very harmful to a partnership. This leads our discussion to the concept of accountability—accountability to each member of a partnership, and accountability to yourself. With no mechanism in place to hold members of a partnership accountable for their actions, there is increased risk for a rocky road ahead. Choosing partners is a tricky business, which is why you must do your homework. Seriously. Even if you are friendly with a person, a business relationship is very different, and a lot more is at risk. Find out everything you can. See if your value systems are compatible. Listen—really listen—to this lesson: *Choose your partners more carefully than you choose your spouse.*

Consider the impact on your family. During the time the Maitland restaurant was under construction, I was also teaching my design class at UCF. One of my students at the time, a little older than the average age of 19 or 20, asked me a very astute question. She wondered how all my activities were impacting my family and my personal life, as I was involved in a number of very time-consuming, demanding projects simultaneously. And while I had a bit of control over some of my other ventures, the restaurant was like a newborn baby—it needed what it needed, when it needed it. It did not matter if I felt like it, or if it was convenient; like a parent, it was our team's responsibility to provide the necessary sustenance. If you are contemplating opening a restaurant, I ask you to consider this student's question. Where are you in your personal life? If you have a family, will they be understanding? Are you fully aware of the sacrifices that may be required, and are you prepared to make them? Do you realize that your anticipated two-year time period for working your tail off may stretch out to four or five years, maybe even more? And if you don't have a family, have you considered that this all-consuming effort might leave little time to start one or to find that special someone? Do you realize that once you decide to go down the restaurant development path, it is very hard to turn around and go back? Directly or indirectly, incredible sacrifices must be made when starting up a new business, especially a restaurant. Whether you miss your child's soccer game or have to cancel a second date, you may have to forfeit your quality of life to pull this off. Is it worth it? Only you can answer that question. I just want to make sure that you thoroughly consider these questions on the front end, before a commitment is made.

Situations evolve. There is an old parable about a frog in a pot of boiling water. If you were to place a frog in a pot of boiling water, the frog would immediately recognize the extreme change in temperature and the risk that the scalding hot water poses to its safety. It would immediately jump out of the boiling water with the speed of an involuntary response. However, if you were to place the same frog in a pot of water at room temperature, and then gradually heat the water to the boiling point, the frog would remain in the pot of water until it died. This phenomenon is significant. While the frog is capable of recognizing drastic changes in a situation, it is unable to recognize major changes that occur gradually — situations that evolve slowly, steadily, little by little. In many instances, we are very much like the frog in that we are able to recognize the drastic changes, but unable to recognize a significant transformation resulting from gradual, incremental changes. Shifting back to our restaurant development efforts, it is easy, in hindsight, to identify a number of examples where situations evolved before we recognized the full impact of our decisions along the way. Think about the delays with our second location and our decision to keep two managers at the first store. Consider the implication of our decision to commence construction in Maitland without a secured loan, and the impact it had on the financial position of our company in its operational infancy. In almost every phase of the development process, it seems, we can find examples where we *allowed* the situation to evolve.

To combat this natural tendency, I encourage you to regularly take stock of where you *are* and to make decisions based on the here and the now. Am I telling you that you should abandon any long-term plans? Absolutely not. Long-term planning is essential. However, there is a balance between where you want to go and where you are. You cannot act exclusively on one and forsake the other. Both are critical. Let's face it: No one opening a restaurant believes they will fail, at least not at the beginning. This overly optimistic attitude can often lead to a dominant focus on the bright horizon, and not enough focus on the current reality. Situations evolve. Be mindful of the frog, comfortable and clueless, in the rising water temperature. Look to the future, but regularly consider where you are, and proceed with balance.

Be patient. Patience is a virtue — another famous saying. Particularly in the restaurant development process, which is full of emotion, there is a strong tendency to allow emotions to drive decisions. Whether in the pursuit of a site, the hiring of your staff, business dealings between the partners, or numerous other examples, emotions play a major role in restaurant development. These emotions, however, must be controlled. Negotiations take time. Nothing happens as quickly as you want it to; everything takes longer than you expected. Remember that a restaurant is a business. Make sound business decisions, even though they may not be what you would prefer from an emotional standpoint. Patience is the key. The best results are often attained with a calm, cool, collected, strategic, and methodical approach.

Expect the unexpected. As long as you are aware that just about *anything* can happen, you will be better prepared to deal with the crises that are sure to rear their heads throughout the development of a restaurant. In my opinion, this is an endorsement for a more conservative approach. By all means, take risks—but take *calculated* risks. Keep in mind that the unexpected almost assuredly *will* happen, so maintain your rainy-day fund. Leave yourself some buffer. If you overextend yourself to maintain the everyday activities, then the very first crisis may be enough to pull you under. I did not expect the SBA to shut down. I did not expect a lawsuit. I certainly did not expect to deal with three hurricanes within six weeks. When I played Monopoly as a kid, I used to hide a few hundred bucks under the board, just in case. That's not a bad strategy, not bad at all.

Everything is negotiable. I may have beat this drum a little too loudly, and a little too often, but it is a valuable lesson. One more time shouldn't hurt. Everything is negotiable. Now, there are an almost incomprehensible number of books, lectures, and professionals dealing solely with the subject of negotiation. I am not about to belittle the subject by trying to cover the intricacies of negotiating in one short paragraph, but I do want to stress the importance of this concept. Consider this: A city government actually waived our impact fees. There are many different techniques to negotiating, and no one technique will work all the time. Each situation is different, and each counterpart in the negotiating process is unique as well. Be fluid, but more importantly, be willing to walk away. If you are unable to walk away, then you are not in a position to negotiate. Think about the landlord's refusal to offer us additional TI dollars when we increased the size of our leased space in Harbor Commons. The landlord refused to budge, but we had already determined that we needed the space. We were not in a position to negotiate. I must point out that this lesson is closely tied to an early lesson we have already discussed: Be patient.

Be tough, but be supportive. No one is going to be as much of an advocate for your needs and concerns as you are. For this reason, owners who are more involved usually get better results. It is unwise for an owner to take a backseat role in the development process. The owner's participation keeps the team of hired professionals focused, builds loyalty among the team, and allows for better decision making. During this process, it is okay to be demanding; a little motivation never hurts. Being too demanding, however, may have a detrimental effect.

Our superintendent, Jim, stated that I was one of the most involved and demanding owners he had worked with in his 30-year career, but I was also, by far, the most supportive. It was a mentality—we were in this together. I can assure you, if I had only been demanding throughout the course of the project, sharing nothing but aggressive expectations and no support, the outcome would have been drastically different. The positive tone on the job site and the willingness of several of the subcontractors to go the extra mile would not have been there.

Don't open a restaurant just to flip it. We began the development of 'Za-Bistro! with the intent to create the concept, grow the company, and then sell it off or hire professional management. I believe that this philosophy was a mistake. Though there are exceptions, I now believe it is generally unwise to establish a business with the primary intent to sell it off later. Most successful companies that have been sold at a profit were good at what they did. The operations—the value that they actually created—came first. The sale was a result of their success, not the reverse.

Plan, don't allow, an exit strategy. My brother-in-law, who is also a restaurateur, raised this very intriguing point with me during a family get-together. Why is it that many business owners *plan* an exit strategy, whereas countless independent restaurateurs do not? Hoping that the restaurant performs well enough to eventually sell it off is *not* an exit strategy. Neither is closing down a restaurant if it fails. Rather, an exit strategy requires proactively identifying milestones when key indicators will be evaluated, and actions that will be taken based on those indicators. To draw a parallel, there is a difference between financial planning that includes a carefully managed portfolio and simply depositing five dollars in a piggy bank on a weekly basis. While it can be argued that both of these methods result in some level of savings, the managed portfolio approach involves more detailed planning and is more likely to yield results consistent with the investor's long-term goals. Restaurateurs should consider an exit strategy from Day One. My brother-in-law has consulted for other restaurateurs. One of the first matters he advises his clients to focus on, when they are just *entering* the restaurant industry, is how they plan to *exit* the venture. This is a wise strategy and sound advice for any new restaurateur to consider before opening for business.

Optimism is great, but maintain objectivity. I deal with first-time restaurateurs all the time through my design practice. Many of them have a confident—bordering on arrogant—demeanor and a strong belief that their restaurant will be successful. This is good, perhaps even necessary, as it is a component of the motivation that leads restaurateurs to start a new business. The beginning of the development effort is full of optimism. It is important, however, not to let that optimism cloud your judgment or lead to unrealistic expectations. I can tell you that in our development process, we suffered from both of these symptoms. We made unwise decisions early in the process, driven more by our belief of success than by any reality. As you now know, our development efforts included a fair number of challenges, and success was anything but guaranteed. As for unrealistic expectations, take a moment and look back at the plan we laid out for the Bistro Managing Partner. Talk about unrealistic expectations! We had not even opened our doors, yet we developed a plan that included a free car for a manager? Based on what? Projections? Did those projections state what would happen if prime costs reached 98 percent? Remember that in order to be successful, you must exceed expectations. If the expectations are set too high, the chance for success on any level is significantly reduced.

Speaking of optimism, many refer to optimists and pessimists in a mutually exclusive manner. It is widely accepted that the optimist sees the glass half full while the pessimist sees the glass as half empty. I am here to tell that you that I am neither an optimist nor a pessimist. I am a realist. I do not see the glass as either half full or half empty. Rather, I see the situation as it is: there is either too much glass or too little water. That is, of course, assuming that the objective is to have a full glass. It could be that the goal is to have no water at all. This may seem like a quick right turn as we run down the lessons learned, but I want to stress the importance of keeping an open mind, evaluating all of the options, and thinking critically before making a decision. You may have more options than appear at first glance. And once the various options are identified, it is essential that the information be evaluated at face value. Many people have a habit of basing decisions on their *interpretation* of the information, and not on the information itself. Evaluating the *information* is part of being a realist.

The upside should outweigh the downside. Closely tied to the concepts of cautious optimism and calculated risk is the management of both upside and downside potential for the new restaurant venture. The personal and financial requirements for opening a new restaurant are substantial. It is easy to quickly take on enormous liability that might, if objectively evaluated, prove to be too great—the downside can outweigh the upside potential of the venture. In other words, the total liability (especially liability that is joint and several) can be larger than the potential profits that may be yielded by the venture. With so many variables and so many moving parts associated with the restaurant development process, constant management of this risk profile is essential.

Business is full of opportunities, not guarantees. I once heard a speaker compare opportunity to waiting for a bus at a bus stop. Busses come along, and it is our decision to either get on the bus or wait for the next one. Each bus represents an opportunity, not a guarantee. Will the bus you choose break down before you get to your stop, making you late? Is there an express coming behind this one that will get you where you are going much sooner? Is the bus that just pulled up the best choice? We don't know. We have to make our choices before we have all of the answers—and then we have to live with those decisions.

FINANCIAL

Consider the reasons for undercapitalization. Undercapitalization is perhaps the most common reason that businesses, including restaurants, fail. I am not sure, however, that most people understand exactly why this undercapitalization occurs. Some of it is easy to explain: There simply was not enough money to begin with. That is easy to fix and falls squarely at the feet of the restaurant developer to do his or her homework. I have come to believe that much of the reasoning, however, is not as intuitive. Take the example of a standard lease, which often includes one ton of air-conditioning for every 250 square feet. This is grossly undersized for the average restaurant, and the remedy for this one oversight can cost $30,000 or more in some cases. The financial impact of this unexpected cost affects the restaurateur only *after* the lease is signed and commitments are made. I am intrigued by this subject, based on personal experiences, and I hope to explore it more in the future. Why do restaurants fail? How much undercapitalization is due to unforeseen expenses during the development process?

If you don't have it, don't spend it. Despite the significant amount of capital we had at the beginning of our development efforts, money was a problem the day we opened our doors. We started construction without first securing our loan, and that was a clear mistake. It was a gamble that had significant consequences, and the gamble did not pay off. Our lack of sufficient funding affected our relationships with the construction team, created tensions among the partners, and led to short-sighted decisions in many cases. You may recall those signs at the fair that read "You must have two tickets to ride this ride." No ticket, no ride — there it is, in black and white. It is not wise to make commitments that cannot be kept or which might adversely affect your new restaurant startup. Interestingly, this ties back to the earlier discussion about values. It should be emphasized that this is one of *my* values and may not apply to everyone.

Two restaurants too soon. Even if we had secured the loan, it was a mistake to develop two restaurants of an unproven concept so close to one another. This is a fantastic example of optimism overtaking logical business decisions. It was a poor decision to commit to both Maitland and Harbor Commons at the same time. We did not allow ourselves the opportunity to apply much of what we had learned. What if a 3,800-square-foot space was too big? What if it was too small? What if we determined that a full bar was essential for our operation, but the space we committed to could not support this additional function? What if our experience determined that we would need more than three pieces of cooking equipment to execute the menu? The development of Maitland was driven by an imminent turnover of Harbor Commons, which never materialized. The negative impacts of these simultaneous commitments were far reaching and significant.

Keep your day job, at least for a while. Once again, I want to pull from my experience as a designer and my regular contact with first-time restaurateurs. I cringe every time someone tells me they just quit their job, and they are about to start the process of opening a restaurant. Yes, I said *start*. They do not have a lease, financing, a menu, a floor plan, a well-developed concept—they don't have anything. My heart sinks, and I find myself in the undesirable position of telling these individuals that the restaurant development process is full of surprises, and that they may want to rethink their decision. They may need some income during the process. I can honestly say that this approach has lost me business, but I believe it is my obligation to look out for the best interests of these individuals, whether it is something that they want to hear or not. Many of these aspiring restaurateurs have proceeded with their development process, unprepared to deal with the delays that are predictable to veteran restaurant developers. As a result, they often tap into their savings to get through the rough beginning. These same individuals frequently find themselves reaching the opening of their restaurant with little or no cash reserves. If you are contemplating leaving your present employment to open a restaurant, I ask you to consider what you will do if you experience delays or unexpected expenses. How will you support yourself, and possibly your family, if the delays continue? What is your backup plan? There is a lot riding on these decisions, so please take the time to carefully consider all possible scenarios and their potential impacts.

SITE

Find the hard-to-find data. Be sure to search for the hard-to-find data. Demographics, average income, average age, and population growth are great, but do not rely on them solely. Let's assume that you want to open a breakfast place, and in your target area, the dominant morning traffic is headed northbound. Perhaps you've found a terrific opportunity on the southbound side of the street. This location, although in the desired neighborhood, could very well be the death of your business, which hasn't even opened its doors yet. It is on the wrong side of the street. This is the kind of data that will not show up on standardized information made available from associations or local government agencies. Talk to local business owners. Observe your potential competitors—frequent their locations and talk with their staff. Attend local organization meetings. Pick up the neighborhood newspaper to find out what is *really* happening. The ability to conduct local research is one advantage independent restaurateurs have over many of the larger chains. Use that advantage. Do your homework, and don't rely solely on the data that is easily accessible.

There is always another site — always. Selecting the location and signing the lease are the first tangible steps toward opening the doors of your new restaurant for business. They are also the most likely parts of the development process to be driven by your emotions when, in fact, they require patience and objectivity. Many restaurateurs have a tendency to force the numbers and justify a site because they want it so much. *Do not* force a site to work. If you find yourself developing a long list of conditions and aggressive projections in order to justify the site, then it is the wrong site. The location is the hardest thing to change about a restaurant. It is better to wait for the right opportunity than to rush the wrong opportunity. You may not *want* to wait for another site, but if the numbers don't make sense, don't do it. Walk away. This may be the hardest, but also the best, decision you will ever make, even if it doesn't seem like it at the time.

Seek natural traffic. I am a strong believer in restaurant sites that are tied to natural traffic generators. Movie theaters, grocery stores, multi-use complexes, and other such businesses bring customers to a certain location. They create a regular flow of traffic — potential customers. Though the restaurant sites in these locations are often a bit more expensive, I believe they are worth the additional money. Whereas the "A" sites cost more, many who have leased "B" sites wind up spending additional money on marketing just to generate the traffic that already exists elsewhere. Unless you are that confident that your concept will draw customers out of their normal travel patterns just to visit your restaurant, I strongly suggest you consider a site in proximity to another business that is already helping to drive traffic. In other words, "B" sites may look less expensive on the front end, but they may be more expensive in reality than some "A" sites when you consider the additional marketing dollars required to drive traffic.

Expect delays. Whether you are looking at an existing site or the construction of a new site, expect delays. I am not just saying they are likely; I am saying you should plan on them. This bit of advice is not based solely on my own experience with 'Za-Bistro! I have seen it time and time again in my design practice. Think about the delays and what you will do if (when) they occur. Consider this when signing the lease with your landlord. How would a delay affect your ability to hire and train, and who (other than you) will be responsible for the financial impact? If you are dealing with a landlord who is unwilling to commit to a specific delivery date or some type of penalty if the delivery date is not met, a red flag should go up. Unfortunately, too many landlords do not care enough about the well-being of their tenants and the impact delays can have on their tenants' livelihoods. While not all delays are within the control of a developer, many of them are, and an extra incentive for the landlord to abide by the original schedule, or face some type of consequences, is in your best interest.

Carefully research the "haunted site." Some restaurant sites are haunted. They repeatedly open and close as different restaurant concepts. If you are considering such a site, I strongly urge you to determine the reasons restaurant concepts tend to go out of business in that space. Ask the landlord. Better yet, if you can, ask the previous owners. They may be more than willing to share some very specific details with you. The worst they can do is to tell you they don't want to talk to you. What do you have to lose? Wait, let me answer that question: plenty!

Leases are serious business. Aside from the partnership agreement, the lease is the document with the longest, most influential impact on your business. The terms are typically set for five years, ten years, or even longer. The terms of the lease could single-handedly determine the success or failure of your restaurant. Don't take them lightly. Read every page of the lease thoroughly. Consult legal counsel. Be creative — propose unique terms and conditions that are mutually beneficial. When it comes to negotiating the lease, remember one of our earlier lessons: Everything is negotiable.

Be sure to carefully tie down all commitments by the landlord in the lease, and include some form of accountability. The lack of a turnover date in the Harbor Commons lease is just one example of our own failure in this regard. If the landlord owes TI dollars, make sure you know when they will be provided and what, if any, documentation will be required to release the funding. Do not assume that the landlord will provide you with your TI dollars just because you ask for a check. Make sure that you and the landlord are both clear about specific aspects of the build-out. *What* will be provided, and *when* will it be provided? What opportunities, if any, will you have to overlap their construction process? Be sure expectations are clearly defined. Assume nothing. The lease is an incredibly important document.

DESIGN

Design-build works. Even though it did not work as planned in our build-out of the Maitland store, the design-build approach is an excellent philosophy to use for restaurant development. The integrated design and budgeting, the inclusion of construction and design professionals in all phases of the process, and the single point of responsibility are clear assets to the ownership team. I am not saying that all services have to be provided by a single company; it can be a joint effort or collaboration by several different firms, in my opinion. The critical aspect is to have an integrated team, with clearly defined roles, involved from start to finish, working on behalf of the ownership.

The design statement should be consistent. It is important to be consistent with all aspects of design in the restaurant. My focus on attractive fixtures in the restrooms stems from this philosophy. The upgraded sink bowls and enclosed stalls were conscious choices to help support the $30 experience we sought to offer. Within the restaurant, we maintained our concept and the desired $30 experience even after all of our budget cuts and cost-saving measures. But while the interior was consistent with the concept, the exterior was not. Though "bold," our exterior color scheme was not a successful design treatment. Customers regularly commented that they were surprised to find the atmosphere we had created on the inside, based on their first impression from the exterior. The design statement was consistent throughout most of the restaurant, but not in all aspects, which definitely influenced the overall guest experience.

Stick to your budget, but not at all costs. Our strategy of spending money where it counts, for the most part, worked extremely well. The upgrades to the oven façade, the display kitchen, and the restrooms were all high-impact elements of our distinctive trade dress, which were successful in their objectives. The use of copper laminate in lieu of real laminate above the oven, where the guest could not touch the finish to feel the difference, was a design technique that served us well. In certain instances, however, our strong desire to save money caused us to be penny wise and pound foolish. For example, we opted to go with a less expensive sign, lit by incandescent lighting, at the front of the restaurant. The other option was a neon backlit sign that would have offered greater visibility at night, but it was more expensive. Our reasoning for the incandescent light at the time was twofold. First, we wanted the signs for Maitland and Harbor Commons to be consistent, and neon signs were not allowed in Harbor Commons. Second, the neon sign was about $2,500 more expensive than the sign we ultimately selected, and would have put us over budget. In hindsight, the additional $2,500 would have likely paid for itself in additional customer traffic, because the neon backlit sign would have been easier to see from the road at night. Although the project came in on budget, the additional $2,500 would have been a wise investment — and worth the budget overrun.

Make sure the logo will look good in all formats. We regularly received positive comments on our logo. For the most part, people really liked it. Some asked us which marketing firm we used to help us develop the logo, and even estimated that we had paid upwards of $15,000 for it. That was not the case, as you may recall. We paid $600 and found our designer through an online logo design company. Early on, though, I failed to consider the implications of the logo's design proportions. The flame and wineglass icon, along with the font styling of the restaurant name, created a triangular shape. Most of the signage space provided by landlords, however, is rectangular. Our logo did not adapt well to many of the signage spaces we were offered. In hindsight, we should have developed an adaptation of our logo that would fit the more rectangular proportions, both horizontal and vertical. Proportions, coloring, presence or absence of a background color, and other such design considerations can impact the success of your logo and its ability to communicate your concept through many different forms of media.

CONSTRUCTION

Lien on me? No thanks. There is a lot riding on the construction effort, especially in terms of dollars. Perhaps the most valuable lesson I learned with regard to construction was the importance of properly dealing with lien waivers as an owner, and checking all of the supporting documentation at each step in the process. You *must* dot all the i's and cross all the t's. Remember that even if you pay your general contractor for the work a subcontractor has performed, you may ultimately still be responsible for paying that subcontractor again, according to the lien laws. A significant amount of liability is riding on these activities. Be careful.

Compare the cost per square foot for each location's build-out. When I solicited the construction bids for our space in Harbor Commons, the cost per square foot increased more than 60 percent over our build-out in Maitland. Some of this had to do with an increase in material costs, even though the pricing for Harbor Commons was completed only a few weeks after Maitland opened. Most of the cost difference, though, was due to lease terms (additional cost for HVAC systems not provided by the landlord) and the complexity of adding a restaurant on the first floor of a three-story building, with two floors of residences above. Maitland was a single-story, freestanding building. In Harbor Commons, the cost of the hood system and its installation were significantly higher than our costs in Maitland. There were also costs in Harbor Commons for items, such as a building sprinkler system, that were not required in Maitland. Despite the additional build-out costs in Harbor Commons, the size of the restaurant and the seating capacity were the same as in Maitland. That is why a review of the cost per square foot for the build-out needs to be completed before the lease is signed. The Harbor Commons store would have to generate a significantly higher revenue stream in order to cover the additional costs of the build-out. This type of information is important to consider on the front end.

Choose a different contract. The hybrid contract I signed with our general contractor was a unique approach. Once the general contractor's fee ceiling was reached, however, the contract was, in essence, a cost-plus agreement with no financial incentive for the general contractor to keep the project within budget. In hindsight, I would have included an additional bonus for the general contractor, made available if the final project was below a certain amount, or perhaps within a certain percentage of that amount. This contract modification would greatly improve the incentive and motivation for the general contractor to stay within or below budget.

Don't make physical changes too quickly. While I was very mindful of the construction budget during our build-out in Maitland, the managers were not as careful with their spending after I turned over the store to the operations team. They were very quick to demand all kinds of changes and additions that they needed "immediately," even though the restaurant had never served a single meal. They contacted the contractor directly and authorized expensive modifications, such as the office millwork. They insisted that a third point-of-sale system would be needed in the dining room, even though it was never added. A sliding window was added in the office for cash-outs. These unnecessary changes drove up the costs at the end of construction. Whether you are planning on running your own restaurant or you are part of a development team that will be turning over the restaurant to an operations team, I offer this advice: wait. Be patient. Live in the space for a little while before making any drastic changes. After 30 or 60 days, *then* you can consider possible changes to the facility. "Urgent" changes to the facility just before opening are a common pitfall for restaurateurs. In most cases the money could be spent in far more valuable ways during the early days of a new business.

MENU

Beer and wine only might have been the wrong choice for us. At one point, our beer and wine sales were regularly averaging roughly 18 percent of total sales, which was pretty good, at least for our concept and location. We had originally debated whether a beer and wine license would be sufficient, or if we needed a full liquor license. When we originally looked at the 18 percent figure, we came to the conclusion that the beer and wine license was the right choice for us. How much more could we have hoped to sell in beer and wine? Eighteen percent was respectable. As time went on, however, we realized that the percentage of sales was the wrong place to focus; rather, we should have focused on the dollars and profit margin. A full bar draws a different crowd. It draws a customer who is willing to spend $10 on a martini and order some appetizers to go with that cocktail. If we were to add a full bar, the percentage of alcohol sales might slip, but we believed that the total sales and profit margin (which is significant on mixed drinks) would increase. Eventually, we added a full liquor license in the Maitland restaurant.

Right-size your portions. As I shared earlier, the comments on the food were consistently positive. Many of our customers were surprised at the quality of the food for the price. The right-sized portions on our plates, however, may have been a bit too far ahead of the curve, particularly with our entrées and bistro specialties. "Right-sized" is not a fancy term to describe unusually small, gourmet portions. The portions were not small, but we did not load up the plates with inexpensive filler ingredients. In certain instances, I believe that the over-sized portions offered by some of our local competitors negatively impacted the perceived value in our restaurant. In other instances, we had some large portions—specifically our salmon salad—which sold for around $10. It was so large that many of our customers would order a salad and split it, reducing their average check and our revenue significantly. Portion sizes are an important part of the menu-planning process.

MARKETING

Give your customers what they want. Restaurateurs take the first step in creating a restaurant, but then we must take a step back and listen to what our customers have to say. Our focus on a female-friendly restaurant concept was dead on. One of our managers even coined a new name for a demographic that frequented the Maitland location: Ladies with Gift Bags, or LWGBs. These are women who frequently meet their friends for lunch, and always seem to show up with a present—in a gift bag, of course—to celebrate a special occasion. They are a loyal crowd who like to "do" lunch, catch up with friends, and socialize. They appreciated the menu, atmosphere, and service, confirming their approval with regular patronage.

There were surprises, however. For instance, it was clear that our customer base had a stronger desire for the entrées and bistro specialties on our menu than they did for our pizzas. There is no use fighting what the customers want, even if it is not what you want. The entrées had a very different food cost model than the pizzas, but our customers did not want to be limited by gourmet pizza. While we originally expected to sell plenty of entrées, the ratio of entrées to pizzas was unexpected. In another example, we found that we were being used for special events far more often than we had anticipated. Despite the fact that we did not view ourselves as a special occasion restaurant, much of our customer base did. We were surprised by the number of rehearsal dinners, baby showers, and birthday parties we booked. Now, this presented us with a unique paradox. Our pricing model was based on regular patronage. If we were viewed as a special-occasion restaurant, were we leaving money on the table with our everyday price structure? Was our price structure too low? Was the interior too formal, or not formal enough? There are no right answers. What I want to stress here is that restaurateurs must allow the concept to evolve. It is about providing an experience that the patrons desire, which may or may not be an experience the owner desires.

Define your concept in one sentence. When people would ask me what kind of restaurant we had opened, I would tell them that it was a European bistro. After my reply, they would predictably ask, "Oh, what's that?" Unfortunately, the second part to that answer wasn't nearly as concise as the first. I would explain the menu, the atmosphere, and the influences. Eventually I would convey the fundamental nature of the concept, but our entire team struggled to relay the essence of the restaurant in a single sentence. In the early days, before word-of-mouth testimonials had a chance to penetrate the local market, I believe this may have hurt our business. Rather than firing people up so they could not wait to try the restaurant, they would leave the conversation with a confused or limited understanding of the concept, and no evident need to see what 'Za-Bistro! was all about. Whether you are creating a unique or a well-known type of restaurant, make sure your concept can be clearly conveyed.

A neighborhood restaurant, for better or for worse. Our decision to be "among the rooftops" was more than a decision on location. It was a marketing decision, tying us into the local neighborhood. That was exactly what we wanted — to be the neighborhood restaurant. I am not sure, however, that we fully understood this decision was for better or for worse. The impact of the hurricanes on our local neighborhood really hurt business for a while. Though our physical structure was not in bad shape, the financial impact on the local community — and, consequently, the restaurant — was significant. Our strategy had pros and cons, and we experienced both.

MANAGEMENT

Expect to be in it for the long haul. The "love 'em and leave 'em" approach I had originally anticipated for my role in the company did not work. I had anticipated that I would be involved in the build-out of the restaurant, as part of the ownership team, and then turn the store over to the operations team with little or no involvement afterwards. Instead, for the first year, I received a call from the managers at the store every time there was a problem with the facility or a piece of equipment. I had provided them with operations manuals, service contact numbers, and preventative maintenance guides, but even the fact that I was over 100 miles from the store did not stop them from calling me regularly to help solve the problems on site. Having a far greater impact on my failed theory, however, was the fact that once you are an owner of a company, you are intimately involved in every aspect of the business, not just your specialty. By both desire and requirement, I was involved in far more than just design and construction for 'Za-Bistro! This was the case for most of the partners, who wound up taking on responsibilities they had not intended to assume at the outset. It is the reality of owning a restaurant, or any business for that matter. "Love 'em and leave 'em" does not work.

Make sure the right systems are in place. If you are not going to be running the restaurant yourself, it is critical to have the proper systems in place so the pulse of the restaurant can be maintained in your absence. When I refer to the "pulse" of the restaurant, I mean the financial health as well as the organizational performance. Both are equally important. Pulling from our experience, we should never have been surprised by significant losses in a single period or prime costs of 98 percent. We should have known this ahead of time. In some instances, we placed too much trust in the operations team without having the proper verification systems in place.

Leaders are born in times of turmoil, not tranquility. It is the hard times that bring out the greatness in leaders. Think of the leaders we revere most, and you will likely find a common thread—a tragedy or crisis with which they had to contend. They were great leaders because they were great during the most difficult times. They knew how to motivate their troops or their supporters, and they accomplished what was possible, but not likely. The business environment provides crises and opportunities for leaders to emerge. We had our fair share of crises, and we learned a lot about leadership.

PERSONAL

Trust that gut feeling. With an assembled team of experts, in many cases I relied more heavily on their experience than on my own instincts when an issue was outside my perceived area of expertise. In hindsight I see that, typically, my gut feeling was right. When I went against my natural inclinations, I was uncomfortable and often made the wrong choice. I am not saying that I was always right; rather, when I went against my gut feeling, I was almost always wrong. Some psychology experts advocate that your gut feeling has a strong scientific basis, made up of complex reasoning and decision strategies that are not readily apparent or intuitive. I am not sure whether that is the case or not, but I can tell you that I have gained a new respect for my gut feelings and listen to them much more closely these days.

Restaurant development is fantastic. The last lesson is a confirmation. I truly enjoy the restaurant development process. From the logo to the menu to the design and construction—I love seeing an idea come to fruition. It is incredibly satisfying to see a restaurant full of people enjoying something that existed exclusively in your mind's eye only a few months earlier. The work to turn these dreams, these *Restaurant Dreams*, into reality is painstaking, draining, and all-consuming. But the results make it worth the sacrifice.

That is my story. If you are bewildered and turned off by the realities of restaurant development, if you have decided after reading this book that opening a restaurant is *not* what you want to do, I have done my job. If, on the other hand, you are chomping at the bit and ready to start developing your own restaurant even after reading about all that the effort entails, by all means follow your *Restaurant Dream*. If you proceed with greater knowledge and understanding of the restaurant development process after reading this book, then, again, I have done my job. I have been honest throughout this book. I have shared information with you that others seem unwilling to share. I shared real problems. I shared real surprises. I shared real successes. As promised, this was not a textbook filled with checklists, to-do lists, and hollow direction. This was real. While the issues discussed in this book were specific to our restaurant development process, the nature of the process and all that we experienced is consistent with the stories of many other restaurant developers.

When teaching my college courses, I would list two course requirements in the syllabus: 1) learn something and 2) have fun. It is my sincere hope that through this story, you have been able to meet those same requirements. I can assure you that I certainly did.

AUTHOR BIO

L **ee Simon** is an award-winning designer, specializing in commercial foodservice and hospitality projects. A graduate of Cornell University's School of Hotel Administration, he has taught *Hospitality Facilities Planning and Design* at the University of Central Florida's Rosen College of Hospitality Management. He is also the author of a column on hospitality design that has been featured in dozens of publications throughout the United States, Canada, the United Kingdom, Hong Kong, India, the Netherlands, Switzerland, Nigeria, and the United Arab Emirates. As a practicing designer, Lee uses his operational experience on a daily basis to assist his clients with the planning of new and renovated foodservice facilities. His past projects, located in the United States and abroad, include all types of foodservice operations.

The Dream Continues

Visit **www.TheRestaurantDream.com**
for more tips, insights, and useful information.

STILL DREAMING?

If you enjoyed *The Restaurant Dream?* and would like more information on opening and operating your own restaurant, here are some additional reference materials available for foodservice operators:

(Set of 3) ~~$239.85~~ **$189.95 SAVE OVER 20% Item # RCT-02**

RESTAURANT REFERENCE SET

THE ENCYCLOPEDIA OF RESTAURANT TRAINING: A Complete Ready-to-Use Training Program for All Positions in the Food Service Industry

THE RESTAURANT MANAGER'S HANDBOOK: How to Set Up, Operate and Manage a Financially Successful Food Service Operation

THE ENCYCLOPEDIA OF RESTAURANT FORMS: A Complete Kit of Ready-to-Use Checklists, Worksheets and Training Aids for a Successful Food Service Operation

TO ORDER CALL 1-800-814-1132 OR VISIT WWW.ATLANTIC-PUB.COM

THE RESTAURANT MANAGER'S SUCCESS CHRONICLES: Insider Secrets and Techniques Food Service Managers Use Every Day to Make Millions

Restaurants are one of the most frequently started businesses, yet they have one of the highest failure rates. A study from the Ohio State University reports the restaurant failure rate is between 57 and 61 percent after only three years. Do not be a statistic on the wrong side; plan for success. There are many books and courses on restaurant operation; this is the only book that will provide you with insider secrets. We asked the successful restaurant owners and operators who make their living on the restaurant floor — and they talked. This new book will give you real-life examples of how successful restaurant operators avoid common pitfalls and thrive. The information is so useful that you can read a page and put the idea into action — today! Learn the most efficient ways to bring customers in and have them return, how to up-sell, cost control ideas, oversights to avoid, and how to steer clear of disappointment.

288 Pages • $24.95 • Item # 9780910627962

FOOD SERVICE MANAGEMENT: How to Succeed in the High-Risk Restaurant Business — By Someone Who Did by Bill Wentz

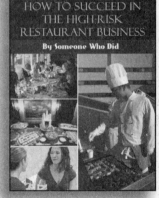

There is so much more to the world of food service than the average patron realizes. This book will reveal all the hidden facets of this fast-paced business and show you how to succeed as a food service manager. The author, Bill Wentz, speaks from experience, making his advice that much more valuable. Wentz truly understands the industry and shares the priceless experiences he had and lessons he learned throughout his career. In this book, you will learn if a food service career is right for you, the many opportunities available in the industry, and where to go for the best training. Food service managers will learn how to predict food costs, how to achieve profit goals, how to conduct recipe cost analysis, and how to realistically price a menu. Wentz shares his philosophies on many of the important aspects of the food service industry and passes on his knowledge in this easy-to-read and entertaining book that not only tells you how to survive in the food service business but also tells you how to be successful.

288 Pages • $24.95 • Item # 9781601380241

THE WAITER & WAITRESS AND WAITSTAFF TRAINING HANDBOOK: A Complete Guide to the Proper Steps in Service for Food & Beverage Employees

This training handbook was designed for use by all food service staff members and covers every aspect of restaurant customer service for the positions of host, waiter or waitress, head waiter, captain, and bus person. The detailed performance of each position is described for different types of establishments and all types of service. It provides step-by-step instructions on hosting, seating guests, taking/filling orders, loading/unloading trays, table side service, setting an elegant table, promoting specials and side orders, handling problems, difficult customers, managing tips, handling questions, handling the check, handling money, and more. Plus, learn advanced serving techniques, such as flambé and carving meats, fish, and fruits. Also, a chapter is devoted exclusively to food safety and sanitation.

288 Pages • $29.95 • English Item # 9780910627474
Spanish Item # 9780910627481

THE COMPLETE WAITSTAFF TRAINING COURSE VIDEO — VHS & DVD

In this 60-minute, high-quality waitstaff training video your staff will learn how to consistently deliver the quality service that makes customers not only come back, but tell others about their memorable experience. This training tape is ideal as a backbone in your training program for experienced waitstaff who are always looking to learn more or for people who have never waited tables and would like to learn the basics. Topics covered include standard American service, alcohol sales and wine service, preparing for service, hosting and greeting guests, taking beverage orders, correct service procedures, suggestive selling, taking the food order, placing the order, picking up the order, proper dish and glass holding, table manners, serving food, completing the service, hygiene and food safety, handling busy times, listening to guest comments, tips, taxes, and more! The training video is on-site and available when needed; you can immediately train new staff and update existing staff right away! Study guide and tests are included. A certificate of completion is available. 60 minutes. Available in VHS, DVD, PAL English, or Spanish.

English VHS Video • $149.95 • Item # 9780910627405
Spanish VHS Video • $149.95 • Item # 9780910627412
English PAL Video • $149.95 • Item # 9780910627429
Spanish PAL Video • $149.95 • Item # 9780910627436
English DVD • $149.95 • Item # 9780910627443
Spanish DVD • $149.95 • Item # 9780910627450
English Certificate of Completion • Item # CWS-CREN • $9.95
Spanish Certificate of Completion • Item # CWS-CRSP • $9.95

To Order Call 1-800-814-1132 or Visit www.Atlantic-Pub.com

ALCOHOL SERVICE POSTERS

Decorative and instructional, these full-color posters will be popular with both your employees and customers. Containing essential information, drink photos, recipes, and more, they will help increase sales and grab attention. Posters are laminated to reduce wear and tear and measure 11" x 17".

Series of 7 Posters
Item # ASP-PS • $59.95

12 Classic Cocktails with Recipes Item # CC-PS • $9.95

12 Popular Cocktails with Recipes Item # PC-PS • $9.95

Types of Beer
Item # TOB-PS • $9.95

Categories of Liquor
Item # COL-PS • $9.95

10 Types of Martinis
Item # TOM-PS • $9.95

Drink Garnishes
Item # DG-PS • $9.95

Common Bar Abbreviations
Item # CBA-PS • $9.95

WINE SERVICE POSTERS

These five color posters cover all the wine basics—from service to pronunciation. Essential information for anyone serving, pouring, or selling wine, yet attractive enough to display in your dining room. Posters are laminated to reduce wear and tear and measure 11" x 17".

Series of 5 Posters
Item # WPS-PS • $39.95

Wine Pronunciation Guide
Item # WPG-PS • $9.95

Proper Wine Service
Item # PWS-PS • $9.95

Red Wine
Item # RWP-PS • $9.95

White Wine
Item # WWP-PS • $9.95

Sparkling Wine & Champagne
Item # SWC-PS • $9.95

To order call 1-800-814-1132 or visit www.atlantic-pub.com

ALCOHOL AWARENESS POSTER SERIES

Alcohol awareness is an important issue. This new poster series covers ten fundamental topics and should be posted in any establishment that serves alcohol. Posters are in full color and laminated to reduce wear. They measure 11" x 17".

Series of 10 Posters Item # AAP-PS • $89.95

Right to Refuse Service
Item # RTR-PS • $9.95

One Drink Equals
Item # ODE-PS • $9.95

Spotting a Fake ID
Item # FID-PS • $9.95

Symptoms of Intoxication
Item # SIO-PS • $9.95

We Check IDs
Item # CID-PS • $9.95

Drinking & Pregnancy
Item # D&P-PS • $9.95

Blood Alcohol Content Chart—Female Item # BACF-PS • $9.95

Blood Alcohol Content Chart—Male
Item # BACM-PS • $9.95

Don't Drink & Drive
Item # DDD-PS • $9.95

Alcohol Slows Reaction Times
Item # ASR-PS • $9.95

To order call 1-800-814-1132 or visit www.atlantic-pub.com